COMPUTER WIMP NO MORE
The Intelligent Beginner's Guide to Computers

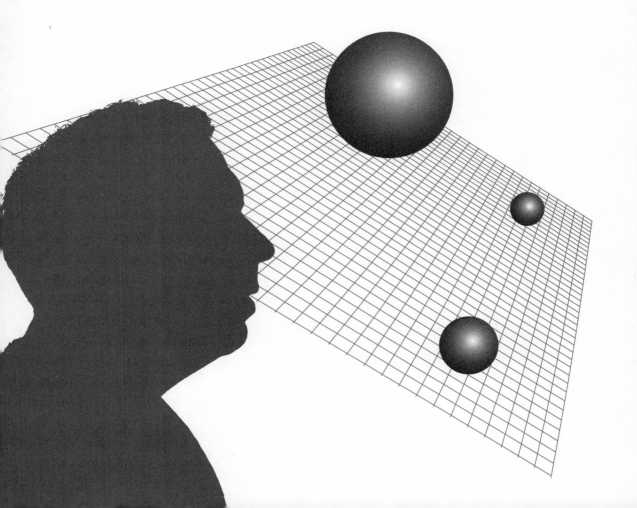

COMPUTER WIMP NO MORE
The Intelligent Beginner's Guide to Computers

by John Bear, Ph.D.
and David M. Pozerycki

with the help of Justine Roberts and Daniel Leduc
and

Margaret A. Bentley | Ginny Brouch | Dolly Clark
Laurence Chu | Nancy Dyson | Ron Kizala
Ramona Lee | Janice Raach | Roger Sinsheimer
| Andrea M. Weisberger |

and

Aileen L. Treadwell
Allen Holland
Aric Friesen
Barbara Barbera
Barbara Iverson
Barbara Warren
Barbi Bennett
Bob Kundrath
Bob Nicolaus
Bonnie Surguine
Boonyarak
   Amnueysuktavon
Bruce Dedlow
Candy Schock
Carol Lastrucci
Charles H. Keck
Charles L. Seaver
Cheryl Butler Long
Craig Griffin
Craig J. Wolf
David A. Lewis
David Ehrenfeld
David Gold
David Hitchcock
David P. Grant
Dennis Bottrill
Diane Milner
Don Schloeder
Don Schneider
Donald G. Hawley
Dorothea Gfeller
Doug Cummins
Ed Cleary

Edward Fagyal
Elaine Schmerbeck
Elihu King
Eliphaletta Jones
Elizabeth Armstrong
Erika Babcock
Estelle Behan
Fran Roberts
Frances Fletcher
Fred J. Gorchess
Gary Rommelfanger
Gladys Kuehmann
Gloria L. Nicolai
Gwen Lenker
Harley L. Sachs
Jack Gaughan
James E. Akins
James L. Parker
James R. Regan
James Fisher
Jean Eichelberger
Jeffrey Norwood
Jill Norden
Jim Clark
Jim Ford
Jim Hoag & Sally Evans
Jim Stevens
John A. Nelson
John A. Salmons
John L. Leander
John C. Dorris
John Salmons
Jon Mir

Julie Cathcart
Katherine A. Phipps
Kathleen Neff
Kenneth Rogahn
Kevin Knudtson
Kevin Quirk
Kitty Purrington
Larry & Yancy Hufford
LaVerne E. Domach
Laura A. Jacobs
Linda Bons
Louis Joline
Louis Lotti
Lynn Mason
M. G. Goddard
Marc de Celle
Mark Monroe
Marilyn Stendahl
Mark Diggs
Mark Monroe
Mark Titus
Mary Helen
   Gearhart-Gray
Mary Jo Sullivan
Mary Van Dyke
Michael J. OBrien
Nancy Merritt
Nick Hennessee
Norman I. Condit, Jr.
Opal Follin
Paul R. Cassidy, Jr.
Paul Zukowski
Phil Black

R. W. Kizala
Ramona C. Lee
Richard F. W. Sadler
Richard Keller
Rick Melton
Robert E. O'Donnell
Robert W. Russell
Roger Nelson
Ron Berryhill
Ron Urbina
Ruby Shultz
Sandy Ryman
Sanford G. Goldstein
Sheila Magdun
Shirley E. Huggins
Shirley Parker
Sonya Cavazos
Sue Kassan
Susan K. Kahn
T. Keith Jones
Terry Strom
Thomas E. Wergen
Thomas L. Vaughn
Todd Hinson
Tom Whiteside
Tony Lesce
V. Lambert
Vincent V. Santiago
Virgil A. Paulson
W. C. Bellows
Walter V. Stone
Walter Blum
Willy Alcorn

Ten Speed Press
Berkeley, California

Ten Speed Press
P. O. Box 7123
Berkeley, California 94707

First printing 1992

Cover and text design by Fifth Street Design, Berkeley, California
Page 184 reprinted by permission © 1982 Ellis Weiner. Originally in *New Yorker* magazine.

Library of Congress Cataloging in Publication Data

Bear, John, 1938-
  Computer Wimp No More : The Intelligent Beginner's Guide to Computers / John Bear
    p. cm.
  Rev. ed. of: Computer Wimp, 1983.
  Includes bibliographical references and index.
  ISBN 0-89815-432-4
  1. Microcomputers. 2. Microcomputers—Purchasing.   I. Bear,
John, 1938- Computer Wimp.   II. Title.
QA76.5.B364   1991
004.16'029'7—dc20
                                                                    91017554
                                                                    CIP

Printed in the United States of America

1 2 3 4 5 – 95 94 93 92 91

Table of Contents

A Message from the First Author about the Other 144 Authors   1
Before Beginning: The Essential Two-Word Glossary   2

PART I

INTRODUCTION   3

Driving a Car *versus* Driving a Computer   5
The Three Kinds of People Who Need This Book   6
Are We Having a Computer Revolution? or The Emperor's New Computer   9

PART II

THINGS TO THINK ABOUT BEFORE YOU TAKE THE PLUNGE   13

Learnability   15
Reliability   16
Repairability   17
Your Ability   18
The Two Kinds of Errors We Make   21

PART III

IMPORTANT ISSUES TO CONSIDER BEFORE YOU BUY   23

1. Never Be the First Kid on Your Block to Buy Anything New   25
2. Plunging Prices   27
3. Improving Quality   28
4. Disappearing Companies   28
5. The "But Wait!" Syndrome   30
Reconciling the "Don't Be the First Kid" Advice with the "But Wait!" Advice   32

PART IV

QUESTION:
Do I Buy the Hardware First, the Software First, or Do Something Else First? . . 35

PART V

ANSWER:
Do Something Else First. Assess Your Needs. 37

Alternatives to Buying a Computer   41

PART VI

BUYING HARDWARE 45

IBM, Macintosh, or Something Else?   47
What Other Factors Do I Take into Account?   51
Bells and Whistles   59
Buying Locally versus Buying by Mail   83
Buying Used or Obsolete Stuff   93
The Shameful Warranty Situation   98

PART VII

BUYING SOFTWARE AND SUPPLIES 103

General Considerations in Choosing Software   105
The Different Kinds of Software   109
How to Learn about Unusual and Special Interest Software   124
Buying Locally versus Buying by Mail   126
Buying Used or Obsolete Software   127
Buying Computer Supplies   129

PART VIII

USING COMPUTERS 131

The One Single Most Important Thing of All   133
Bulletin Board Services   139
About Programming   143
How Do You Learn More?   150
You Are Smarter Than You May Have Thought (A Short Pep Talk) 156

PART IX

PROBLEMS WITH COMPUTERS 159

The Inherent Fragility of the Machinery   161
The Dreaded 99% Factor   169
Other Incompatibility Problems   171
Software Failure   174
Don't Ask Why, Just Keep On Going   176
Evil People: The Problem of Computer Viruses   178
Psychological Problems   180
Communication Problems: The Matter of "Technobabble"   187

PART X

SOLUTIONS TO COMPUTER PROBLEMS 189

Finding a Support Group   191
All About RYFMS   192
Computer Repair   194
The Last Resort: Computer Consumer Karate   202

PART XI

THE DARK UNDERBELLY OF THE COMPUTER WORLD 207

1,000,000 Mistakes Per Second: The Problems of Being Fast, Dumb, and Big   209
"Maybe I Could Just Die Early:" Fear of Computers   212
Health Hazards of Computers   216
Piracy: Dealing with the Decision Whether or Not to be a Pirate   220
Stealing Computers and Computer Time   223
The Sledgehammers of the Night: Computer Sabotage   225
Computer Crime   228
The Jangling Can: Computers and Invasion of Privacy   232

PART XII

WHERE, THEN, ARE THINGS GOING 235

Spanish Ladies on Bicycles: Computers and the Economy   237
The Future: How Computers Might Really Change Things   240
My Computer Autobiography   241
Glossary   245
An Available Consulting Service from the Authors of this Book   257

HERE IS YOUR $200 BONUS

THE PRACTICAL PERSONAL COMPUTER BUYER'S GUIDE 259

Note From John Bear:
I. Introduction   262
II. The Steps   263
III. Appendices   274

A Message from the First Author about the Other 144 Authors

In the early 1980s, I wrote my computer autobiography, under the title *Computer Wimp: 166 things I wish I had known before I bought my first computer!* It became one of the better-selling computer books of the '80s. Nearly a decade later, the publisher came to me and said, "How about a *new* book: a practical guide for all those people thinking about computers, but who are not quite sure where to start. For the intelligent beginner, shall we say."

"I was a wimp when I wrote *Wimp*," I replied. "But I am no longer an intelligent beginner. Intelligent? Well, until Mensa requires annual retests, I'm in good shape. But beginner? No way. I've been messing with these machines for nearly 20 years now. My finger is no longer on the pulse of a technologically uncertain America."

For our solution, we went to the method used by the computer industry itself: a new product development team. Nationally syndicated computer columnist Bob Schwabach invited readers of his *On Computers* column to join the Computer Wimp Development Team. From a carload of applications, we selected five hundred people who had the qualifications of (a) beginnerhood, (b) some level of articulateness, (c) good ideas, and (d) a willingness to do a bunch of work for almost nothing: a free autographed book, a neat certificate, and getting their name on the title page of the book. The 11 most helpful team members were promised special prizes.

The Development Team came through in pretty much the same fashion as computer industry teams come through. About a quarter of them checked in with useful, helpful suggestions, that have formed much of the basis of this book. The rest took the free loot and were never heard from again.

The most helpful team member, Dave Pozerycki, was elevated to coauthorhood. The two next most helpful (decision of the judge, me, was final), Justine Roberts and Daniel Leduc, achieved "withhood" on the title page. The next nine in the pantheon got slightly larger typeface, and the other 133 kind and helpful souls are herewith gratefully thanked.

Before Beginning:
The Essential
Two-Word Glossary

1. HARDWARE
2. SOFTWARE

I am as annoyed as anyone with "technobabble"—the tendency of computer writers to disdain the use of comprehensible English when writing about computers. But there is no point in evading the two most common words in this field, so before anything else, let us be sure that we are all clear on the meaning of both of the above-printed terms.

Hardware is the machine itself. The physical equipment: the computer, or the disk drive, or the printer, or the monitor (television screen), and so on.

Software is the changeable stuff: the programs; the electronic information, contained on disks, tapes, and other carriers, that tells the hardware what to do.

The simplest and closest analogy is in the world of home electronics.

Hardware includes tape players, CD players, turntables, speakers, amplifiers, radios, television sets, and so on.

Software includes cassette tapes, CD disks, phonograph records, videocassettes, and so on.

The same *hardware* is capable of accepting a wide range of *software*. Your tape deck probably doesn't know whether you are playing Mozart or Sid Vicious. Your hardware reads the information contained in the software, and somehow sound comes out of your speakers or pictures appear on your screen.

Not all stereo hardware can accept all stereo software (please do not try to force an 8-track tape into your Walkman). Kitchen hardware (e.g., toasters) can accept some kitchen software (e.g., sliced bread) but not others (e.g., tomato soup). And not all computer hardware can accept all computer software. If it could, there wouldn't be nearly as much need for a book like this.

PART I

INTRODUCTION

Driving a Car *versus* Driving a Computer

Driving a computer should be as simple as driving a car. You learn to drive in a matter of hours. It's easy. You can enjoy your car even if you don't know how to change the oil or rebuild the transmission. And the skills are readily transferable from one car to another. If you trade in your Yugo on a Rolls-Royce, you will be able to drive the Rolls and, in a pinch, probably a Mack truck or a school bus as well.

It is only when they go wrong that machines remind you how powerful they are.
—Clive James

But would you buy a car
* if it came with a 600-page instruction manual;
* if it took six months to learn to drive in first gear and another year to get up to second;
* if it came with a 90-day warranty, and had to be sent to Minnesota to be repaired;
* if there were hundreds of thick books in every bookstore with titles like *Mastering Your Chevrolet,* or *How to Drive Your Ford;* and
* if you needed to attend meetings of your local Toyota Users Group to gain valuable insights on how to open the trunk and turn on the headlights?

What has gone wrong in the world of computers?

The machines are basically sound and reliable. They can do wonderful things, in the home and in business. And they really aren't that formidable, once you get to know them.

Yet we have millions of intelligent, well-meaning computer users (or would-be computer users) who have grown confused, angry, frustrated, and/or despondent when all they want to do is drive the damned machine.

Who are these people?

The Three Kinds of People Who Need This Book

Because of my computer writing and my talk show appearances, I get a great deal of mail from intelligent but frustrated people. They fall very evenly into these three categories:

Category 1. "Where is the diving board?"

Just because 'everyone else' is doing it doesn't mean that you have to do it too.

About a third of my correspondents tell me that they are really interested in taking the computer plunge, but they have been having a lot of trouble finding the diving board or even the pool itself. They were almost hopelessly confused by the number of different brands out there, the thousands of available software packages, the advertising (many of them miss the days when life was simpler, and computers were being sold on television by Charlie Chaplin, Bill Cosby, and the cast of M*A*S*H); the magazines, the shows, and copious advice and counter-advice from friends and relatives.

Millions and millions of people who could genuinely benefit from having computers in their lives don't have them, because they simply *don't* know where to begin. They ask (or should be asking) questions like these:

- What can computers do for me, in my business or in my personal life?
- How do I find out more about computers without devoting my life to study, or embarrassing myself in front of a computer salesperson who looks to be 14 years old, has been using computers since he was three, and probably knows more than I ever will?
- Exactly what computer should I buy? How much should I spend? How much software should I buy? (What *is* software, anyway?) What kind of printer? What kind of accessories? How do I even know what questions to ask of myself, much less of a salesperson?
- And if I ever could decide, do I go to a computer store or a discount house or do I buy at discount by mail or a used computer from a classified ad in the Penny Saver?

Category 2. "I've got this $4,000 doorstop."

Another third already have small computers, and are not totally thrilled by the experience. They have been disappointed by their hardware, their software, or, most commonly, their inability to make the computer a truly important addition to their lives.

For them, it's like having a 78-passenger bus, and using it only for making short trips to the grocery store a few blocks away. It's like having a Ferrari and never driving over 25 miles an hour. The great majority of computer users, however well intentioned they may be, make use of only a tiny percentage of all the things a computer could be doing for them.

Millions of people have computers that either sit collecting dust in the closet, or are being used to do only one or two of the hundreds of things they are capable of doing.

Some of these people are casualties of the computer wars. Their buying, learning, and using experiences to date have been sufficiently unpleasant that they have no wish to go on.

Others just don't have the time or the know-how to march forward. They are using their computer *just* for writing letters, or *just* for doing the bookkeeping, or *just* for shooting down invaders from the planet Xarxx, and they are uneasily content to do only that, although at some level they are aware that it might be fun to drive the Ferrari on the freeway once in a while.

Category 3. "I've never tried computers because I don't like them."

The final third of the people said, in effect, "Do you mean that I really don't *have* to join the computer revolution? I won't be arrested as a draft dodger?" These people expressed a tremendous feeling of relief when I reassured them that they could probably live out their lives in peace and harmony without ever setting finger to keyboard or eye to screen. Nonetheless, I had the strong feeling that many of these people might well have benefited from computers, if only their initial attitude were just a little different.

Years ago, the manufacturers of Guinness Stout did some market research showing them that a great many people were not buying their product because they had a clear preconception of what it tasted like—but they were completely wrong! Once these folks had their first sip, they became enthusiastic. The company thereupon came up with this brilliant slogan: "Guinness Stout: I've never tried it because I don't like it."

In much the same way, there are millions of people who have never considered owning or operating a computer, because they are absolutely convinced they would never learn how, or that it would do nothing useful for them. They've never tried computers because they don't like them.

Now, in an endeavor to ward off a battery of annoyed or angry letters, it is essential to point out who this book is *not* for.

Category 4. "You disparage my machine, I break your face."

These people have turbo-powered machines, hard disks, all the software one could ever want, most of it actually legal. They have track balls, modems, full-page display screens, and accelerator cards. Their nimble fingers fly across keyboard and banks of switches keeping them in touch with their business and personal lives, their accountants and lawyers, their friends and relatives, their bail bondsmen and dealers. Every time I write that computers may not offer the solution to all the problems of our planet, they fire off "how can you say that, dude" letters, virtually threatening to send goons to my house to break my typing fingers if I continue to disparage these fantastic tools.

If we are having a computer revolution, they may not be the generals, but they are surely the advance scouts. I wish them well, but this book is not for them.

Are We Having a Computer Revolution? or The Emperor's New Computer

Remember the story called *The Emperor's New Clothes,* in which dishonest tailors persuaded the vain Emperor that he was dressed in finery, when he was in fact stark naked. As the Emperor marched along in a royal parade, his courtiers and followers loudly praising his magnificent outfit, it was a little child who called out, "The Emperor has no clothes."

Before we turn our attention to computers themselves, we would do well to look at the so-called computer revolution and see whether or not this particular emperor is wearing any clothes, and if so, what sort: a brocade robe, a pair of Frederick's of Hollywood briefs, or something in between.

To be sure, *something* is happening out there, but it may not be exactly what many of us have thought.

What has happened is that approximately 1% of the adults on earth have bought a small computer.

In the United States of America, the wealthiest and most technologically advanced nation on earth, by 1991, 15% of the households actually had a computer, which means that 85% did not. According to a 1991 report from the Bureau of the Census, 28% of American adults have used a computer. According to my calculations, that means 72% have not.

Are we having a computer revolution? Yes and no.

Yes, to be sure, with regard to the giant "mainframe" computers that handle our credit card accounts, run the telephone system, fight wars, design airplanes, and fill our mailboxes with personalized "junk mail." Is it not a miracle that you can stick a small plastic rectangle into a slot outside a bank in Fiji, and within seconds learn that your checking account back in Ohio is overdrawn?

No, with regard to small personal computers: the Apples, IBMs, Compaqs, Tandys, Amigas, Ataris, and others that we buy for a few thousand dollars and set up in our homes or businesses. There may well be a revolution in their design and capability, but with regard to their *usage,* the revolution is on hold because of three factors: the gen-

Voice recognition is a developing science.

eration gap factor, the disappearance factor, and the where-are-we-going factor.

The generation gap factor

If we *are* going to have a genuine computer revolution, we may know for sure in another 15 to 20 years. Major changes in society rarely happen all at once to everybody. When large numbers of people emigrated to America from Europe, Latin America, and Asia, many of the older ones never really did learn English well or fit into "the American way of life." The younger ones learned pretty fast. And the babies born in America grew up utterly American.

So it is with small computers. We middle-aged folks will never, ever feel as comfortable or be as knowledgeable as today's teenagers. And *their* children will probably routinely use computers of all kinds–often without even knowing it, due to the disappearance factor.

The disappearance factor

I am fond of Bob Wachtel's analogy between the invention of the electric motor and the invention of the computer. When Nicola Tesla came up with the first practical electric motor about a century ago, the public was fascinated by it. The yuppies of the late 19th century acquired electric motors simply as a curiosity. Their friends came over for white wine and cheese and they watched a wheel spinning around, with Vanna White nowhere in sight.

But the *real* growth of electric motors came as they were incorporated into all kinds of other machinery. No one says, "I'm going to buy a vacuum cleaner plus an electric motor," (or a motorized washing machine, food processor, water pump, or typewriter). The motor is taken for granted. It has disappeared. Even though the average home has something like 28 electric motors, they are all inside things. None of them is sitting on the coffee table or collecting dust in a closet.

So it seems to be happening with computers. When you set your stove or your microwave to turn on at a certain time, you are using a small built-in computer. When your camera "automatically" adjusts the lens and the shutter speed for the existing light, it is a computer that does the job. Tiny computers can already be found in vacuum cleaners, video cameras, doorbells, burglar alarms, and throughout the family car. When you use the automatic teller machine at the bank or that "end user communication terminal" you may call a telephone, you are tapping into huge computers that could be thousands of miles away.

But all of these computers are invisible. They have disappeared into other things. The time may well come when the "freestanding" computer sitting there on the kitchen table may be as rare as a freestanding electric motor is today.

Or that time may *not* come. The simple fact is . . .

No one knows just where we are headed.

In 1948, Thomas Watson, the President of IBM, predicted that as many as 12 companies might someday have their own computers. Six years later, the estimate was expanded to 50 companies. In the late 1960s, I attended the opening of the AT&T Picturephone booth at Grand Central Station in New York. At the time, AT&T predicted that by 1980 more than 500,000 homes would have picturephones.

Anyone who thinks that *anyone* can predict our technological future with any accuracy is well advised to read back issues of science-oriented magazines. Experts really aren't very good at forecasting the future. Two examples will suffice; others can be found in marketing professor Steven P. Schnaar's book, *Megamistakes: Forecasting and the myth of rapid technological change,* which reviewer Justine Roberts has likened to "the other side of *Megatrends,* . . . all of the wrong predictions regularly issued by think tanks, politicians and market researchers."

In 1967, *Popular Science* magazine told us that "a few years ago, when people thought about household computers at all, they thought of some small, inexpensive individual unit that would keep track of the family checking account. . . . Now we know it won't be like that at all. It will be far cheaper to build one monster computer with thousands or even millions of customers hooked to it, than to have small individual machines in individual homes."

A year later, *Changing Times* magazine, noting that the banking industry has been "poised to leap into the cashless, checkless, electronic money world" for a quarter of a century, lamented that we would not see this development until the mid-1970s.

One exciting reason no one can predict the future evolves from Arthur C. Clarke's hypothesis that half the great inventions of history were long anticipated (airplanes, television, movies) while the other half were complete surprises, quite unexpected until they happened (phonograph, nuclear power, lasers).

My great grandfather grew up without telephones. My grandfather grew up without planes and cars. My father grew up without radio. I grew up without television. My daughters grew up without computers. What are *their* children going to grow up without? Will astonishing breakthroughs revolutionize the revolution we've already got going? Or will computers "merely" continue to get smaller, faster, cheaper, and more versatile? Stay tuned.

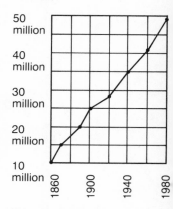

DATE: March 3, 1860
PROJECTED NUMBER OF HORSES IN AMERICA, 1860–1980

This projection was 25 times too high. Unexpected events play havoc with any long-range forecasting.

One last thing, before plunging in.

As it happened, I was living in England when that country undertook one of the major social-technical changes of the century: the largest country ever to switch over to the metric system.

Years of planning, study, public relations, advertising, and consumer education were undertaken. And then one day, soon after the changeover, I needed a piece of wood. I studied and rehearsed what I was supposed to say. I headed for the lumberyard, and said to the man in charge,

"I'd like a 5-centimeter by 10-centimeter board, 2 meters long, please."

Without hesitation, he turned and shouted, "Alvin, get this bloke a 6-foot 2 b' 4."

Somehow, I knew everything was going to be all right.

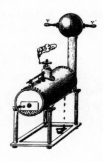

MARK I

MARK II

MARK III

PART II

THINGS TO THINK ABOUT BEFORE YOU TAKE THE PLUNGE

Simply put, the computer is unlike any other machine you have ever dealt with. As we go through life buying machinery—cars, lawn mowers, refrigerators, television sets, washing machines, and the like—we have developed certain expectations about what it is like to deal with a new machine in our lives.

These expectations relate to:

- its learnability: how long will it take before the machine is up and running, and how long will it take to learn everything there is to know about it;

- its reliability: how often can we expect things to go wrong;

- its repairability: what happens when things *do* go wrong; and

- its role in your life: your ability to adjust to being a computer owner and user. How will life be different, for better or for worse, because of this machine?

In each of these four respects, dealing with a computer is quite different from any machinery experience most people have ever had before. Understanding and acknowledging these differences will make the experience far more positive, if only by helping to reduce the frequency and the duration of the periods of distress and anguish that inevitably will occur.

The computer can, in a fraction of a second, work out the shortest of 10,000 alternate routes between Windsor Castle and St. Paul's, but it can never say that if a detour is made through a garden in the spring, this is one of the things that make a journey seem shorter.

–John Hargreaves

Learnability

If you are all through with school, and unlikely to take up brain surgery or differential calculus as a hobby in your later years, learning to use a computer is probably going to be the most complex and difficult mental activity you will experience between now and the end of your life.

There is nothing wrong with this—indeed, for some people, the intellectual challenge is more stimulating and satisfying than the end result. But for people who have grown accustomed to plugging in a refrigerator and immediately filling it with food, or buying a new car and spending at best a quarter hour with the owner's manual to learn how to work the radio, air conditioning, and six-way power seat, there is a rude awakening in the realization that it will be many hours, more likely weeks or even months, before one can drive the computer slowly around the block.

Another factor to consider—more psychological than educational—is the fact that no matter how hard you try, you will probably never be as skilled in using a computer as thousands and thousands of teenagers are right now.

For people who are accustomed to becoming good at things they do, the feeling can be quite debilitating. I have heard more than a few people say, in effect, "If I'm never going to do it well, then I don't want to do it at all."

A foreign language teacher once told me that he no longer brings into his class small children who are native speakers. When a person who has been struggling for five years to speak Japanese suddenly realizes that she will never speak it as well as that seven-year-old child, a pall of gloom descends over the learning process.

But things *are* getting better, pall-of-gloom-wise, as the computer industry begins to acknowledge that people really do want things to be simpler. For some peculiar reason, most people would much rather press a button that says "Make a copy of this disk" than engage in a lengthy and complex series of steps, including typing in several lines of instructions, to achieve the same end.

There is already an acronym for this development: GUI, or the Graphic User Interface. It is the way people who can't let go of a need for some obfuscation are saying, "We will visually (G) make it easier for ordinary human beings (U) to use our equipment (I)."

Men have become the tools of their tools.
—Henry David Thoreau

Everyone is claiming to be the most "user-friendly" while no one but an expert can even begin to fully utilize the products that are so billed.
—Charles Chickadel, computer consultant.

The first popular computer to move in this direction was the Apple Macintosh. And as the originally-scorned-by-serious-users Macintosh became more and more popular (more Macintoshes were sold in 1990 than IBMs for the first time), the rest of the industry could be heard muttering, "Hey, how can we make our stuff more like their stuff?" The arrival of programs like Microsoft Windows for the IBM and Open Look for Unix computer systems heralds easier times ahead for all of us.

Reliability

As buyers of machinery of all kinds, from can openers to pickup trucks, we have come to expect a certain level of performance, and we have developed a set of behaviors to deal with unsatisfactorily performing machinery.

In fact, the State actually intervenes in certain common machinery-failure situations, as in the so-called "Lemon Laws" a number of states have passed, which require a car dealer to replace or refund the purchase price on a new car that needs repairs four or five times for the same problem.

The bad news is that these expectations do not apply to many aspects of the computer experience. Whether the failing is in the machinery, the programs, the instruction manuals, or the human being using the equipment, the number of failures is likely to be much higher than for any other kind of electrical or mechanical equipment.

To be sure, "failure" can mean anything from a 15-minute delay while you try to figure out what the manual is attempting to say, to a two-month delay while a part is returned to Korea for adjustment.

The good news is that things are definitely better than they were a few years ago. IBM and Apple have established industry standards for reliability, and many other manufacturers can match or exceed their MTBFs. MTBF? Oh, doesn't everyone know that it means Mean Time Between Failures? (I didn't until about three days ago). An MTBF of 50,000 hours for certain computer equipment is not uncommon. Of course that is little consolation to the poor soul who has an MTBF of 20 minutes. One is reminded of the statistician who drowned in a river with an average depth of six inches.[1]

---

[1] The MTBF concept has relevance in the educational system as well. "Carstairs, your MTBF is three weeks; we're putting you on probation."

Repairability

Once again, we mortals who never quite understood why refrigerators get cold, or whether the toast in the toaster rises due to magnetism, levitation, or a catapult of some sort, have grown accustomed to a certain procedure in getting machinery repaired. If it is heavy, someone comes to the house and fixes it. If it is light, we take it in (or mail it in) to be fixed.

The small computer industry does not have established standard procedures for getting stuff repaired, especially once the generous 12½ week warranty period is over. (Happily there is a trend toward longer warranties, but rarely more than a year).

To begin with, one is often unsure what needs repairing. This is a major nuisance when it could be any one of six different things, and one has to go to six different dealers, manufacturers, or mail-order suppliers for repair.

The problems are rarely insurmountable, and often trivial. Just don't expect it to be as easy as taking your food processor in for its five thousand soufflé checkup.

This matter is discussed in some detail, beginning on page 194.

Sirs, I have tested your machine. It adds a new terror to life, and makes death a long-felt want.
—Sir Herbert Beerbohm Tree, when asked to write a testimonial for the new gramophone

Your Ability

This is not a trivial matter. We humans respond in many different ways to new and difficult situations, whether it is dealing with the aftermath of a car accident or with the sudden appearance of $5,000 worth of cardboard boxes delivered to our front door.

A child is hit by a car. While one witness may go into hysterics or stand around in shock, another will rush up to administer first aid, while a third may already be formulating plans to start a citizens' group against drunk driving.

It is surely the case that the process of learning to use a computer will produce a large number of moments that may range from mild frustration to severe anguish to black soul-shattering despair—quite frequently all in the same afternoon.

The *causes* of anguish, despair, and/or frustration are considered on page 180. Here we will look at the four basic ways that people deal with their ability to take a computer into their lives. The better prepared you are to understand this matter of dealing with something new and complex, the less likely computers are to be, quite literally, hazardous to your mental health.

People fall into four categories in this regard. I call them *Pollyannas, Wimps, Patners,* and *FCUs (Former Computer Users).* Let's look briefly at each.

Pollyannas

The original Pollyanna always saw the bright side of everything, and no matter what misfortunes befell her, she just *knew* that everything was going to turn out all right in the end.

We are all Pollyannas when we buy our first computer. Oh, sure, we're vaguely aware that some people have had some problems, but we've read the glossy brochures and the friendly, well-written advertisements (if only the ad writers and the instruction manual writers would change jobs!), and if all those legions of bright nine-year-olds are getting along so well, surely an intelligent, motivated grown-up can (etc., etc.).

And then things start going wrong. Maybe it is just that the speed of learning is so much slower than expected or hoped for. Maybe it is a minor thing like a bad cable connection or a flickering screen or a "5" key that simply broke off the keyboard, or a disk drive with a funny high-pitched sound (to name four things that have happened to me so far this month). Maybe big things, confusing things, mysterious things.

With the first problem comes the quite reasonable attitude: "It must be something minor, and it is undoubtedly my fault for not reading the instructions properly." To be sure this *is* often the case. (See page 190 on 'RYFMs.') And sometimes it is *not* something minor. Like it or not, some small sores *are* incipient cancers.

With the second and third and perhaps up to the 20th or 30th problem, Pollyannaism persists. But eventually, anywhere from a few hours to a few months into the computer experience, most new users start moving (sometimes slowly, sometimes abruptly) into one of the other three categories about to be discussed.

The category chosen (or evolved into) will determine the level of success or failure in your relationship with computers for years to come.

Wimps

Some people, for whatever reason, are natural victims. They actually seem to thrive on pain, distress, or anguish. They take whatever is dished out, and never complain. Some actually seem to seek out situations in which their wimpishness will come to the fore. For these people, to their "traditional" arsenal of lusting after unattainable love objects, supporting fringe political parties, flying regularly on certain midwestern commuter airlines, and the like, can be added a new diversion: getting into computers.

It no longer surprises me how many people there are—I have heard from hundreds—who have had the most devastating problems, over and over again, and keep coming back for more. A dialogue not unlike this one occurs, in one form or another, time after time:

Friend: But why? You have had actual use of your computer for less than 30 days in the last year. It has been in the shop nine times. Your business is suffering. You are breaking out in hives again. Why do you persist?

Wimp: But they said if I bought a new RAM card and had my connections replated in gold, that should take care of the problems.

Friend: Yes, but didn't they tell you a month ago that your problem was dirty disks and a too-slow baud rate on your modem?

Wimp: Admittedly—and before that it was either the wrong version of the software or that I didn't love Jesus. But don't you see, I've got to keep trying.

And so he or she will . . . at least until such time as things either get much better or much worse, propelling the wimp upward or downward into another category.

Patners

Many years ago, in Chicago, I had a friend named Marshall Patner, who was a very active and very dedicated public interest lawyer. In the era of the first Mayor Daley, there was a great deal for a public interest lawyer to do in Chicago and Marshall, it seemed, was trying to do it all: filing suits and countersuits, seeking injunctions, and otherwise trying to deal with corruption and evil-doing in government, law enforcement agencies, and huge corporations.

An extremely high percentage of the things he tried to do failed. Cases were lost on appeal. Witnesses disappeared. The political machine rolled on.

One day, following a particularly devastating courtroom defeat, I asked Marshall Patner how he could go on tilting at this unfair world of windmills. A big smile came onto his face, and he said,

"Ah, but you must understand that the personal satisfaction from each victory overcomes the despair of a hundred defeats. And with each victory, the world improves just a little. Even with nine steps backward for every ten forward, you eventually reach your goal."

A hundred defeats? Well, for me it would be more like three. But the Patner philosophy was often the only thing that kept me going. Once I spent the better part of a day trying to figure out how to make a straight line, using one of the most popular computer drawing programs. It came out curved. It came out too thick. It disappeared from view. Of course I could have done it with a pen and a ruler in less than a minute. But the feeling of joy when it finally did work right was so strong, so uplifting, that it gave me nourishment to survive the next dozen problems in good mental health.

Patnerism is a healthy attitude, especially in the early days of working with computers. Take heart. For most people in most situations, things can only get better. And if they don't, we move sadly to the fourth category.

Former Computer Users

More than a few people have written to me to tell me that their anguish, despair, or frustration quotient was exceeded, and their solution was to become a Former Computer User. There is nothing wrong with this, although it is sad to see it happen. Quite often, there might well have been satisfactory alternatives, that would have involved keeping the computer, had there been sufficient understanding or proper advising.

An American who speaks perfect, accentless Japanese was once talking to a business acquaintance in Tokyo. "What a shame," the Japanese was saying, "that you Americans do not take the time to learn to speak Japanese." "But honored sir," replied the American, "we are *speaking* Japanese." And so they were, and had been for an hour.

There are none so blind as those who cannot see. Or hear. Or compute. I think of this when I am communicating with someone who has been having devastating problems with his or her computer. "But honored victim," I think of saying, "have you noticed that it is permitted to dispose of an unfriendly computer?"

So many people seem to have the feeling that they are wedded to their computer, for better or worse, until death do them part. It somehow never occurred to them that there were relatively simple ways out of their dilemma, including:

• *Change horses.* Switch over to a comparable computer system that can run the same programs and use the same files and records you have been using. Even get another of the same make and model, if you are satisfied that your lemon is a truly rare event.

• *Start over.* If you're not ready to give up on the *idea* of computers, go back and start from scratch, utilizing all you have learned from your experience (and mine), which should make round two a happier experience than the first round.

• *Give up entirely.* Become a former computer user. Thousands upon thousands of people have done this, and lived to tell the tale. From the letters I get, it seems that more often than not their mental health improved, their social standing did not suffer[2], and their bank accounts grew healthier.

The Two Kinds of Errors We Make

In life and in computers, there are two kinds of errors: stopping too soon when it would have gotten better; and continuing too long when you should have stopped sooner, thereby making it worse.

Whether you go on suffering, look for the silver lining, or give up entirely is, in large measure, a matter of personality. The better this is understood before taking the initial plunge, the better the likelihood of surviving nicely as a Patner, and that is not only the best for which one can hope, it is actually not bad at all.

---

[2] I wonder if people who have given up computers repose in the same social niche as people who have voluntarily given up telephones. The only person I've known to live an urbane and busy life without telephones, the attorney Dinty Warmington Whiting, claimed never to have had regrets, other than that he missed a last-minute opera invitation once, and that he was generally known as "Dinty-Whiting-the-lawyer-without-a-telephone."

PART III

IMPORTANT ISSUES TO CONSIDER BEFORE YOU BUY

Before you spend one cent on anything other than this book, you should spend time considering these six important issues. Not every issue is crucial to every person or every buying situation.

Please note that these are issues that are relevant to *any* buying situation: computers, printers, software, probably even waffle irons and Buicks. Specific advice on buying hardware, software, and how to decide which to buy first, comes in the following chapters.

1. Never Be the First Kid on Your Block to Buy Anything New

If I were asked to do the *Reader's Digest* supercondensed version of this book, and only had room for two pieces of advice, this would be one of them. (The other will be found on page 257.)

The First Kid On His Block.

The temptation is almost overwhelming to buy the newest, the latest, the most clever computer or software or electronic gadget, machine, or program. As one who has long subscribed to the "He who hesitates is lost" school of life (as contrasted with the "Look before you leap" school, just down the road), I have, time after time, acted quickly (detractors might say "impulsively"), buying some computer-related wonder, and been very sorry for it, anywhere from nine seconds to a few months later.

There are four good reasons to resist this sort of temptation. The first is by far the most important, but the others bear consideration as well.

Bugs

New technology, whether hardware or software, is almost certain to have bugs, or flaws, or problems. Because of the difficulty in detecting all the problems at the factory, and because of considerable pressure from the marketing and financial departments to get the item out on the market before someone else comes along with something similar (or better or cheaper), it is quite common for flawed or defective computers and computer software to be offered for sale.

Sometimes the manufacturer knows *specifically* what is wrong, and hopes that it is not wrong enough to cause most buyers to return it. Much more often, however, the manufacturer can be pretty sure that *something* (or, more likely, *many* things) are wrong, and he is going to let the early customers be the guinea pigs to find and report the flaws.

Once, a remarkably candid service department manager who was checking my machine for the fifth time for the same problem (disk drives that were supposed to read both sides of a disk, but were reading only one side) said, "You know, when they came up with these drives, they figured it would take at least six months of testing to be sure they had it right. Rather than deprive the public of them for so long, they decided to release[3] them at once, and let the early customers do the testing for them."

Gee, that's great. I was a guinea pig and I didn't even know it. Here's a creative concept: how about an ethical marketing department saying, "We're looking for five hundred customers to try out our new Whatever for six months. We'll sell it to you at 30% off, and give you a year's free service for your help." Sounds great, but the Vice President for Ethics would be overruled by the Vice President for Marketing. "We can't do that, Larry. We know that three of our competitors are about to release similar products, and *they* aren't going to wait to get all the bugs out."[4]

Alas.

It isn't little back-alley companies that engage in this behavior. More than a few of the industry giants have indulged in this kind of marketing. The Apple Lisa and the IBM PC jr leap to mind as examples, along with more than a few now popular software programs that were less than wonderful in some earlier versions.

---

[3] "Release" is the word computer marketers use for putting things out on the marketplace, as if they are setting them free from cages.

[4] One refreshing exception was the Ashton-Tate company, that offered a word processing program called FullWrite by saying, in effect, "We're not quite ready, but if you buy our test version ['betaware' which is one step down from the presumably perfect 'alphaware'], we'll give you a free copy of the final version, as soon as it is on the market."

2. Plunging Prices

Computer prices have fallen quite incredibly since the days, a generation ago, when a million dollars bought a room-sized machine that literally was able to do less than a shirt-pocket-sized Hewlett-Packard 12C financial calculator. Computer people are fond of pointing out, and correctly, that if automobiles had followed the same performance versus price pattern as computers, we could now buy a 400-miles-per-gallon Rolls-Royce for 25 cents.

So even if you were convinced (or could somehow rationalize away your concerns) that a new product was genuinely bug-free, it might make good financial sense to wait at least a little while to see if the laws of the marketplace (competition; supply and demand; volume manufacture) will work to bring the price down quickly and dramatically.

The same argument applies equally to hardware and to software. In 1975, I paid about $7,500 for software that would store and manipulate a mailing list for my mail-order company. (It never worked very well. If David Sexton is reading this: Never mind, David; we gave it away years ago; all is forgiven, or at least forgotten). A few years later, I bought, for $750, off the shelf, a mailing list program that was more sophisticated than the first (and it worked a little better). Now I'm using a $200 program that is vastly more versatile than either of the first two. And there are some pretty good $50 programs available through mail-order discount houses as well.

Here's another way to look at this phenomenon. The first portable[5] computer made its appearance in 1980, and you would have had to work 900 hours at the minimum wage to buy one.[6] Within a year, there was a smaller, more sophisticated, more feature-laden portable, selling for about seven hundred hours of work. Today the so-called "laptops" or portable computers, with many more features, can be bought for less than two hundred hours of minimum wage work.

As autos boomed into a mass market, the Peerless, the Hupmobile . . . and many other early starters fell by the wayside. . . . Nothing is more uncertain than the early days of a giant market.

—Kathleen K. Wiegner

---

[5] That was the manufacturer's optimistic term. With battery pack, it weighed in at 56 pounds. The word "luggable" ["schleppable"] in some parts of the country] was more often applied than "portable."

[6] In order to avoid the confusion of comparing 1980 dollars with today's dollars, I have converted the prices to a more inflation-free standard: hours necessary to work at the minimum wage to buy the item. This is not the place to speculate on whether someone earning the minimum wage would be likely to buy a computer.

3. Improving Quality

As prices come down, very often the quality (sophistication, reliability, cleverness, speed) goes up, as competitors vie with each other for the share of the market carved out by the original innovation.

4. Disappearing Companies

What a blow it is to write or telephone the manufacturer of your computer or program, and learn that it no longer exists. But it does happen all the time, both with computer manufacturers (although not nearly as frequently as the turbulent mid-1980s, when computer manufacturers were failing at the rate of two or three every week!), and, more commonly, with software companies.

It is not just the little guys, like Akbar and Jeff's Computer Hut[7] that fold. Giants like RCA, Xerox, Exxon, AT&T, and Singer[8] all went into the small computer business and then went out of the small computer business.

Companies don't necessarily disappear because their products are poor or faulty. More often, it is their finances that are one or the other. Here is an all-too-typical scenario of events that actually happened a few years ago.

a. A small group of earnest technicians came up with a model of a slim briefcase-sized box, into which they had built a fairly sophisticated computer, a full-sized keyboard, a disk drive, a battery pack, a large illuminated screen, and a printer.

b. They hand-made a few dozen of these wonders, then rented space at a big national computer show, offering the computer at a price based on what they *hoped* to make them for, if they got thousands of orders before the money ran out.

c. The money ran out.

d. Those who bought one—the "first kids" on that block—are now like the legendary art collector who badgered Picasso for a little draw-

---

[7]Fictitious name used by Matt Groening. A real company would never be called this. There seems to be a rule that grandeur of a company name is inversely proportional to the size of the company. Wang and Digital and Tandy and Apple and IBM are billion-dollar companies, while the probability is high that International Cosmotronic Industries is run from someone's back bedroom.

[8]Real names.

ing one day on the beach at Cannes, whereupon Picasso took a stick and drew him a beautiful picture—in the sand, at low tide. They have something quite wonderful right now, but they know its days are numbered. When the tide comes in, when the first major repair is needed, they may have themselves a $3,000 bookend.

Relevant antiques.

5. The "But Wait!" Syndrome

Even though small computers are being sold by the millions, I am convinced that sales would be double or triple their present level were it not for the "But wait!" syndrome.

The number of people frozen into total immobility by the serpent-haired Medusa has nothing on the vast legions who are paralyzed each month upon picking up the latest issue of their favorite computer magazine.

Here is how it works—an actual case history, chosen from scores that I have observed:

A few years ago, my friend Bruce decided that he needed a small computer. Bruce is a writer, and thought he would like to use a word processing program. He is also an investor, and believed that a computer would be desirable for tracking stocks, performing various calculations, and perhaps doing his income taxes.

Bruce had pretty well decided to get a Macintosh 512, or possibly an IBM PC jr. As he was reflecting on the relative merits of these two systems, someone said to him,

"*But wait!* Apple is coming out with a 512E (for enhanced) computer in a few months, and it will be much more versatile than the plain old 512." Bruce waited.

Just about the time the 512E was coming into the stores, Bruce read an article that said, in effect,

"*But wait!* Radio Shack has just announced the Model 100, a really nifty battery-powered briefcase-sized computer with all kinds of software built right in." Bruce put off the writing project he was about to begin and waited. After all, it would be pointless to write a book on an old-fashioned typing machine.

Well the Radio Shack finally came out, and all Bruce had to do was walk into his local store and buy one. But the devil in disguise said to him,

"*But wait!* I know a man in Texas who can get it for you wholesale. You'll save $400." Bruce delayed starting his next novel one more time. The deal in Texas dragged on and on, and while it was dragging,

"*But wait!* Amiga is coming out with a computer that does everything the Apple and the Radio Shack can do, and it can do it in full living color." The Amiga finally appeared, only a little behind schedule, but the software was very limited, and the nearest dealer to Bruce was three counties away, and anyway,

"*But wait!* Apple is rumored to be coming out with the Macintosh Plus, which will render the 512E obsolete overnight."

And so it goes, and goes, and goes. Apple this. IBM that. Tandy the other. Rumors of crystal memories and bubble memories and there was that article about protein memories, and some major breakthrough in Czechoslovakia which will make *everything* obsolete, and prices are plunging and and and and and . . .

Poor Bruce. Five years have passed since he decided to buy his first computer. He actually sold his old IBM typewriter somewhere along the way, and he has not written a thing—except letters to computer companies asking when such-and-such a model, rumored to have been shown at the South Korean Computer Fest, will be available. It is painful to see Bruce bicycling home from the post office with his weekly fix of computer magazines, newspapers, and newsletters, ready to absorb information about at least a dozen new "But waits."

Reconciling the "Don't Be the First Kid" Advice with the "But Wait!" Advice

What, then, is the intelligent consumer to do? You definitely don't want to be the first kid on the block, nor do you want to be the last. It's one thing to be cautious; it's another to drive your horse and buggy down the interstate freeway.

There is a sensible path to be steered between "first-kid-ism" and the "But wait!" syndrome. Some guidelines:

• Wait. If you see something wonderful that you must have, but can live without for a short while, promise it to yourself in, say, 120 days—and during that time, watch the literature, talk to people who did buy one (users' groups and bulletin board services are excellent resources here), and try to get a feel for where it is going.

• Search for equivalents. The wonderful new "X" may be one company's answer to the more tried and proven "Y" that has been on the market long enough to get the early bugs out.

• Address the feeling, all too common, that there must be something wrong with a person who goes along with the pack. Save your uniqueness for the way you look, dress, invest, drive, etc. There is nothing wrong (and a lot that is right) with being Macintosh or IBM customer number ten million instead of International Cosmotronic customer number three.

• Rent. You can rent both hardware and software (see page 41). If something turns out to be horrendous, at least you can return it at the end of the month.

• Do not be frozen into immobility. If there are no alternatives to what you must have, then cross your fingers, knock on wood, offer up a prayer to St. Silicon, and go for it. One man required a program to deal with management of his stud farm. When he discovered stud farm management software from a small private developer, clearly one of a kind, his only choices were do it, or do nothing. He did it. A year later, he was moderately happy. He had survived many glitches and breakdowns, but he saw the horse at the end of the tunnel. A quite common outcome.

• Finally, and significantly, watch out for "vaporware." Vaporware is a product (software or hardware) that has been announced, but doesn't actually exist. In effect, a false "But wait!" report. All too common a marketing ploy is to announce an imminent arrival that is but a gleam in a designer's eye, to see how the marketplace will react. An announcement is sent to scores of newspapers and magazines. If extreme interest is shown, if switchboards are flooded with people wanting to place orders, then the company *might* consider going into production. If not, they will quietly abandon the whole idea, and the only memory of it will lie with the Bruces of the world who will go about telling their friends,

"*But wait!* I've heard that International Cosmotronics is just about to . . . "

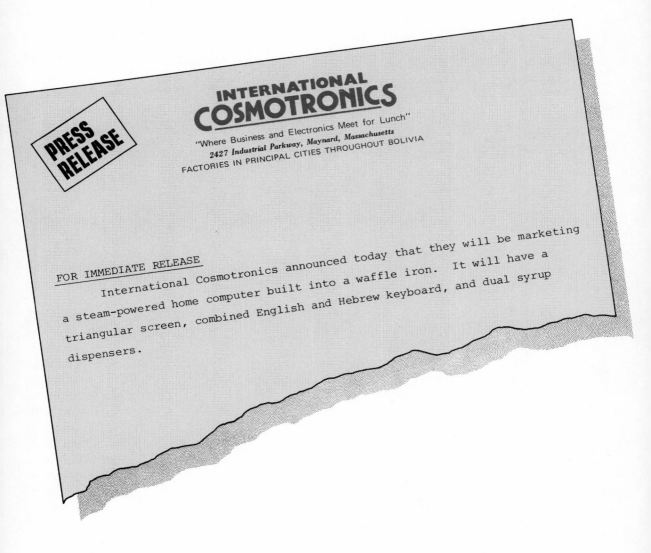

PRESS RELEASE

INTERNATIONAL COSMOTRONICS
"Where Business and Electronics Meet for Lunch"
2427 Industrial Parkway, Maynard, Massachusetts
FACTORIES IN PRINCIPAL CITIES THROUGHOUT BOLIVIA

FOR IMMEDIATE RELEASE
    International Cosmotronics announced today that they will be marketing a steam-powered home computer built into a waffle iron. It will have a triangular screen, combined English and Hebrew keyboard, and dual syrup dispensers.

PART IV

QUESTION:

Do I Buy the Hardware First,
the Software First, or
Do Something Else First?

For the first decade or so of the small computer era, the conventional wisdom declared that you should choose your software first, then find the hardware to run it. The reason for this was that on the one hand, there were half a dozen or more totally different and mutually incompatible kinds of computers, and on the other hand there was a relatively limited amount of software available.

Therefore, if you found the perfect software (to organize your stamp collection; to keep track of your political mailing list; to run your beauty salon or stud farm, whatever), you should have bought that first, and then you would have bought a computer that runs it.

Here's an analogy: some cars run on unleaded gas, others on leaded (but they work sort of OK on unleaded), some on diesel, some on propane, some on electricity. I once knew a man who lived in a remote part of Alaska, where the only fuel available was diesel. Obviously he had to buy a vehicle that matched the available fuel. A gasoline-powered Buick might have looked lovely in his driveway, but unless his mother mailed him buckets of unleaded from Seattle, he would have had nothing more than a two-ton windbreak.

But things have changed (with regard to computers, not necessarily Buicks). Three significant changes in the last ten years:

1. There are many fewer kinds of computers. There are still many brand names, but essentially only four major different kinds: Macintosh, IBM (and compatibles), Amiga, and Apple II (that's a "two" not an "aye-aye").

2. Even among the four kinds, there is increasing compatibility. Some Macintoshes can read IBM disks, and occasionally but not commonly vice versa. That sort of thing.

3. Most importantly, there is so much software out there that if something exists for the Macintosh, it (or something very much like it) almost certainly exists for the IBM and perhaps for the Apple II. There are still some exceptions, usually in the area of extreme specialization. The elaborate software for running a horse stud farm exists (I have been told) only in Macintosh format. A sophisticated program that assists in translating from Old Icelandic into English exists only in IBM format.

So if your main or only purpose in needing a computer is running a stud farm, you probably should get the Macintosh. If you are running an Old Icelandic stud farm, you may be in big trouble.

Thus the answer to the question of which comes first, the hardware chicken or the software egg, the answer in nearly all cases would be the hardware.

But (see the title of this section), there is something even more important that comes before buying either the hard or the software.

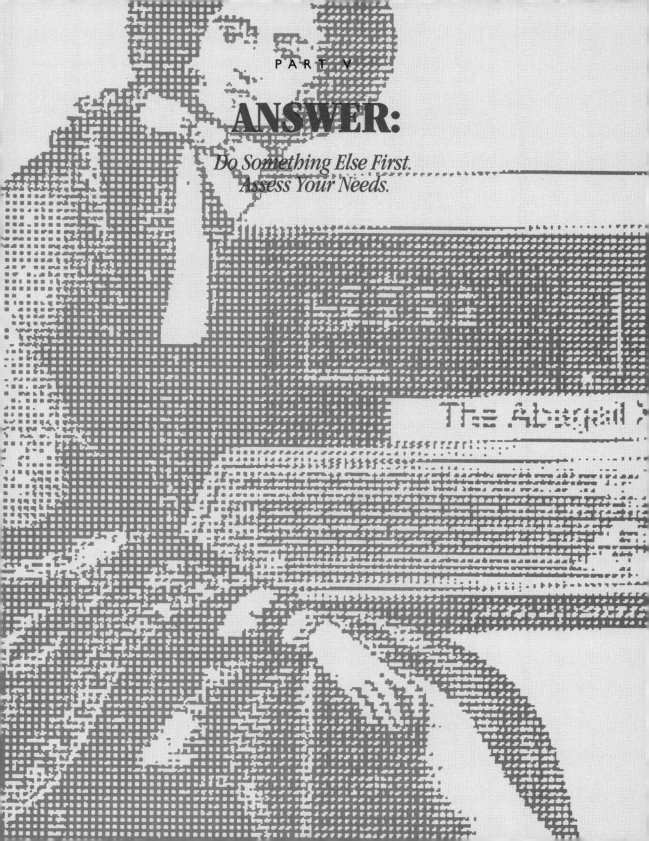

PART V

ANSWER:

Do Something Else First.
Assess Your Needs.

Before you decide what computer to buy, ask yourself the question that far too few people ask themselves at this stage: do I really need a computer at all? And if so, do I really need it sitting there on my desk or table, or are there other places it might sit (like in a service bureau two thousand miles away)?

Many of the needs for which people buy computers can be handled in other ways: either by alternative technology, or by using other people's computers. Consider, for instance, the seven major ways in which people use computers (which are discussed in some detail in the section on buying software, starting on page 103), and how those people without computers deal with the same matters.

COMPUTER USAGE	NO COMPUTER
Word processing	
Writing, editing, spelling check, grammar check; storing documents for later use, etc.	Typewriter; pencil with eraser, dictionary, thesaurus, file folders, secretary.
Data base	
Store lists of people and things; add and subtract names, print labels, etc.	3 x 5 cards, Rolodex, address book, filing cabinet with color-coded folders.
Spreadsheet	
Store and manipulate numerical data for accounting, business planning; loans, P&L forecasts.	Calculator. Lined paper and pencil with eraser. Dust off that old slide rule.
Graphics	
Drawing, drafting, page design and layout, illustration.	Ruler, pens, drafting table, white-out fluid, copier.
Communications	
Interacting with humans, other computers to send messages, retrieve data, etc.	Telephone, fax, postal service, public libraries.
Games	
Games on your own computer; interactive games with people or computers in other locations.	Monopoly. 20 Questions. Charades. Hide and go seek. Double crostics. Chess. Etc.

In response to my standard question, "How are you using your small computer," a Chicago businessman proudly told me that he was using his IBM PS/2 to keep track of his neckties. He could tell at a glance how many striped, patterned, and solid color ties he had, what they had cost, when they were last cleaned, and how often he had worn each one.

I dared to hope that he had found a few other uses for his thousands of dollars worth of machinery, but that was the one he wanted to talk to me about.

This kind of situation is extremely common. No, I don't mean cataloguing your garments. I mean the equivalent of using your 1938 Hispano-Suiza 12-cylinder touring car solely to go buy your morning newspaper. As *Time* magazine pointed out, "for many household operations . . . microcomputers are clearly inferior to simpler and less expensive devices. Like fingers."

Consider three simple examples of people who might have been (or were) better off by analyzing their needs, and then deciding not to buy a computer.

1. Educational trivia

An elementary school, already equipped with Apple II computers in the classrooms, purchased a not inexpensive geography learning program. It did little more than show a map on the screen and invite the student to identify the state or country and name its capital city. A $10 box of flash cards could have done as well.

There are many creative uses for what is called CAI, or computer-assisted instruction, but this is not one of them. The same tedious uncreative people who gave us tedious uncreative textbooks are now giving us tedious, uncreative computer programs.

As David Grady put it in an article entitled *A Hard Look at the World of Educational Computing,* "With a world full of good books to read, songs to sing, and pictures to paint, computer-based exercises should have to earn their way into the school day by delivering at least as much value as whatever they replace. . . . Sad to say . . . the replacement of existing tedium with the latest most up-to-date tedium is an activity as old as the schools themselves."

2. Personal finance

Many computer people tout the merits of using a computer to keep track of personal finance: accounting, bookkeeping, bills to pay, income tax data, and so forth. Indeed many people talk about this as one of the justifications for having a home computer, but not all that many actually do it. Perhaps they agree with *Money* magazine that "family finance programs generally either are unnecessarily complex or simply duplicate what you can do with a $30 calculator and a little patience. . . . Probably in less time than it takes to set up the budget program and tally monthly totals for income and expenses, you could do the same job with a calculator and a ledger."

James Fallows, writing in *Atlantic Monthly,* did the appropriate calculations: "At the end of the year, I load the income-tax program into the computer, push the button marked 'Run' and watch as my tax return is prepared. Since it took me only about six months to learn . . . I figure this approach will save me time [in eleven years]."

3. Inventory control

The *Wall Street Journal* reported on a clothing manufacturer who purchased a $10,000 computer system, "but he prefers to use clipboards to keep track of things. . . . The computer could track the inventory, but it is simpler and quicker to subtract each day's shipments from what's on hand to keep a continuous inventory account . . ." The *Journal* also describes how American automobile manufacturers have developed very expensive and sophisticated computer systems for keeping track of inventories of parts in warehouses all over the country. Japanese auto manufacturers, on the other hand, build their parts factories right next door to their car factories, thereby eliminating not only the need to keep track of inventories, but even the need for inventories themselves.

The Abagail XZ-2700

Alternatives to Buying a Computer

Once we lived in a fancy Chicago suburb. Every Saturday morning a certain ritual began. As far as the eye could see, up and down the streets, similarly-attired men went to their garages, fired up their power lawn mowers, and spent the next 15 minutes trimming their one-eighth of an acre of grass.

The thought often occurred to me as I played my role in this pageant, that I was looking at thousands of dollars worth of lawn mowers on my street alone. What if some enterprising soul had gone 'round to all the houses and said, "Why don't 50 of us chip in $20 each and we'll buy one really good professional quality mower that each of us can use a few minutes a week. We can sell the lawn mowers we have now and donate thousands of tax-deductible dollars to worthy charities."

While such a mower entrepreneur may well have been accused of latent socialism and banished from the neighborhood, the philosophy makes sense, and is often applied in the computer industry. With that in mind, let us look at five alternatives to buying and using a computer.

1. Renting or leasing a computer

This is the least risky and most thorough way to find out if you really want to enlist in the computer revolution, such as it is. In most larger and some smaller cities, there are companies that rent small computers, printers, and other equipment on a month-to-month basis, often with only a one or two month minimum. Even though you may be paying between 5% and 10% of the cost of the equipment each month, renting gives you an unparalleled opportunity to find out, on your own premises and with your own data and your own needs, whether you wish to computerize at all, and if so, whether this particular equipment is good for you.

Some rental companies will apply a percentage (often 50%) of rental fees to the purchase price, should you decide to buy that which you are renting.

Some rental companies provide software along with the hardware. If not, there are some mail-order software rental companies you can deal with; they generally advertise in the back of computer magazines.

2. Renting a chair

The chair should be one that sits in front of someone *else's* computer. There are commercial by-the-hour rental services, often in copy shops and sometimes connected with computer stores or service bureaus. The going rate is roughly one percent of the value of the computer for three or four hours of time, typically five to fifteen dollars an hour for the computer and use of a wide array of available software.

The chair could also be in front of a computer of a friend or business associate. Most businesses are closed more than three-fourths of the time (128 of the 168 hours in a week). More than a few people have written me that they made arrangements with a local business to come in after hours or on weekends and use a computer, for an hourly or weekly fee.

3. Time-sharing

Think of it this way. Suppose you wanted to own 50,000 books for your business and pleasure reading. The cost is out of the question, so you get thousands of your neighbors to go in with you for a few dollars a year. You buy a building, and fill it with books, to which you and your neighbors have access whenever you want. You might call it "The Public Library." By pooling your resources, all of you can have something that none can afford alone.

The same thing works with computers, both hardware and software. You would like to work on a $50,000 machine—so you and lots of others all agree to pay an hourly or monthly fee, and the money collected enables an entrepreneur to buy the big machine and make it available to all of you.

"Available" means that you buy (or rent) some very simple and modest equipment, which lets you interact with the big machine over the telephone lines.

There are hundreds of publicly-available services, to whom you can pay an hourly, monthly, or per-item fee, for the privilege of making their huge computer, and all that it contains, a part of your simple, inexpensive home or office equipment.

Some of these services are highly specialized, containing only information on real estate investing, or the entire contents of *The New York Times* back to the year one. Names and addresses of all gynecologists. Airline schedules. Tax preparation information and programs you can use to prepare your own taxes with their information.

Is it better to time-share, or to buy your own equipment or software? There is no simple answer. You will find advocates of both—and of doing some of each. Using other people's hardware or software certainly increases your repertoire of available programs. Your start-up costs are lower, although you may end up, over the years, for instance, spending $7 an hour for a hundred hours' use of a general ledger program that costs $350 to buy for your own.

In older times (the 1980s), there were often problems in the accuracy of data transmission, due to the vagaries of the phone lines. You are still at the mercy of the telephone companies and your own "modem" device that connects your computer into the phone lines, although things keep improving technically (a hardware circuitry known as MNP is said to be 100% error free). You may suffer in terms of loss of privacy (see page 232) and you may risk damage from computer viruses (see page 178).

4. Let someone else do it

Hanging on the wall at the famous little advertising agency that gave me my first real job were the agency's three mottoes. One of them was "Never do anything that someone else can do better."[9] This philosophy is especially important for people considering computerizing their lives or their businesses. There is something psychologically satisfying about having all your possessions within arm's length, as it were, instead of worrying about your precious words and numbers stored in someone *else's* computer, perhaps thousands of miles away.

Please Patronize
LES & DICK'S
COMPUTER
SERVICE BUREAU
★ ★ ★ ★ ★ ★ ★
PROMPT
ACCURATE
FRIENDLY

Also, some people find it very difficult to delegate responsibilities, and they fear that some hired hand can never treat their data with as much loving care as they would.

Still, many people use computer service bureaus, either instead of or in addition to their own computer. Service bureaus do the computer work for you. They type your words and numbers into their machines, using their personnel. Then they crank up their computers and supply you with your payroll, your reports, your mailing labels, etc.

You have none of the fears of machines failing (most bureaus have backup equipment; this is a question to ask when screening them). It is like taking your clothes into a Laundry Service Bureau: you don't really care what equipment they use, who does the work, or what brand of soap has been selected. You just want your clothes back nice and clean.

5. Don't buy one at all

As indicated earlier, one of the serious options to consider as an alternative to buying a computer is not to computerize your life at all. It is surprising how many people fail to consider this option.

---

[9] The other two mottoes probably also have relevance for some computer enthusiasts: One was "Anything worth doing is worth overdoing." The third, espousing the philosophy that there are some things that are so perfect, one should never tamper with them in an attempt to improve them, was "Don't put raisins in the matzohs."

PART VI

BUYING HARDWARE

OK, so you have probably decided to go ahead with this madness and buy one. Now you have only four major decision areas left:

1. What should I buy: IBM, Macintosh, or something else?
2. Are there factors other than the computer itself that I should take into account?
3. Which model; which bells and whistles should be added?
4. Do I buy in a retail store, by mail-order, or in another manner?

Since this is (or could be) a really big deal, considerable time and attention will be spent on each of these four matters.

After growing wildly for years, the field of computing now appears to be approaching its infancy.

—Opening line, President's Science Advisory Committee on Computers, 1967

IBM, Macintosh, or Something Else?

Embracing a computer is not unlike embracing a religion. People who have already made their choice cannot imagine why anyone in their right mind would choose anything else. So listen to your IBM zealots and your Macintosh zealots and even, if you know any, to your Amiga, Atari, Commodore, and Illyushin Motorized Slide Rule advocates. Listen politely, and try to determine if they are familiar with other brands, or if they have been sitting there with blinders on, as the world went trotting by.

Here is a brief history of how we got to where we are.

The first widely distributed small computer was the Apple II, that miracle that emerged in the late 1970s from the garage of two young men in northern California.

A few years later, International Business Machines looked down from Olympus on this little upstart machine, decided there was a market worth pursuing, and launched the IBM PC (for Personal Computer).

There was a significant difference in marketing philosophy between Apple and IBM.

Essentially, Apple said, "No one can copy our operating system. If anyone else tries to make a machine comparable to the Apple, they can expect a phalanx of lawyers on their doorstep within hours."

IBM, on the other hand, said, "Here we are, world. You can imitate us, duplicate us, replicate us. You can build machines that look like IBMs, sound like IBMs, run like IBMs, and we will rejoice, because we believe that the more IBM-like machines there are out there, the more likely it is that IBM will become the business standard."

Thus the word "clone" entered the computer lexicon.[10] An *IBM clone* is some other manufacturer's product that behaves pretty much, or exactly, like an IBM. An *Apple clone* is nonexistent. To be sure, some companies tried, in Brazil, in Taiwan, even in New Jersey, but Apple was true to its word, and its lawyers fanned out across the planet, briefcases full of injunctions and cease-and-desist orders.

Literally hundreds of other companies joined the fray, all but a few in the IBM clone direction. For a very confusing and complicated few years in the early 1980s, there was some doubt as to whether we would end up with one standard, two, three, four, or many. It was as if

Grant, O God, that we may always be right, for thou knowest we will never change our minds.

—Old Scottish prayer

---

[10]But the first clones came much earlier. Pascal apparently built and marketed a little calculating engine, gears and levers and all, called the Pascaline. It was so popular and so much coveted that others built nearly identical ones, some even giving the public what they *really* wanted: a fancy case with nothing inside, at a reduced price.

each of a dozen record companies was pushing for the 33 rpm standard, the 37 rpm, the 45 rpm, the 53, and so on. In a five to seven year span, companies like Osborne, Timex, Sinclair, Kay-Pro, Attaché, Epson, Franklin, Cromemco, Casio, Seiko, Jonos, Otrona, and dozens of others, came and, for the most part, went.

Flushed with the success of the Apple II, Apple labored mightily and gave birth to two stillborns in a row, the ill-fated behemoth Apple III (this one could have been pronounced oy-yoy-yoy), and the almost-there-but-not-quite Apple Lisa. The Lisa was like a soft drink called Six-Up or a car named the Ford Palomino. Close, but no cigar.

Relatively fast learners, the Apple company took all that was good and creative and innovative about the Lisa, threw out much that was bad, and packaged it into a little cubical box called the Macintosh.

The Macintosh was slow to be accepted by the traditional business world, but when one of the biggest accounting firms bought 10,000 of them and the Air Force bought 20,000 of them, others began to take notice. IBM (or at least its stockholders) could not fail to have noticed that in 1990, for the first time, more Macintoshes were sold than IBMs. (Of course vast numbers of IBM clones were sold as well, and, because Apple was sticking to its guns, zero Macintosh clones were sold). Then, in the summer of 1991, Apple and IBM jointly announced that in the future, there would be more compatibility between their products.

And so, as we march toward the Third Millennium, we find that the seers of SRI (Stanford Research Institute) may well have been right, in the early '80s, when they predicted that three of the then hundreds of computer companies would be dominant: IBM, Apple, and Sony. (Although Sony's computers faltered by the wayside, they hold the basic patents on the 3-inch plastic-encased disk that has become the industry standard, so they are doing quite well, thank you.)

We have the Macintosh (and still the Apple II, clinging on by its fingernails, the Old Beloved Warhorse We Cannot Put Out to Pasture; it is used mostly in elementary and some secondary schools).

We have the IBM, and a dozen or more major competitors making IBM-compatible computers. Compaq is among the largest, along with Tandy (formerly Radio Shack), NEC, Dell, ZEOS, Everex, Epson, Packard Bell, Hyundai, Toshiba, Mitsubishi, and roughly 230 others.

And we have a few major companies who make machines that are essentially incompatible with either IBM or Macintosh; ones that sell quite well in Europe and elsewhere, but not all that well (except as game-playing tools) in North America. Amiga and Atari are foremost in this category.

For virtually all buyers, then, the choice comes down to Macintosh versus IBM (or IBM-compatible). And this is where we get to "computers as religion." You would not ask the Pope whether it is better to be

Recommending the right computer is a little like recommending the "right" religion. People tend to like the system they've ended up with. The most important point about computers, more so than about religions, is that the difference between a good one and a bad one is tiny compared with the difference between having one and not.

—James Fallows

a Catholic or a Jew. (You probably would not ask the Pope about IBM versus Macintosh either, for while he is apparently able to type, it is believed he has not entered the computer age.)

The main reason for Macintosh's rise to fame and glory was that it was much easier to learn to use. The most telling bit of evidence I have ever seen on which one to buy was a fairly extensive survey done around 1990.

This survey determined that the average IBM (or compatible) user was familiar with two or three major programs (such as writing and accounting), while the average Macintosh user was familiar with eight or nine major programs (writing, accounting, list management, drawing, poster making, menu planning, etc.)

The second most telling bit of evidence is to offer an example of what happens when you insert a disk that has not been initialized into the computer. (Computers need to format a disk in certain ways: add electronic signals to it, before it can be used.)

When you insert an unformatted disk into an IBM, you get a screen message saying that this disk cannot be used, but it does not tell you why. To format the disk, you must type the following: "Format b: /n:9/ T:80."

When you insert an unformatted disk into a Macintosh, you get a screen message saying that this is not a formatted disk, and do you want to format it? If you say yes, the job is automatically done for you.

When you are asked to name a file in an IBM computer, you get 8 letters, a dot, and three more letters. Your Christmas letter to Aunt Helene might thus be called LTRANTHL.XMS. Your checking account data might be CHKACT92.BKP.

When you are asked to name a file in a Macintosh computer, you get 31 letters and numbers, and the luxury of spaces. In the above instances, your files could be named "Christmas Letter to Aunt Helene" and "Checking Account Data for 1992."

While IBM plodded stodgily along, an independent company, Microsoft, run by the world's youngest billionaire, came up with some ingenious software, called Windows, that had the salubrious effect of making an IBM run pretty much—not quite, not exactly, but pretty much like a Macintosh. And that one invention, Windows, seems to be enough to lift IBM (and the compatibles) out of the doldrums, and put it back in the race with Macintosh.

It is as if an independent supplier came up with an inexpensive replacement engine, transmission, and body for the Yugo, which made it look and run not unlike a Porsche. Not quite, but a heck of a lot better than it was before.

What it really comes down to then are factors other than the computer itself. As long as you heed the "Don't be the first kid on the block . . . " advice offered earlier, you really can't go wrong with either choice. They are by no means completely interchangeable (although I would bet we will see that day before too long), but there is very little one can do that the other cannot.

It is time, then, to pay attention to the other factors that will affect your buying decision.

What Other Factors Do I Take into Account?

1. Power limits

Elevators generally have notices in them giving their maximum capacity. Of course this doesn't mean the elevator will plunge to earth if it goes one pound over the limit—but I would not be overjoyed to be a passenger in an elevator near its limit if a 350-pound person was about to leap on.

Whether it is airplanes, kitchen mixers, lawn mowers, or computers, machinery is less reliable and more likely to fail or cause other problems when operating at or near the limits of its specifications. With computers, the problems are generally those of either power or speed.

Power of the computer

Theoretically there is no upper limit to the number of peripherals, or additional things, that can be hooked into even a small home computer. Many computers have "slots" into which can be plugged the additional electronics needed to run a hard disk drive (or two or six), several printers, monitors, scanners, voice synthesizers, and so forth.

This is similar to plugging more and more appliances into the same wall socket. They will all work up to a point. They may all work at reduced power or efficiency. Then they may all fail at once.

Some manufacturers make devices which make it easier to overload the system. These electronic equivalents of the extension cord permit even more extra units to be plugged into the computer than the manufacturer intended. For instance, my old Macintosh Plus had all its slots filled: hard disk, printer, telephone modem, mouse. I wished to add on an external big-screen monitor. One manufacturer figured out an ingenious way to build an extra jack into a hole in the rear of the Macintosh which Apple thoughtfully provided to pass a security cable through, to tie the computer down (presumably in an insecure office or a high wind). The good news is that I was able to add this splendid big screen. The bad news is that my computer suffered a major power failure a month later. Was it caused by "tampering" with the basics? Some experts would say yes, others no. It is hard to know what to do when experts disagree. San Francisco has been wrestling with this problem for 30 years, with regard to building a second deck on the

> It is said that one machine can do the work of fifty ordinary men. No machine, however, can do the work of one extraordinary man.
>
> —Elbert Hubbard

Golden Gate Bridge. For every structural engineer that says yea, the opponents come up with an equally well-credentialed one who says nay. What's a fella to do?

The two things to do are this:

1. Anticipate, to the extent possible, all the things you may be running with your computer and buy with that in mind. (Overloading the computer may actually void the warranty).

2. Acknowledge that the more you add on, the more heat will be generated, so a good cooling fan (which may or may not be a part of the original equipment) is a wise investment.

Power in your plugs

In North America, computers, along with most other electrical objects, require 120 volts of power, courtesy of your friendly neighborhood electrical utility. The problem is that electricity is not quite so constant as we might wish. One moment you may be getting 120 volts, another 117, and when everyone in that condo down the road turns on their air conditioning at the same moment, you may drop to 90 or 95, or indeed at times to zero.

These so-called brownouts or even blackouts generally cannot damage a computer, but they can play havoc with the files or data you are working with at the time it happens.

The more serious problem, albeit very rare, is that of power surges. Whether due to lightning or problems at the power station, a great surge of power can come coursing over your lines. It may last only a fraction of a second, but that can be enough to cause permanent damage to your computer or any peripherals plugged into it.

Some people believe that surge protectors—special boxes into which you plug your computer, and which in turn are plugged into the wall—may protect you from these problems. But there are also intelligent, serious computer experts who believe that most surge protectors are of little or no use; only those with sophisticated (and more expensive) circuitry can do the job. Everyone agrees it is sensible to unplug your computers during an electrical storm.

You may wish to consider these factors if you live in an area subject to brownouts or blackouts. If you are concerned about surges, some power companies will temporarily install, on your line, a device that measures surges. If there is a problem, the most common solutions (other than moving) are:

• using battery-powered computers (the so-called laptops, which typically work from batteries or by plugging in, are fast becoming the most popular kind of small computer sold);

• using sophisticated surge protectors;

• using devices powered by storage batteries that provide an even level of power, not too low or not too high, no matter what is coming over the lines from the power station. They are constantly recharged by the volts arriving from the electric company. They have the advantage of keeping all your equipment going, even during a blackout, for long enough for you to close everything down without losing data (5 to 10 minutes is common).

Speed

Different models of computers operate at very different speeds, and there is not always consistency in the way this happens. One computer may take forever to sort a list of 10,000 names into alphabetical order, but run a spelling check on a 200-page novel in a matter of minutes. Another may do just the opposite. Speed is often a combination of the workings of the computer itself and the cleverness of the software it is running. Computer magazines will often do "bench tests" in which they will have 10 or more different computers doing the same exercise with the same software. The results are often extremely varied: for what machine A does in 30 seconds, machine B takes 12 minutes; that sort of thing.

Sometimes excessive speed doesn't help, and may even hurt.

There are ways of adding on to a computer to make it run faster in certain contexts: "accelerator cards" and additional internal memory that can be plugged in.

There is (as with most things) no one single answer best for everyone, but speed is a factor to take into account when shopping around or talking things over with your local or telephone sales counselor.

2. Ergonomics

Ergonomics has to do with how human and machine and environment interact. Four of the relevant factors to consider here are size, climate, power grid, and lizard droppings.

Size

I once wrote at length with the admonition never to buy anything you couldn't lift. I had more than a few dismal experiences staggering up flights of stairs to a repair depot with an 80-pound object in tow. But this was back in the days when there were no "desktop" computers; most were desk-sized themselves, thus, presumably, "floortops."

Size is really only a factor if a computer is to be installed in quite a small space, and/or moved a good deal, since, as I maintain elsewhere, computers are actually more fragile than most manufacturers would like you to know. It is best if you do not move a medium-sized desktop unit (20, 30, 40 pounds) about regularly, either from table to floor because that is also your dining table, or from home to office.

Some repair people have told me that it is sometimes the very *smallness* of a computer that results in behaviors causing damage. People are used to swinging their briefcases or attaché cases around, setting them down without great care, and lobbing them onto airplane luggage racks or into car trunks. You just can't do that with a small computer and expect its disk drives to remain aligned and its soldered joints to hang together.

Regarding so-called portables (now happily down from their earlier 30-pound weight to less than half that), here is a rule of thumb I have just made up: Never plan to carry anything that weighs 10% or more of what *you* weigh for a distance greater than 100 meters. Having once carried a "laptop" from the check-in counter at O'Hare Airport, Chicago, to a gate so distant I believe I walked halfway to my destination of Cedar Rapids, I believe to this day that as a direct result one arm is an inch longer than the other.

Climate and lizard droppings

In the early days of computers, they used to be installed in special climate-controlled air-conditioned dehumidified rooms, with elevated static-free floors. And the sad news is that they still should be. But no one is going to put in tens of thousands of dollars worth of remodeling to house a $2,000 machine.

Heat and humidity are the twin enemies of computers. I know whereof I speak. Indeed as I type these words, I am living in what is by a wide margin, the rainiest city in the United States (over two hundred inches last year), and one of the hottest to boot. When one of my computers failed a few months ago, it was devastating to view its internals at the repair depot. It reminded me of those horror pictures of tobacco-scarred lungs that one sees from time to time in antismoking articles. How could my nice shiny little tan box look so hideous inside: rust, corrosion, grime so thick you could scratch a novel in it.

Reluctantly, but necessarily, within hours, I ordered air conditioning for my office. The dehumidifier comes next. Well, actually moving to a more sensible climate comes next, but that's another story entirely.

Oh, and about lizard droppings: That happens to be a problem I have. Gecko lizards, fresh from bombardier class, scoot across the ceiling, aiming their droppings with remarkable accuracy into my keyboard and printer. Of course I have gotten plastic covers (for the computer, not the geckoes), but let this serve as a reminder that the most unexpected environmental factors may be worth taking into account. Remember that the original "bug" in a computer was, in fact, a moth that shorted out a giant computer in Washington.[11] Had it been a creature of a different kind, we presumably would be referring to "worms" or "mongooses" or "Republicans" in our computers.

---

[11] The actual insect was carefully preserved by its discoverer, Admiral Grace Hopper, who showed it to the press some 40 years later.

Comfort

Getting accustomed to a computer is very much like buying shoes. A pair that feels fine in the store may be causing great miseries a few weeks later. Or a borderline pair that you bought anyway because they were on sale may evolve, with time, into your most beloved and comfortable footwear.

There are three kinds of comfort that are important for me in using a computer:

1. *The keyboard.* "Keyboard action" is an extremely personal thing. People talk about the "great feel" of a certain keyboard: the "action," the "response," etc. All that can really be said is that keyboard action differs greatly from brand to brand, and if you are going to be typing a lot, you will want to spend as much time trying it out as possible.

Many people feel that the demise of IBM's highly-touted bottom of the line computer, the PC jr. (commonly known as the Peanut) was accelerated by a keyboard that neither humans nor orangutans (surely they must have tested it on someone) found tolerable.

2. *The screen.* You will spend a great deal of time staring at the "TV" screen, or monitor. (Safety considerations are discussed on page 216; the concern here is with comfort only.) Is it big enough? What about full-color versus two-color? And among two-color screens, there are those with white letters on a black background, black letters on a white background, orange on black, green on black, etc. Some screens have nonglare glass or filters.

Does the screen show all the work? Or does it act like a window on the work, in which you can see, for instance, only the top half (or top 8 or 12 lines) of a page, and you must "scroll" up and down, using keyboard commands, to see the rest of your page? Some people don't mind this (they are known as "Macintosh owners"[12]); others find it a nuisance.

3. *Sitting down.* I continue to be baffled by the extremely common practice in which people spend thousands of dollars for equipment at which they will be sitting for literally thousands of hours (if it and they survive), and then they end up doing that sitting on a cast-off dining room chair, a thrift shop wonder, or some other object condemned by the American Spine Protection League. This is one case where an extra $100 to $200 for a good chair can immeasurably increase the pleasure (or, more accurately, greatly decrease the pain) you will get from your computer.

---

[12]Now only the least expensive Macintoshes have small screens, and even with those, one can buy a full-page- or even a two-full-page-sized add-on monitor.

3. Buying something that duplicates something else

In the complex and convoluted process of trying to decide which computer and which software to buy, an important consideration—some would say the most important—is to buy stuff that is a duplicate of stuff that is available to you. This means, for instance, buying for home what you already have in the office; or buying for the office what others in your building have. That sort of thing. There are four good reasons for this:

1. *Pretesting.* If you can use the actual programs on the actual machine for a significant period of time—not the few minutes generally available in the computer store, or the zero minutes available by mail-order—you will have a much better idea of whether they are right for you.

2. *Office in the home; home in the office.* For many, it is a great convenience to be able to continue a project at home (or the office) that was begun in the office (or at home).

3. *Diagnostics.* If you have access to an identical system, when problems arise, you can substitute each component into the duplicate system to see if it works.

For example, once when nothing was working right, all I knew was that I had a problem with (a) my computer, (b) my disk drive, (c) my printer, or (d) my software. Because we had two identical systems in the office, we set them side by side, and substituted parts one at a time. Often this works; in this instance it didn't, until we made the clever discovery that we hadn't substituted (e) the cable connecting the computer with the printer, and there, indeed, was the problem—solved promptly with a few dollars worth of wire, instead of a long delay and perhaps a big repair bill.

Of course it will do you little good to have the same machine as your neighbor, should she sell it, die, move away, or refuse to cooperate because you sawed off the limb of her avocado tree that was encroaching on your backyard. Fortunately, there is good diagnostic software, available for "industry standard" machines such as IBMs running software known as MS-DOS (the most popular sort).

4. *A backup machine.* Ultimately, a breakdown will occur which will mean you may be without your equipment for a few days or more. At such times, it is highly reassuring to have access to a backup machine. It may simply be a duplicate in the same office, or it may be an arrangement with a nearby user of the same general equipment. Not many enthusiasts use their computers all 168 hours of the week, so even if it means coming in nights or weekends to use the duplicate, at least you will get your necessary work (or necessary games) done.

4. Tryout time available

Many years ago, I was in charge of marketing for the world's first water bed company. We found a great deal of sales resistance. Most people were fascinated by the concept, but after a bounce or two, followed by a smirk or two, the typical customer said, "Thank you very much; I'll think it over," and was never seen again.

At the other end of the scale, and equally a problem, were those people who *did* buy one after the two-bounce test, and then returned sadly or angrily a few days later, to report that they simply couldn't sleep (or do whatever else they had expected to do) on their water bed.

The obvious answer (we eventually came to realize) was that there are some things in life that require more than a two-bounce test. (Our solution, which may be the reason you can find water beds today in Sears, Macy's, and other formerly-sneering retail stores, was (a) to install as many water beds as possible in hotels and motels, and (b) to offer a 30-day free home trial).

There are close parallels between small computers and water beds. Not many people report that their sleep or their love life improves after buying a computer (quite the contrary in a distressing number of cases). But they share the problem of not having enough time to try it out in the store.

Will a computer, or a new piece of software, do what you want it to do, in your home, your business, your life? Buying computer products on the basis of reviews, hearsay, and the manufacturer's literature is very much like going to a movie on the basis of reviews. Sometimes you will be delighted; sometimes you will be extremely disappointed. But if you don't like the movie, you can walk out, and you are out only a few dollars and a few hours of your life. An unhappy computer experience can multiply both figures by a factor of hundreds, even thousands.

Realistically, you cannot expect to sit in a computer store for many hours, entering data, to see how a computer performs in ways you will actually use, rather than in flashy demonstration programs prepared by the manufacturers to show things off at their best. Nor can you know what it will feel like sitting at that particular keyboard staring at that particular screen for hours, even days on end.

Some defects can be seen during a short demonstration. I was once checking out a mailing list program in a store, and it was immediately clear that this program did not allow for nine-digit zip codes. I could reject it at once.

Other defects may take months to become apparent. The mailing list program I *did* get worked absolutely fine when there were only a few hundred records that needed to be sorted into zip-code order. But when I got up above 5,000 names, sorting took an impossibly long time: something that another program might have done five or ten times as fast.

There is no one best solution to this problem, but it can be minimized in one of the following ways:

1. *Homework.* Learn all you can about any given hardware before you visit a dealer or talk to a mail-order company. Read reviews in the various computer magazines. Many of them rate products, the way *Consumer Reports* does with cars and canned asparagus. Ask the dealer for the names of other local individuals or businesses who are using similar equipment, and talk to them.

2. *Renting hardware or software.* As mentioned earlier, there are companies that rent both computers and software on a short-term (as little as one month) basis. Some dealers rent, with a portion of the rental applied to purchase.

3. *Ask for return privileges.* No, it is not common, but yes, it is done. If you can honestly persuade a dealer that you almost certainly want this equipment, but need to put it to a longer test, you may be able to work out a deal enabling you to return it, for any reason, within a month. People who have told me they have done this typically agreed to a 10% "restocking" fee for returned equipment. No harm in asking.

Bells and Whistles

Back to the faithful car analogy one more time. Even after you decide to buy a certain brand of car, you still have many decisions facing you: color, engine size, number of doors, air conditioning, radio, and so on. So it is with a computer. There are two kinds of decision areas: the "Yes, but what kind?" and the "Yes or no?"[13]

The "Yes, but what kind?" category includes, among other things,

- the amount of memory,
- the kind of disk storage,
- the kind of printer
- the kind of keyboard
- the kind of monitor

The "Yes or no?" category includes, among other things,

- do I want a modem?
- do I want a mouse?
- do I want a scanner?
- do I want a CD player?
- do I want to chuck it all in and go live in a monastery in Tibet?

Let's look at the various aspects of these decision situations.

Amount of memory

One of the more important variables in selecting a small computer is the amount of memory it has built in. I have heard apparently intelligent and undoubtedly humorless salespeople in computer stores say to sincere but clearly unknowledgeable potential customers, right off the bat, "How many 'K' of RAM did you have in mind?" This is akin to asking the little old lady who wanders into the new car showroom how many cubic centimeters of cylinder displacement she requires in her new sedan.

All computers have built-in memory of some sort. The memory is the place where the computer remembers, electronically and *temporarily*, what you have typed into it, or otherwise fed into it. "*Temporar-*

---

[13]It can be argued that there is a third category, "Yes, and what else?" Just as one car manufacturer used to list the rear seat as an "optional extra" in order to keep the base price of the car down, there are likely to be additional bits and pieces of hardware not figured into the original price, but which are either essential (like cables and jacks) or desirable (like fans and multiple outlet boxes).

Bubble memory is one of the new technologies now showing up in some small computers. This photomicrograph, magnified at least 4x, helps explain how it works.

ily" means that when you turn the computer off, the memory disappears, just as the picture on a television screen disappears when the power is turned off. And just as you can save television pictures forever on a videotape, so can you, if you wish, save the contents of your computer memory on a disk.

This temporary memory is generally called RAM, which stands for Random Access Memory.[14]

The amount of memory in a computer is measured by the number of characters (letters, numbers, symbols) it can hold. Since computers wouldn't be as mysterious or special if they didn't have their own words for everything, each character is called a "byte."[15] From metric usage, the prefix "kilo" means 1,000, and so a "kilobyte" means 1,000[16]

---

[14] Computer people talk about the "RAM and ROM" of a computer. You really don't need to know or worry about ROM, the "Read Only Memory" which is the permanent, unchangeable memory built into the computer, storing the permanent instructions that tell it how to operate.

[15] Another word you do *not* need to know, but which keeps cropping up in books and discussions about computers, is "bit." A bit is one of the electronic units that makes, in effect, a part of each given letter, number, or symbol. It always takes eight of these electronic signals to identify a complete letter or number. Hence eight bits equal one byte. Now forget this.

[16] Actually, to computer people, but to no one else in the world, a "kilo," which should be 1,000, is actually 1,024. Thus "16K" is *not* 16,000 but actually 16,384 bytes. Don't worry about this; it makes no difference to you.

bytes: 1,000 letters or numbers. "Kilobyte" is usually abbreviated as "K" as in "This file is 16K long" meaning it has about 16,000 letters or numbers in it, roughly 5,000 words.

The prefix "mega" means a million, so a *megabyte* is about one million characters, or about 200,000 words, or about the length of a James Michener novel.

There are two kinds of things to consider when it comes time to worry about what size RAM, or memory, to get with your computer: necessity and convenience. While important, the RAM decision is not utterly crucial, because it is relatively easy to add additional RAM to a computer after it has been purchased.

Necessity

The programs necessary to make your computer do things are also made up of letters, numbers, and symbols. A simple program, perhaps to calculate a mortgage payment or play a game of hangman with you, might require only a few thousand characters, or bytes. A typical word processing program or bookkeeping program might require several hundred thousand bytes, and more than a few graphics, page layout, and other complex programs need a million bytes (a megabyte) or more.

These programs are permanently stored, either on removable floppy disks (which hold roughly one megabyte), or on a hard disk (which can hold 100 megabytes or more). When you want to use them, the computer electronically transfers the programs from the floppy or hard disk into its RAM memory—*if there is room*. If your RAM can hold 1,000,000 bytes, there clearly is no way you can transfer in a program containing 1,100,000 bytes.

This concept, the difference between RAM memory and disk memory, is so often misunderstood, let me say it one more time, in a different way.

Let us say you have a briefcase that can hold 10 books. That is the equivalent of your changeable RAM memory. And let us say you have a bookcase at home that holds 1,000 books. That is the equivalent of your permanent disk storage. When you leave home in the morning, you can take 10 and only 10 books with you in that briefcase. That is your temporary storage capacity. No matter if your bookcase at home can hold 1,000 books or a million, your temporary operating capacity is 10.

So it is with the computer. If your RAM briefcase can hold one megabyte, it matters not whether you have one or 10 or 1000 megabytes of programs stored in your hard disk bookcase, you can only use one megabyte at a time.

The most important consideration, then, is whether the computer has at least as much RAM memory as that required by the largest program you are likely to run. Some programs are clever enough to load a part of themselves into the RAM memory, then, when needed, unload some of itself and reload other parts, so that, for instance, a one megabyte (one MB) program may only require half a megabyte (500K) of RAM. How can you possibly know? All competently marketed products will state their RAM requirements, usually on the outside of the box.

How much RAM memory do you need? The only possible answer is: More than the minimum required by whatever software you may wish to use. The cost of additional memory keeps dropping. At this writing, it is roughly $50 for each additional megabyte. There are limits to how much additional memory you can add to the RAM of a computer. Older Macintoshes, for instance, came with as little as 512K, but could be upgraded to as much as four megabytes. Newer models can go higher.

Keep in mind, also, the concept of multitasking: of keeping more than one program open (in the active RAM memory) at the same time, so you can switch back and forth instantly between, say, your accounting program and your writing program. Keeping a 500K and an 800K program open simultaneously requires 500 + 800 = 1.3 megabytes of RAM.

Suggesting a precise number is the surest way to make this book obsolete before its time. In 1983, to my lasting embarrassment, I wrote that one MB was all the memory I could ever imagine anyone needing. Within three years, people were laughing and pointing at me on the street for making such a silly statement. The computer on which I am writing this book has four MB of RAM, and there are already times when I wish I had more.

Convenience

Many programs are considerably larger than the amount of the RAM in the computers that run them, and that is often a real nuisance. A popular page layout program for the IBM MS-DOS system, for instance, comes on thirteen floppy disks. Even with a fairly large amount of RAM, only a small fraction of this huge program can fit in the RAM memory at any one time. The program is smart enough to tell the user when to trade disks, but is not only a nuisance, but quite time-consuming as well. The bigger the RAM, the less of this would have to go on.

I once figured when I was in this sort of situation that I was spending about four minutes a day switching disks around. That came to 20 hours a year, and a hundred hours over the next five years. By investing $100 in additional RAM memory, my problem would be eliminated. Is my time worth $1 an hour? I decided it was, and bought the additional memory.

One message from this kind of situation is that hard disks have really become a necessity for many people, not just a pleasant time-saver. At least those 13 floppy disks could be permanently stored on a hard disk, which means no more constant disk switching. But remember, no matter how large the hard disk may be, it is the much smaller size of the RAM memory that determines the size of the programs you can work with.

Let us return, then, to that incomprehensible question posed by the computer salesperson at the start of this section, namely "How many 'K' of RAM did you have in mind?" Although the best answer might have been, "Please speak to me in English, young man," another answer is, "Let me first consider which programs I am likely to be using, and how much memory they require."

Kind of disk storage

In the same way that sounds are stored on a tape cassette and sounds plus pictures are stored on a videocassette, computer information (which can include sounds and pictures, but most often words, numbers, and operating instructions) is stored on disks.

Disks are round plastic wafers, generally encased in paper, plastic, or metal housings, onto which electronic signals can be recorded, and from which they can be played back. There are three varieties, several configurations, and half a dozen sizes.

Varieties

Floppy Disks. The basic coin of the small computer realm is the floppy disk, typically either a 3½"-diameter disk encased in a square plastic holder or a 5¼"-diameter disk encased in a square heavy paper or plastic holder. They are called "floppy" because the disks themselves bend, even if the holders don't. The smaller disks hold as much or more information than the larger ones, and they fit nicely into a shirt pocket. They would probably take over entirely, but for the fact that there are millions of computers out there already with the 5¼" disk drives.

One floppy disk can hold anywhere from 400K (400,000 bytes, or 400,000 letters or numbers, thus about 80,000 words or four hundred pages of typing) up to well over 1,000K (one million bytes, or one thousand pages of typing). Floppy disks are about as fragile as tape cassettes. They should be protected from extreme heat or cold, from being dropped or bent, having things spilled on them, being gnawed on by small animals, and from being left in the proximity of magnets, including those found in hi-fi speakers. (While the X-rays used at airports are unlikely to damage disks, there are magnets in X-ray machines which may do the foul deed).

Sometimes disks are identified as being "single-density," "double-density," "high-density," "single-sided," or "doubled-sided." These all refer to the capacity of the disk, and the only consideration is to be sure that your disks match what your computer disk drive can handle. A double-sided disk drive can also read single-sided disks, and a high-density disk drive can also read disks of lesser density.

Double-sided disk drives are essential, and that is all you would ever find on a new machine anyway. Higher density, higher capacity disk drives are handy but not essential for most users.

With the price of all kinds of disks comfortably under a dollar each, the cost of disks is no longer a factor in deciding what kind of disk drive to have.

Hard Disks. Hard disks (they are less flexible, less floppy) work on exactly the same principle as floppies, but they are somewhat larger, and store a great deal more information. They are in sealed boxes. Nothing can be removed. If you are lucky, you will never see the inside of your hard disk case. Hard disk capacities are referred to in megabyte (one million byte) units. Hard disks start as low as 20 megabytes (20 million bytes, or about 20,000 pages) and go up into the hundreds of megabytes.

Hard Disk Cartridges. The third alternative combines the convenience of floppy disks (remove them, copy them, store them in safe places, mail them to people) with the storage capacity benefits of hard disks. These are, in effect, hard disks in which the disk portion is removable, on a cartridge, typically containing 40 megabytes of memory and up. With each small cartridge holding the equivalent of 30 or more floppy disks, storage and organizational problems are minimized.

Configuration

Hard disks can either be built into the computer, or sit in a separate box alongside the computer. Built-in ones generally cost a little less, but are less easy to remove, either because you are getting a larger size, or because of the need for repair. External hard disks cost a little more, and take up more space on the desk or table (or, as computer lingo would have it, they have a larger footprint).

Most computers permit having either or both configurations. A computer with a built-in hard disk can still have an external hard disk (or hard disk cartridge unit) plugged into the back.

Also, it is usually possible (especially in the Macintosh world) to "daisy chain" two or more hard disks together: Drive #1 is plugged into the computer, Drive #2 is plugged into the back of Drive #1; Drive #3 into the back of #2, and so on, up to a total of six in the chain. This, however, is quite rare. Most people choose a hard disk of a certain size, and stick with it until it is time to turn it in on a larger one.

Size

Hard disks start as small as 20 megabytes (roughly 20,000 pages of typing) and go well beyond one million megabytes (one million megabytes equals one gigabyte, which is the equivalent of about 10,000 novels).

Here are three factors to consider in choosing the size of a hard disk:

1. *Cost.* It rises very slowly, such that a 40-megabyte drive might cost less than $100 more than a 30-megabyte drive; a 60 less than $100 more than a 40, and so on.

2. *What you will store on it.* The above capacity examples were in terms of words: eight million of them on a 40-megabyte hard disk. But some people store other things, including pictures and sounds, both of which use up a great deal of disk memory. For instance, one elaborate drawing or photograph might take up as much space as several hundred thousand words; a few minutes of music, even more.

3. *Parkinson's law for computers.* Professor C. Northcote Parkinson proposed that work expands to fill time. However much time one has to do a job, the job will expand to use up all the allotted time. So it is with disk storage. When you have a great deal of it, you will use it, albeit not always efficiently. When you have written a long letter to Aunt Louise, printed it out, and sent it, you will think, "Maybe I should save it on the hard disk, in case she doesn't get it. Or, since her memory is failing, I can print it out and send it to her again next Christmas, she'll never notice." And so that letter is saved, along with dozens, soon to be hundreds, even thousands of other items that you may never see again . . . until the day you notice that your hard disk is nearly full (with some computers, each time you turn the computer on, you get a message telling you how much space remains on your hard disk), and then you will start electronic housecleaning, wondering how you could have ever saved this, and that, and all those others.

Do you need a hard disk at all? In almost every case, the answer should be yes. It is virtually a necessity. More and more software can only run on a hard disk, since it takes up more room than a single floppy disk. Your computer life will go faster and more efficiently. Also, the more software you keep on your hard disk, the less often you have to find, insert, and boot up floppy disks.

What factors do you consider? Speed, reliability, and size. The first two are much less important for beginners and indeed most other users; differences are relatively slight. Hard disks are regularly reviewed in computer magazines, for those who wish to reflect on every possible variable. Yet the differences between the fastest and the slowest; between the most and the least reliable; are not that vast, as long as you remember the "Don't be the first kid on the block" philosophy.

Size *is* an essential factor. The trite advice is to buy the smallest size that will accommodate your needs for the foreseeable future. But how do you know? In the late 1980s, the most common size was 20 megabytes. In the early 1990s, it was 40 megabytes. I sit here using one with 65 megabytes (and it is nearly full; there is probably an 80 or a 100 in my future). It probably makes sense to calculate, as best you can, everything you might want to keep on such a disk ("Let's see . . . PageMaker needs 4 megabytes, Word Perfect needs 600K, the novel I plan write will use 450K, the bowling league mailing list . . ." etc.) and then double or triple the end result, and you should be set for a while.

Obsolescence-avoidance disclaimer

As I wrote the previous section in 1992, disk storage (in the various configurations described) was the storage method of choice. There have long been rumblings about other cheaper-faster-better storage technologies involving bubbles, crystals, and, most commonly, compact disks. Sometime between next Tuesday and Armageddon, there is likely to be an inexpensive "read-write" CD. Now they are read-only (you can play them but you can't record on them) or they are WORMs (you can Write on them Once, then Read them Many times, but not write any more). Since one CD can hold the equivalent of hundreds of floppy disks, it would indeed be a revolutionary event, were we able to store all the data we would ever be likely to need on one, or a small handful of CDs. (We would also have the unparalleled opportunity to lose or destroy everything all at once, instead of a little bit at a time. Making copies, and copies of the copies, and storing them in different locations [not all in the back pocket, please] will become more important than ever.)

Printers

There are four major factors to think about in choosing a printer: appearance of what is printed, speed, price, and noise level.

Appearance

There are five common technologies used to put words, numbers, and pictures onto paper. The one (or ones) you select will depend in part on the intended purpose of having a printer in the first place (camera-ready copy for a commercial printer; important letters; casual memos;

rough drafts; finished artwork, etc.); and in part on the other three factors: price, speed, and noise.

In order of increasing quality of output, here are five alternatives:

1. *9-pin dot matrix printer.* There is a print head containing nine tiny little wires, in a vertical row, that moves back and forth across the page. As it moves, some or all of the wires are thrust forward, pressing through a ribbon onto the page. To make a capital "L," first all nine wires come forward, then just the one on the bottom several times in a row. This happens at the rather amazing rate of 20 or 30 times per second. The 9-dot-high letters are certainly readable, but not lovely. (Some people report that photocopying 9-dot output helps sort of blend the dots together, making the letters look better.)

2. *24-pin dot matrix printer.* Same technology, but now there are 24 even tinier pins in a vertical row, so that the letters look much more as if they are a single line, rather than a bunch of closely packed dots. Sometimes this technology is called either NLQ (for "near-letter-quality") or, more optimistically, LQ, referring, a bit anachronistically, to the quality of the IBM Selectric typewriter of ages past. This is a little bit like referring to a new car as NMTQ, for "near-Model T-quality."

One charming feature of dot printers is that you can install a four-color ribbon, and when your software permits, you can designate that certain words or drawn objects are printed out in any of eight or nine colors (yellow printed over blue = green). The quality is almost as good as color postcards produced in 1912.

3. *Ink jet printer.* Instead of little pins coming out to strike a ribbon, ink jet printers have a row of impossibly tiny nozzles that squirt ink directly onto the paper, as the print head moves quickly back and forth. Because of the number of nozzles and the fact that the inked dots sort of flow together, the quality of the output is at least "letter-quality" and perhaps a bit more. Some ink jets use waterproof ink, which will smear when wet, but which dries within seconds. The ink is supplied through a small replaceable drop-in or snap-in cartridge.

There is, at this writing, one full-color color ink jet printer of surprisingly good quality, at price only double that of the black and white, that is to say in the vicinity of $1,000. (Details in the Buyer's Guide in the back of the book).

4. *Laser printer.* A laser beam, controlled by the computer, moves rapidly and precisely over the drum of the printer, temporarily "etching" the letters, numbers, and designs onto the drum, which in turn bonds the black powder onto the paper, not unlike your standard office copying machine. The letters are still formed of tiny dots, but now they are so close together (typically from 300 to 600 dots per inch, or DPI) that for most people it looks just like typesetting, but purists would insist it is NTQ, or near-typesetting-quality.

5. *Phototypesetter.* The finest quality output comes when the computer is used to drive a professional phototypesetting machine, which is what is used for producing most books, magazines, and other printed materials. Phototypesetters also print in dots, but now we have anywhere from 1,200 to 3,000 or more per inch, and it is only with a magnifying glass that anyone could tell there are any dots at all.

Two other technologies in use are the thermal printer, used primarily for relatively low-cost full-color printing and the now obsolete daisy wheel (or even golf ball) typewriter, controlled by the computer and limping along at a mere 200 to 300 words per minute (still far faster than any human has ever gone, using the fingers alone).

Speed

Speed of printers used to be measured in CPS, characters per second, and it used to be a major factor in choosing a printer. Now most printers are rated in PPM, pages per minute, and the differences are relatively small: a range of 2 or 3 pages per minute, up to perhaps 10 or 12. But since printing can go on "in the background"—the printer can be working away while control of the computer is returned to you, to continue doing other things with it—the actual speed doesn't matter for most people in most situations.

If speed is a factor, be aware that "rated speed" is to actual speed as advertised miles per gallon is to real miles per gallon. I may type at 200 words per minute for the fraction of a second it takes to type the word "the" but at about 9 words per minute when I am typing "17,397 zebras @ $21.56 ea. less 10% = $337,571.39." Thus my rated speed is 200, even though my true average speed is perhaps 73.

Price

Printer prices, like so many other prices in this field, have been plunging most pleasantly. People are still alive who can remember the first laser printer coming on the market at more than $7,000 (in the late 1980s). Now many are under $2,000 and their quality is rivaled by some ink jetters well under $1,000. The 9-pin printer that cost me $800 in 1981 was $150 ten years later, and that's not factoring in the decline of the dollar.

You must also take into account what it will cost to operate a printer, since they all require supplies that have a nasty habit of getting used up.

Ribbons for a dot printer cost two or three or four dollars (more for color), and are good for 100 pages on up, but of course each page will be just a tiny bit lighter than the one before it. Figure two or three cents a page.

Cartridges for ink jet printers are in the $15 to $20 range, and will last for 400 copies on up, depending on how much blackness there is on the average page. Figure three to five cents a page.

Cartridges for laser printers will last for 3,000 copies or more (sometimes a good deal more), and sell for $100, give or take $20. Figure two or three cents a page.

All three of the above technologies are renewable, which is both ecologically and economically sound. Ribbons can be reinked (you can buy an under-$100 gadget that does it for a few pennies per ribbon, but I must report my fingertips are, I think, permanently darker than they used to be, following my flirtation with such a machine a few years ago). There are services that insert new perfectly inked ribbons in the ribbon cartridge for a fee lower than buying entire new ribbons.

Ink jet cartridges can be refilled with a little hypodermic-like device for less than half the cost of buying a new filled cartridge.

Laser printer cartridges can also be refilled at about half the cost of a new one, although any given cartridge can only be refilled four or five times before other parts start wearing out in it. Services that refill cartridges can be found in the Yellow Pages of the phone book, and in the small ads in the back of many computer magazines.

One interesting bonus of refilling ribbons, ink wells, or laser cartridges, is that you can change colors. Ribbons, ink, and laser powder are commonly available in red, green, blue, brown, and occasionally other shades.

Noise

The sound printers make can range from almost inaudible (in the case of some laser printers) to, as one reviewer said about one otherwise well-regarded machine, "not unlike the sound of a wildcat being tortured to death."

Should you be stuck with a loud printer in a place where the sound will annoy you or others, sound-deadening insulated boxes are available, whether for your printer or your wildcat research laboratory.

Making your printer decision

All four factors are ones you can get a good handle on relatively quickly in the computer store. Even if you are thinking of buying by mail, you should see the quality and listen to the noise level before investing money. And when you are ready to invest, you will see that, in general, the more you spend, the better the quality and the less the noise.

Printer Enclosure

SO QUIET, YOU CAN NEST A CHICKEN ON IT!

The Keyboard

Unless you have a very personal relationship with your disk drive, the keyboard is the part of the computer you will be touching the most, and so it should be something you feel very comfortable with. Some computers come with a keyboard as part of the package; with others, you must buy your own keyboard, from a small assortment of styles available.

The main factors to consider in choosing a keyboard are the feel, the number of keys, and the configuration of those keys.

Feel

The most important consideration is the feel. How does it feel typing on it: not just a couple of renditions of "The quick brown fox," but for half an hour, an hour, or more. There is no universal standard for size, shape, or distance between keys, and there are quite a few slight variations. One otherwise wonderful portable computer drove me nuts, because the keys were about 1/16th of an inch closer together than I was used to, and my stubborn fingers refused to adjust, forever hitting the wrong keys.

Keyboard Actual

Part of the "feel" as well is the key action. Is there a clearly-defined "click" when you depress a key, or is it sort of mushy, like pushing a sugar lump into a bowl of gelatin?

Then there is the angle of the keyboard. Some sit almost flat on the desk; others are slanted upwards. Some offer an adjustable angle, with one or more settings. A few actually fold on hinges, to assume different angles that more closely match the angles of your hand and wrist.

Another variable is the size and shape of the keys themselves. Some are square, some are oval or nearly round. A few people with long fingernails have told me they prefer the oval. Some have especially large and prominent shift keys or return keys. Some have keys of different colors, which may be helpful to "hunt and peck" typists. Some have tiny raised dots on two "home row" keys, presumably so your fingers will know when they are in the right place.

Number of keys

An old fashioned typewriter has about 45 keys, thus 90 characters, using the shift. I once had a *really* old fashioned typewriter that had "shift" and "double shift" with three characters on each key—a clever idea of the early 1900s that pretty much disappeared until computer people came up with the "control" or the "option" key. A control key is a special key on the keyboard that changes what all the other keys do. In effect, it doubles the size of the keyboard without adding new keys. For instance, if I strike the key labeled "Y" on my keyboard, I produce either an upper case (Y) or lower case (y) letter. But if I hold down the control key, and then hit "Y" I get either a yen sign (¥) or, when shifting, a capital A with an accent mark (Á), for writing in European languages. In other words, four characters from a single key.

Some keyboards offer two, or even three separate control keys, thereby doubling, tripling, or even quadrupling the potential number of characters that can be produced.

Some keyboards offer an extra row of keys, known as F-keys, or function keys, either along the top, or at the side. With the appropriate software, usually provided along with the keyboard, these F-keys can be simply programmed to carry out various functions at a single keystroke. For instance, if you were a secretary and your boss was named Throckmorton P. Gildersleeve, you could program a single F-key such that when you pressed it, the entire above-given name would appear on the screen. A great time saver. An F-key can carry out an entire script that you write for it: call a certain telephone number of a bulletin board, wait for an answer, type in your name and password, and then go to the section on the latest sports scores.

Configuration

Number pad. A keyboard feature some people demand, and others have little or no use for, is a separate number pad: the numbers from 0 to 9, along with the +, -, and other mathematical keys are all repeated in another place on the keyboard. For people who enter a great many numbers, this is a real convenience; for others, typing in the numbers from the top row of the regular keyboard is generally good enough. A few enlightened keyboard makers have noted that not everyone is right-handed, and offer the choice of the number pad at either the right or the left, or perhaps interchangeable.

Duplicated keys. Some keyboards have duplicates of certain much-used keys. The shift and shift-lock key, for instance, the return key, and sometimes the aforementioned control key or keys, may appear on both the left and the right side of the keyboard. For people who must type with only one hand, this could be a necessity. There are times, for instance, when one needs to hold down the "control" key and type an "o" (as, on my keyboard, to produce the Scandinavian letter "ø." If the two keys that must be pressed simultaneously are on opposite sides of the keyboard, there is a problem. (Apple has addressed this problem humanely, by offering free "Easy Access" software, that can add a time delay to any keyboard stroke, such that hitting "control" then "shift" then "Y" one after the other is treated as if they were all hit at the same time.)

Finally, do not take for granted that the letters will always be in the place that your fingers have come to expect them. One woman bought a popular make computer from a Frenchman, and learned to her dismay that in France, the "A" key is on a different row from its "standard" American and British location. Specialized keyboards featuring alternatives to the "QWERTY" arrangement of letters have been offered from time to time, especially for the Dvorak revised layout, which nearly everyone agrees is (a) much faster to learn and type on, and (b) unlikely to catch on in our lifetimes. (If you wish to try out a Dvorak keyboard, software is available that will change the electronic linkages, in effect, so that when you hit the "W" key you will get an "X" and so on.) (Have fun. Amuse your friends. Sneak in and change their letters around while they sleep. What fun they will have trying to type the next day. Yossiroobeb.)

The Monitor

The monitor is the "television" screen on which your letters, numbers, artwork, etc., appear. Some computer systems, such as the less expensive Macintoshes, come with the video tube built in (but you can still add on an external one). Many others offer you the choice of size and color, which are the two main variables.

Size

The range is from some screens that can only show a few lines at a time, up to those that show two full pages, side by side, at actual size. Smaller screens do not usually show smaller images; the letters and numbers will be the same size regardless of screen size. Instead, they act as a window onto a larger page, but you have to scroll (move the text in the window) to see the entire page.

Imagine, for instance, that you are looking through a 5½"-high window onto a standard 11" high page. You could only see half the page at a time; if you were looking at the top half and wanted to see the bottom half, you would have to move your page up to get it under the window.

So it is with small-screen computers. The entire document is always there, but to see it all, you have to move it around underneath the window. The bigger the window, the less moving you have to do.

If your main activity is dealing with simple text, it is less important to have a large screen than if you are designing full pages, creating a newsletter, doing artwork, or even looking at long financial tables.

As with many other accessories, the cost of a full-page add-on screen has dropped dramatically in recent years. I had been craving one for years, when the cost was around $2,000, and I vowed that if it ever dropped below $500, I would indulge. It did, I did, and it was a good thing to do. Sort of like upgrading from coach class to business class on the airplane. It doesn't get you there any faster or more safely, but it is, well, just a nice thing to have done.

Many people are satisfied with a full-page-size vertical screen. Some, who do a lot of layout of multipage documents need or prefer a two-page-wide screen. At least one model rotates 90 degrees, so it can either be a vertical screen for page layout or a horizontal screen for dealing with charts and tables. The image on the screen actually "snaps" from vertical to horizontal as you rotate the screen.

The question often arises: what about using my television set as a monitor? The answer for most people in most situations is no. Unless the television was specifically designed to be a computer monitor, the resolution will not be good enough (small letters will be illegible), and your lifestyle will become more complex. ("Can I watch the game?" "Not until I finish entering these recipes, and updating the mailing list for my club.")

Color

Some people find the colors on their screen to be an important factor in computer happiness or misery. If green and orange do not top your personal hit parade of colors, then a screen with orange letters on an green background (I have seen such a thing) might have you reaching for the Dramamine as often as for the mouse. Once you have tentatively decided on a monitor to buy, it is nice if you can actually sit at it for a few hours, to give it a decent test, both for eyes and for stomach.

The available options include ordinary two-color, special two-color, ordinary multicolor, and special multicolor.

Ordinary two-color. The most common pairs are black letters on a white background, white on black, green on black, and orange on black.

Special two-color. Some black and white monitors are designed to show a great many shades of gray, so that photographs seen on the screen look as good as glossy black and white photos straight from the darkroom developer. Indeed, the main users of such monitors, generally quite expensive, are people who produce or retouch or edit photos, and people who deal in computer pornography (a rather sizable industry on the dark underbelly of the computer world).

Ordinary multicolor. Simple "full-color" monitors can show as few as 8 or 16 separate colors. These are useful when the reason for color is to make the programs you are running easier to work with. If the debits on your accounting program actually appear in red; if editing changes you have made in a document appear in green; if special instructions for manipulating a page design program always appear in a yellow box, then the color is a nice thing to have, and you will not feel the need for 36 shades of blue; one is enough.

---

[17] This phenomenon is called WYSIWYG, or What You See Is What You Get. It is pronounced "WHIZZY-WIG" and, despite claims to the contrary, it doesn't always happen. More than once in your life, What You See will *not* be What You Get, whether in terms of color, design, type styles, page layout, or even fonts used.

Special multicolor. When color is important to the content of your work, as with the need to edit a color photograph, or design the cover of a book that must look on the screen just as it will look in real life,[17] it is necessary to have a color monitor capable of producing either thousands or, in some cases, millions of different colors.

These are the things you must have with your computer: storage, a keyboard, a monitor, and, almost always, a printer. Next, a few words about the four most common "bells and whistles" that are nice to have, but not always essential.

Do I want a mouse?

Consider the cursor. The cursor is an indicator on the screen that shows you "where you are." In writing, for instance, it marks the place where the next letters you enter will appear. In drawing, it shows where the electronic pen will begin creating a line. In accounting, it points to the place where the next numbers will be entered, or to the numbers that are to be added to, subtracted from, etc.

Until the mid-1980s, the way you moved the cursor from one place to another on the screen was by means of striking keys on the keyboard. Often there would be up and down arrows and left and right arrows, as well as other keystrokes with shorthand messages: move cursor to the beginning of this document; move cursor to the start of the next paragraph, etc.

Then came the mouse. The original ones were small and gray, with a "tail" wire connecting the small rectangular box to the computer, hence the name. By rolling the mouse around on the desk by your computer, you move the cursor around on the screen. Move the mouse up and to the right; the arrow (or other indicator) on the screen goes up and to the right.

The advantage of a mouse is that it can be a lot faster for certain maneuvers. If, for instance, you are editing a text and you wish to move the cursor 6 lines up and 42 spaces to the right, you can either punch your up arrow and your right arrow enough times so the cursor finally gets there, or you can move the cursor with the mouse to precisely the point you want, click the button on the mouse, and your cursor is in the new place.

The two main drawbacks of the mouse are that it is slower for certain operations, and some people will sneer at you.

Speed: On my computer, if I wish to print out a page I have just typed in, I have the option of moving the cursor with the mouse to a place on the screen where there is a box labeled "Print," and click the mouse button—or without moving my hands from the keyboard, I can type the "control" key and the letter "P" for print. I do have the choice. The mouse is usually "backed up" by available keyboard commands. It probably takes me 6 times as long to use the mouse: perhaps three seconds, instead of a half a second. Insignificant, perhaps, except that I probably do this exercise 200 times a week, which means a savings of 500 seconds a week, or more than 144 hours over the next 20 years.

Sneering: For some reason, macho computer users developed a disdain for the mouse, more than likely because they didn't have one.[18] They used to make noises about being so important, they couldn't afford the additional 30 or 40 square inches of desk space needed to roll a mouse around on. But now that nearly all computers are available with mice, there is much less mouse envy, and most of the "Real Men Don't Use Mice" T-shirts have been packed away.

There are several alternatives to the mouse: technologies that also permit moving the cursor around without laying finger to keyboard.

Track ball

Instead of a mouse that you roll around on the table, there is a stationary unit housing a billiard-ball-sized hard ball. As you rotate the ball in various directions, the cursor on the screen follows suit. The advantages are less desk space used, and fewer times your hands have to leave the keyboard vicinity. (Some track balls are actually built into the right or left sides of keyboards). The main disadvantages are added cost and a slightly longer learning curve to get used to moving the cursor in that manner.

Joy stick

The joy stick is a vertical rod a few inches high, grasped by the fist. When it is moved forward, the cursor (or other object on the screen) moves up; backward is down; left is left, right is right. Most joy sticks lack the precision available in mice and track balls. Their primary use is in game playing. Since joy sticks are primarily used by people under the age of 12, joy stick envy is not an identified psychopathology at this time.

Graphics tablet

'Graphics tablets' transfer drawings directly into a computer.

A flat drawing surface and a styluslike "pen" are connected to the computer. As you move the pen around on the tablet, the cursor moves around on the screen. This technology is especially useful for precision drawing, or for tracing existing drawings that have been taped to the tablet.

There are other cursor-moving technologies, including the human voice ("Cursor up," you say; "Cursor left, cursor stop, cursors foiled again," and so on); and an infrared beam-sending headset, in which the motion of the head moves the cursor on the screen. To avoid social

---

[18] See my forthcoming paper, "A Freudian Look at Mouse Envy in Western Man," to be published in *Eeek: The Journal of Mouse Technology*.

gaffes, be sure to remove this unit before leaving the computer; otherwise you might hear people saying, "Excuse me, sir, but I believe a beam from your hat has just opened my garage door."

Do I want a modem?

A modem is a device that converts computer output into a form that can be sent over ordinary telephone lines. The word (pronounced "MOE-dumb") used to be a contraction of "*mo*dulator/*dem*odulator" (just as "RADAR" used to be a contraction of *ra*dio *d*etection *a*nd *r*anging, but both have evolved into words in their own right).

Using a modem is, in theory, quite simple. You plug it into a small computer, dial the number of another computer that has a modem, and the two machines can interact, whether they are across the room or across the world from one another.

Speed: The main variable to consider in choosing a modem is speed: the speed with which your information (words, numbers, pictures, whatever) is transmitted to the other computer. Speed is measured in units called "baud" (rhymes with "fraud" and stands for "Big Al's Universal Delivery" or perhaps something else). While some older modems can be found with a baud rate as low as 300, a range from 1,200 to 4,800 or even 9,600 is common. Baud rate numbers translate roughly into that number of words per minute, even though it measures something else entirely. Thus sending the 235-word Gettysburg Address from Gettysburg to Vicksburg at 1,200 baud would take less than a quarter of a minute. Sending the Bible from Jerusalem to Rome at 2,400 baud would take more than three hours and might better be accomplished by FedEx (*Fed*eral *Ex*press) or the PoOff (*Po*st *Off*ice), unless time is really of the essence.

Accuracy: Consider two people standing on opposite sides of the Grand Canyon wishing to communicate. A loud yell can be faintly heard at the other side. If you shout slowly and clearly, all the words should get through to my ears, but if you shout faster, or if a plane goes by ("noise" in the system), some words might be lost. If your message was "I'm now pregnant; meet me at the wedding place at noon," and what I hear is "I'm not pregnant; meet me at the bedding place at noon," those two tiny errors could be rather significant.

Same situation with modems. If the bookkeeping data you send your accountant has a few sevens that turn into nines during the transmission, we're in trouble. The faster you send (or shout), and the more noise in the system caused by the phone lines or faulty equipment, the more problems there will be in getting messages through with great accuracy.

When total accuracy is absolutely essential, the solution is to get what is called an MNP modem: one with Microcom Networking Proto-

Hats can become cats when electrical impulses get interfered with.

col, which is nearly infallible. It is the equivalent of having a third party sitting there on the rim of the Grand Canyon, reading your lips through a telescope. When the word "hat" comes through, he says, "Wait a minute, I think she said, 'cat'; have her try again." Retransmission is requested, until he tells you things are right.

Alternatives to a modem

Computers in the same general vicinity (same office, even the same building) can "talk" to one another over locally-installed wiring. But a modem is the only way to tap into the giant computers of the giant information services (GEnie, The Source, CompuServe, Prodigy, On

Line America, etc.). Still, you don't need a $50 million computer to determine Snuffy Stirnweiss' batting average for the Yankees in 1947.[19] A couple of minutes with a reference book or a phone call to the public library might do as well.

Sneakerware and the postal modem: The other way to get your data (letters, numbers, artwork, etc.) from your computer to someone else's, or vice versa, is, obviously, to cause the disk physically to move. This method of transmission has been called "sneakerware" (you run it from one machine to the other) or "the postal modem" (you mail it).

Pigeonware: There is one other alternative, albeit not in widespread use: The Lockheed company needed to send information regularly from Sunnyvale, California across the mountains to Felton Air Force Base. A special phone line for the computers was too expensive. The solution: carrier pigeons. I asked the military man who told me of this if he was worried about the pigeons being intercepted by trained Communist eagles. I think he took me seriously. So if you see a pigeon with a tiny briefcase chained to its leg being escorted by a jet fighter . . .

Trained Communist eagle.

But what do I do with a modem?

Glad you asked. Since the modem is the tool that turns a small computer from a pleasant little appliance around the home or office into a gateway to the universe, thereby making it one of the better reasons to consider buying a modem *and* a computer to hook it to, it would be appropriate to spend a bit of time on this matter, which is done on page 77.

Do I want a scanner?

A scanner is a device that transfers information (words, numbers, pictures) from a sheet of paper into electronic information in the computer. If, for instance, you scan a photograph of Michael Jackson from a fan magazine, it will appear in your computer, ready to be edited (you can give him another nose job, electronically), resized to any size you wish, or pasted into a document (like a term paper, a newsletter [watch for copyright violations!], or a letter to Aunt Helene in Florida).

If you scan text, whether from a book or magazine, a typewritten page, or even very neat handwriting, it can appear in your computer, ready to be edited, incorporated in another document, printed out, etc.[20]

Scanning is a luxury for some, a game for others, and an absolute necessity for many artists and most lawyers.

---

[19].256

[20] All the scanner does is make a picture of the thing, inside the computer. It then takes some very clever and sophisticated software to figure out whether the "thing" is a bunch of squiggles that make a drawing of a centipede, or a different bunch of squiggles that form the actual word "centipede." Such software may not come with a scanner, but must be acquired separately.

There are three approaches to scanning technology:

Flatbed scanner: The book or artwork or whatever is to be scanned lies on a flat plate. The moving lens passes over it, sending information into the computer. Such scanners begin in the vicinity of $1,000 and go up from there.

Hand held scanner: A small squeegeelike device is manually rolled over the art or text. The relatively low cost ($300 and up) is off-set by the smaller width (most are four or five inches wide, so they cannot deal with a typed page), and the occasional distortion caused by moving the device at a nonconstant speed.

Thunderscan: There is one unique technology, in which the ribbon cartridge in a dot matrix printer is replaced by a scanning head, which moves back and forth across the original as it is rolled through the printer. The quality is good, the cost is low (well under $300, but you must already have the printer), but the speed is very, very slow.

Do I want a CD player?

Compact disk players can play through a computer, and there are hundreds of available disks, some with immense amounts of information on them: entire encyclopedias, the "Guinness Disk of Records," thousands of public domain drawings or photographs, hundreds of type fonts, and so on.

Although you cannot (at this time) store information on compact disks, you can transfer information (pictures, fonts, articles, etc.) from the compact disk into your computer's hard disk memory, and then edit and store for further use.

The CD players themselves start in the vicinity of $500, and the disks themselves from $50 on up into the thousands, but there often seem to be special "bundle" deals. I got my $500 CD player and an alleged $2,500 worth of software for about $900 total. This is only a good deal, of course, if you can use the software. I am pleased to have lots of fonts, drawings, and, I guess, a 20-volume U.S. history series, but I am not too sure what to do with Encyclopedia Bulgariana.

There is some very clever technology in use here, in which you can buy an inexpensive CD disk with a huge amount of information on it, but only a tiny bit of the information is accessible to you until you pay more. For instance, one disk might have 700 type fonts, but only 12 are usable. If you want more, you call a toll-free number, at which you are given a secret code to type into the computer, which "unlocks" the additional material you want, at the very instant your credit card is being charged for same. This is financially the computer equivalent of "900" phone numbers or the "pay per view" movies available in hotel rooms: you get immediate gratification, and don't

No machines will increase the possibilities of life. They only increase the possibilities of idleness.

–John Ruskin

appreciate how much damage you've done until the bills come in next month.

Some CD units will play computer disks through a computer and music disks through a hi-fi system, but unless you keep your computer by your stereo, there could be some annoying disconnecting and reconnecting.

Specsmanship

This is a message for those people who are used to buying goods based on the printed specifications. They use such information, for instance, to compare a stereo with 100 watts per channel and 10-inch speakers with one that has only 80 watts per channel but 12-inch speakers. This car has an 8-valve engine, a digital speedometer, and a 6-way power seat. This one has 16 valves, an analog speedometer,[21] and a 4-way power seat.

The problem with this method of comparing and buying is that there is sometimes little relationship between the specifications and what the thing is actually like. That's why most people *listen* to stereos and *drive* cars before buying. (Sometime I could tell you about the Model A "replica" car I once bought solely because of its glorious brochure, full of utterly misleading specifications.)

With computers, matters are more complicated. Not only is "test driving" harder, especially for the beginner, but the specifications writers seem, at times, to be quite carried away with enthusiasm.

The good news is that the industry has become much more standardized in recent years, so that the only two computer specs one needs to fret about are speed and number of bits. (Specs of printers, modems, scanners, and the like, have been alluded to earlier.)

Speed

Most small computers work at a speed of somewhere between 5 million and 33 million cycles per second. One simple operation is performed with each on-off cycle. For many users, the difference between an 8 million-per-second machine and a 16 million-per-second is very much like the difference between a Chevrolet that can go 90 miles an hour and a Maserati that can go 180 miles per hour, when what you mostly do with your car is take your mother to her Harvest Years Aerobics Club.

The performance of a "slow" computer that can perform 100,000 complex calculations *per second* and a "fast" one that can do 250,000 calculations per second is not anything most users need to worry about.

---

[21] This seems to be what car brochures now call the old needle-swinging-past-the-numbers type of speedometer. Gee, and my grandfather carried a pocket watch all those years, and never knew it was an analog chronometer.

The speed of computers, incidentally, is usually given in mH, or megaHertz. One megaHertz is one million cycles per second. One megaAvis is presumably a little slower.

Number of bits

A "bit" is a single unit of information: a single "off-on" switch in the computer's memory. (Bits and bytes were briefly explained on page 60). Older computers (until the early 1980s) were able to deal with 8 bits at a time. Then came 16-bit machines, and then 32-bit machines. While a 32-bit is ostensibly four times as fast as a 16, in reality it is even faster, because of some improved design features. But some of the literature on the newer machines leads one to believe that using a computer with fewer bits is like flying in the Wright brothers' biplane. Not so. It is, perhaps, closer to flying in a 4-engine propeller craft. Not as fast or as powerful, but it will get you there nearly as well. (Alternative image: a 32-bit ladle may empty the soup pot faster, but an 8- or 16-bit ladle will get the job done). Don't feel sorry, yet, for the poor old 8-bit machines. If *you* could do something—anything!—10 million times a second, you would not need to be pitied.

Buying Locally *versus* Buying by Mail

There are persuasive arguments for and against the two main ways people buy computer hardware, but they can generally be summarized in the following nine words: buy locally for service; buy mail-order for price. But there are some important exceptions to these rules. So let's look in some detail at both options.

Buying locally

Through much of the 1980s, computer stores were spawning like salmon, and offering jobs to far too many people whose aluminum siding or desert land sales careers had become temporarily side-tracked. Thankfully, things have gotten much better. Thousands of miserable retail stores have fallen by the wayside, and the ones that remain are, by and large, helpful, not too unreasonably priced, and likely to be there to help you with your problems after the sale.[22]

The salesperson is very important . . . but you may never see him or her again

My mother, whose only nautical experience was a trip on the Staten Island ferry, once bought a five-year subscription to *Popular Boating* magazine. Her helpless explanation was the salesman at the door was so nice, and he needed just one more sale to win a trip to Disneyland.

People often buy things, including computers, for all the wrong reasons. The advertising genius Howard Gossage put it this way: "You should never confuse the thing *promoted* with the thing *itself.*" In other words, the buyer thinks that he is buying a macho image; a rugged, masculine bit of the old west; a piece of history; something that makes him a real man. The outside observer sees that he is buying a tube of dried, shredded tobacco leaves. (And does anyone else remember when Marlboros had red tips so ladies, virtually 100% of Marlboro smokers at the time, wouldn't leave ugly lipstick stains on their cigarette butts?)

If there is a technological advance without social advance, there is, almost automatically, an increase in human misery.
—Michael Harrington

"Would I lie to you?"

---

[22] A separate category of retail, to keep in mind, is the college or university bookstore. Major computer companies regularly offer huge price discounts to students, staff, and faculty, on both hardware and software. For instance, the page layout software called PageMaker 4.0, with a retail price of about $800, was sold in college bookstores in a special student version for $49.

The only computer "expert" a lot of computer buyers ever talk to is the salesperson in the retail store. Who is this person? Often, he or she is likely to be a commissioned salesperson, who can only earn a decent living if sales are made. Many will conscientiously learn all they can about their products. Some know little more than what is in the superficial promotional materials provided by the manufacturers. And some, especially in discount stores and buying club outlets, know literally nothing about the product, other than the price.

One thing a lot of salespeople know is that even if you make your initial and primary purchase at the store, there is a good chance any further purchases will be bought by mail or at other stores, based on price. So you must watch out for the tendency to be oversold. Here are two case histories:

Two elderly sisters told me that they were thinking about a computer to do some of their genealogy and family history work, such as storing family tree information. They shopped around a bit, and found an ever-so-helpful young man, who sold them a super-powered IBM with an 80-megabyte hard disk. He could probably have sold them a Maserati, skydiving lessons, and a double lifetime ballroom dance course.

A small kindergarten and nursery school wanted to keep track of student records. A persuasive sales team sold them a Macintosh LC (not a bad choice), and then talked them into paying a princely sum to have special programs written specifically for their needs, when a couple of hundred dollars of "off the shelf" software would have done just fine.

Most salespeople are reasonable and helpful. But never forget that it is a buyer's market, and always will be. So if you are uneasy with either the feeling of the store, or the apparent knowledge level or pressure of the person you are talking to, move on. You are buying a computer, not developing a lasting personal relationship with a salesperson.

One reason that retail computer stores may not be paragons of helpfulness, especially if they detect a lack of determination on your face, is that they secretly worry that you might be a SHABE.

The matter of SHABEs

"SHABE" is the acronym for "Shop Here And Buy Elsewhere." You are just about to buy a nifty new printer for $799 by mail, but you really want to check the amount of noise it makes. So you stop by your friendly local computer store, where you can get the full demonstration. Then, when you say, "Thank you very much; I'll think it over," the salesperson thinks, "There goes a SHABE."

Is there a middle ground here, that is fair to the retailer and fair to the customer? I think so. But first it is necessary to discuss the matter of buying hardware by mail.

Buying hardware by mail

The pages of almost every computer magazine are filled with big ads of companies that sell all manner of computers and accessories by mail, generally at prices roughly 35 to 40% lower than retail.

Why are they so much cheaper? To begin with, they don't have to worry about a fancy retail establishment, and can operate from more austere quarters in the low-rent district. They don't have to support a staff of demonstrators and customer's hand holders. Many of them don't offer after-the-sale advice, help, and support—and even for those that do, it is through short and efficient phone calls, not dealing with a near-comatose customer staggering through the doors. Many of them do business in such huge volume, they can get by with a very small profit per sale. And, perhaps most significantly, they don't have to worry about SHABEs.

The matter of sales tax

OK, I promised Verenda Smith of the Illinois Department of Revenue that I would put this in, so here it is. Most people think that one of the big advantages of buying by mail from another state is that you don't have to pay tax. Not so. Even though you do not pay *sales* tax, you are obligated to pay a *use* tax, equal to what the sales tax would have been. When I once wrote about the "don't pay tax" benefit of mail-order purchasing, Ms. Smith wrote me, politely asking me not to perpetuate this myth. So be it.

What this means is that when I buy a $10 box of disks from a supplier in another state, I should immediately waltz into my state tax office and demand to pay them the 42 cents that my state lost on this transaction.

Of course when you look at the big picture, the billions of dollars worth of stuff shipped across state lines each year, the tax losses are indeed significant. A few states are fighting back, by demanding (and getting) customers' records from some of the major mail-order houses. Thus your state might discover that you bought a $3,000 printer from someone in another state, and they will politely request their fair share of use tax, which you are well advised to pay, or they can also go after you on tax evasion charges. ("Whaddya in for, Kid?" "Murder, assault, and arson. What about *you*, Baldy?" "Aaah, they got me for buyin' a 40-megabyte hard disk by mail without I paid the tax.")

Eventually, I suspect, mail-order companies will collect tax from people in every county and state, and then have to disperse to each of

> You keep adding components until you exceed your yearly income.
>
> —James Warren,
> Computer Consultant

thousands of separate jurisdictions. Prices will then escalate, as much because of the increased paperwork as the need to pay the tax.

The matter of $CALL

In many mail-order discounters' advertisements and catalogues, you will see listings like this:

Macintosh Classic.....................................$875
Macintosh LC ....$CALL

Just how much is "$CALL?" This designation is reserved for items that are heavily discounted, highly competitive, and/or filling up the warehouse. The price can vary from hour to hour, even during the course of the phone call. (On one $CALL I made, the chap on the phone actually said, "Make me an offer." I did. "You gotta be kidding," he said).

The matter of the gray market

Paradox:

• IBM and Apple will not sell their computers to unauthorized dealers.

• IBM and Apple do not allow their dealers to resell their computers to other dealers, or to sell computers by mail.

• One of the largest mail-order and retail sellers of discount Apples and IBMs in the United States is an unauthorized dealer, 47th Street Photo of New York,[23] followed closely by half a dozen huge Texas discount houses.

How can this be?

The answer lies in understanding the nature of the so-called "gray market"—an important consideration for anyone thinking of buying a computer by mail, or over the counter from a discount house.

Apple, IBM, and others generally do not allow their products to be sold through discount houses. Cheapens the image, they say. To reinforce this policy, they require all their dealers to sign a pledge that they will not resell their own stock to a discount house.

The dealers smilingly sign this pledge—and then they ignore it.

Consider a typical dealer for a major brand. If he or she buys five or ten computers from the manufacturer, the discount might be 30%. But if the order is for 100 or more, the discount goes up to 50% or more.

Thus dealers all over the country are buying far more computers than they can possibly sell, in order to get the big discount, then shipping most of their order out the back door to New York or Texas.

---

[23] They are also among the more interesting of America's businesses. Probably the only $100 million plus business run from premises upstairs over a delicatessan, the core of the business is a room in which dozens of Hassidic Jews, equipped with yarmulkes, side curls, and long-distance telephones take orders from all over the world for electronic gadgetry.

Often they make no profit whatever. Sometimes they even take a loss, in order to get needed cash, or to avoid the carrying costs for their excess inventory. Then the discounter turns right around and sells the computers at a 35% to 40% discount to the public.

It appears to be perfectly legal for the general public to buy from these discounters. At times, some manufacturers have tried to "get even" on their customers for doing this foul deed by refusing to honor their own warranty. This is potentially a major problem for the largely innocent buyer, but fortunately it is not a common one. It can't hurt to ask your mail-order supplier to confirm, in writing, that the equipment you are buying comes with an honorable warranty.

Two reasons to buy hardware by mail

1. *Low prices.* They will almost always be 20% to 40% lower than prices for identical equipment from local authorized dealers, and often lower than discount houses as well.

2. *Greater availability.* Because a huge mail-order house may do five hundred times more business than a local store, their inventory at any given time will be vastly larger as well.

Seven reasons not to buy hardware by mail

1. *Lack of set up.* If you buy locally, you can ask for (and usually get) the dealer to come to your office or home, set up the equipment, and check it out. Your mail-order purchases will be delivered by a uniformed representative of your Federal government, but he or she is unlikely to help unpack your computer. (In this regard, there are sometimes bits and pieces that you have to order separately, like connector cables or multi-plug outlets, which a local dealer will remember to include, and may even throw in at no extra cost.)

2. *Lack of technical expertise and advice before purchase.* Some mail-order sellers do have help and advice lines for potential buyers; many others do not have the time, inclination, or knowledge to counsel customers as to which machine best meets their needs.

3. *Lack of technical expertise and advice after purchase.* Again, some mail sellers do, many don't.

4. *Lack of service.* Although some mail-order houses also offer mail-order service, most do not. Computers can always be brought or sent to an authorized dealer for repair, whether or not bought there, and whether or not still under warranty or service contract. But there are retailers (even some who sell to the discounters in the first place!) who are reluctant or unwilling to service gray market machines.

Man is the lowest 150-pound non-linear all-purpose computer system that can be mass-produced by unskilled labor.
–Apochryphal NASA report on why we send humans to the moon instead of robots

Anything you can't spell won't work.
–Will Rogers

5. *Harder to bargain*. Bargaining or negotiating is not possible when you are dealing with a telephone order taker, whereas in a face-to-face situation at the local dealer, you can haggle to your heart's content.

6. *Lack of speed*. Minor problem, nowadays. Some mail-order sellers can get most things to you by overnight delivery service, often for only a few dollars extra. But if you want (or need) something at 10 this morning and go to your local store, you can have it by 10:05, instead of waiting a day or more.

7. *Lack of windows to soap*. If you have bought locally and you are very unhappy about something, at least you have a nearby place to go and squawk, pound on counters, soap windows, picket, etc. (see the section on Consumer Karate, page 202).

All right then, retail or mail-order, how do I decide?

Is it ethical to shop locally, then buy by mail? Each person must, of course, make his or her own decision. Some won't do it. Others do it but feel guilty. And many do it without regrets, believing it to be a logical extension of our free enterprise system.

For whatever it is worth, here is what I often do. The strategy doesn't always work, but the risks are small and the benefits, if it works, are considerable.

Assumptions

1. Retail prices will be 20% to 40% higher than mail-order prices.

2. The higher price goes, in part, for a support staff to install the computer and give assistance after the sale.

3. Retail stores are also in business to make a profit, and the less after-the-sale time they have to spend, the more profit they will make.

4. Retail stores have some interest in repeat and referral business.

The kinder gentler dialogue

Bear: "I have now decided I wish to buy this IBM 386SX with a 256-color VGA monitor and a 40-megabyte hard disk. Your price on this package including tax is $2,700. Here is an advertisement from a mail-order house that will sell me the identical package for $2,300 including shipping.

"Now, I am willing to pay you more than I would pay these people in Texas or New Hampshire or wherever, because I fully expect that you will bring it to my office, set it up, give me splendid service, expert advice, help me out with a loaner machine in times of need, and generally be available for aid, assistance, and consultations at all reasonable hours. In return, I shall do my best to be a sensible user; I will try not to be a 'RYFM' [see page 192]; I will tell my friends, coworkers, and the guys at the tennis club about you; and I will be back for more goodies as my business grows. On that basis, will you split the difference and accept this check I am waving at you, for $2,500?"

Some retailers will go for this, some won't.

The hard-nosed dialogue

Young:[24] "Look, you're asking $2,700 for this pile of crud. You know and I know that I can buy it by mail for $2,300. I can't see paying you four hundred bucks for at best a few hours of your time. But I am willing to give you an extra $100, here and now. So if you sell it to me for $2,400, we have a deal. Otherwise, it is off to the telephone I go."

It is OK to haggle

Whether you do it politely or gruffly, bargaining is really OK. No one pays the "sticker price" on a car. Even people (like me) who hate bargaining will "make an offer" when buying a home. But few people feel comfortable dickering over the price of a refrigerator or a computer, and I only know one person who would probably try to negotiate the cost of a Slurpee at the 7-Eleven.

Perhaps the word "haggle" is a bit harsh, with its connotations of the Turkish marketplace. But it is entirely reasonable and proper to negotiate the terms of your purchase, if not the price itself. Most people don't do this. But those who do tell me that it almost always works—and when it doesn't, they go to another supplier who is willing to deal.

These are the areas that can be negotiable:

The total price. Some dealers would rather make a few hundred dollars than lose a sale entirely, knowing that satisfied customers are likely to return.

The terms. Some dealers carry their own contracts; most have working arrangements with local banks, leasing companies, or the various manufacturers. Some are open to creative financing. One man told me he wanted a $6,000 system. "Look," he told the dealer, "I won't haggle on the price, but I have cash flow concerns. I will give you $2,000 today, $2,000 in six months, and $2,000 in a year, but I want the equipment now." He got it.

Try-out period. A purchase can be made subject to your satisfaction, with the option to return everything for a full (or 90% or other negotiated percentage) refund within, say, 30 days.

Delivery and installation. Some people don't want or need help; the cost should be less.

Warranty length. If the dealer also does repair work (and why are you even talking to a dealer that doesn't?), it is not unreasonable to

---

[24] Not Bear; I am not comfortable doing this, but clearly many people are.

say, "I'll buy this if you personally extend the warranty by one year" (or two or three, for that matter).

Training. Some dealers and distributors offer classes in the use of the equipment, lasting from a few hours to a few days. If this is not available, or if you feel the need for more personal instruction, you may wish to ask for 5 or 10 or 20 hours of teaching as part of the deal—your place or theirs.

Seven ways to pay for a computer

Here are four 'traditional' ways people pay for their computer systems, and three less traditional ways.

1. Banks and finance companies

Many traditional lenders will make computer-buying loans payable over a period of three to five years, at as many points over the prime rate as they can get away with. A last-resort method.

2. Seller carries contract

All larger and many smaller computer companies are capable of doing this. Often a 20% or 25% down payment is required. The interest rates are usually comparable to what banks offer.

3. Credit card

If the total purchase price exceeds your credit limit, the dealer may agree to charge a certain amount now, let you take the equipment, and then charge you an agreed-upon amount per month until the total is paid. The dealer would retain legal ownership until payment in full is made.

But the best reason to buy by credit card is if you have a card (many now offer this) that "automatically" doubles the length of the warranty, and even pays you if the purchase is lost, stolen, or destroyed during the first 30 to 90 days. (Throwing it, in disgust, from your 34th-floor condo balcony doesn't count.)

4. Lease purchase plan

Leasing companies buy the equipment from the dealer, then lease it to you for a monthly payment equal to anywhere from 3% to 10% of the purchase price. After one to five years of making payments, you own the equipment (or have the right to buy it for a small amount). The main advantage is that there is little or no down payment. There may also be tax advantages.

The toughest decision a purchasing agent faces is when he is about to buy the machine that will replace him.

—Laurence J. Peter

5. Get someone else to buy it for you

A surprising number of people told me stories about how they acquired their computer equipment for little or no out-of-pocket expenditure. Three brief examples should suffice.

• A small company specializing in data entry (typing other people's information into a computer) was charging 15 cents to type in a customer's name and address. They approached their largest client with this proposal: We want to buy new equipment for about $4,000. You buy it for us, and we will type in your next 40,000 names at no cost to you. The client agreed, and got $6,000 worth of service for their $4,000 investment, and the data entry firm got a "free" computer.

• A computer typesetting company suggested to a major client that if that client bought them 1,000 new fonts stored on a hard disk (about $2,000 worth), they would get all their typesetting at half price for a year. Another deal that made everyone happy.

• A bookkeeper wanted to computerize her business. She suggested that each of her 30 clients put up $100 in advance to finance her purchase of necessary computer equipment. In return, she agreed to deduct $10 from each of their monthly statements for one year. The purchase was made, financed ⅟30th by each client, who hardly noticed the monthly deduction and got back a 20% return on the investment to boot.

6. Become an informal commissioned salesperson

People who would never think of trudging from door to door with a sample case have nonetheless made some very successful arrangements in this regard, typically with a local retailer rather than directly with a big company. For instance, one woman who wanted a flatbed scanner made this deal with her local store: they "installed" a demonstrator model in her studio. $200 was credited toward the price for each person who bought one after seeing it in action there. After 10 sales, most of them to business associates and friends, she owned her "demonstrator" free and clear.

7. Become a demonstration site

Some enlightened companies or dealers acknowledge that it is virtually impossible to get an adequate demonstration during a short visit to a store. They are willing to make equipment available under favorable terms to users who will permit potential buyers to come in and see the equipment in operation. The county I used to live in made such a deal with a major manufacturer, who made all kinds of financial concessions in return for the right to bring people from other government agencies in to see their machines in action.

This approach has worked for equipment worth thousands and for equipment worth millions. A small mail-order company in Chicago, for instance, bought its mailing list computer for half price in return for allowing four "visitation" inspections a year. A hard disk manufacturer offered its new product on extremely generous terms to early buyers, in return for evaluations and testimonials.

Buying Used
or Obsolete Stuff

Used or obsolete hardware

Buying used computer equipment involves taking something of a risk—but, all things considered, it may be not too much greater a risk than buying new equipment, and the cost savings can be immense. There are two crucial factors to consider: Why is the last person getting rid of it, and how useful will it be to you.

There are, logically, only four reasons why computer equipment finds its way onto the used machinery market:

Be suspicious of used computers for sale.

Previous owner stepped up

If a computer user is happy with his or her equipment, but decides it would be nicer or necessary to have something faster or more powerful or with more features, then that person's old equipment is well worth considering. A happy and satisfied user is more likely to have taken good care of the equipment and treated it well. Indeed, one sees used-computer-for-sale ads in the classified ads that specify "owner upgrading."

Previous owner fed up

I telephoned a lot of people who were advertising used computers for sale. I found quite a few who simply had given up, and decided *not* to computerize their businesses, homes, or lives after all. Some of the prices quoted by such people seemed remarkably low. When I remarked on this, one man replied, "It's an albatross around my neck. I just want the damned thing out of here by Saturday." This is the computer equivalent of throwing your golf clubs in the water hazard. You may well regret it a few minutes or a few hours later.

It really **is** *a lemon*

Some people give up and sell their computers because they are genuine certified lemons (the computers, that is, not the people). Sometimes they mention that they have "had a few problems," and sometimes they don't. There are some deceitful computer-selling practices akin to unscrupulous used car sellers putting diesel oil in the crankcase to make a miserable engine sound OK—for about three hundred miles. One example: a not uncommon problem is a misaligned disk drive, which can only, in effect, read misaligned disks, created on that drive. So one can see a nice functioning computer, but as soon as one gets it home and puts one's own disks in, the lemonhood becomes apparent.

The good news is that most computer hardware can be checked out with relative ease. More on this in a moment. Unhappily, not too many buyers do this. They either are too trusting or too dazzled by a few simple tricks they see the computer do.

It is being sold by a dealer or broker

Many computers are "sold" to insurance companies. Once the insurer has paid off on a claim, they are eager to dispose of the stuff as quickly as possible, generally to dealers. The two kinds of events that lead to this situation are (a) stolen computers that have been recovered after the victim has already replaced them; and (b) computers damaged in a fire or other disaster.

One dealer with a large business in used computers told me she often picks up computers that were sprayed by fire extinguishers. They look awful, but more often than not, when she cleans them up, she finds they work fine, and she sells them for five to ten times the "fire sale" purchase price from the insurance company.

Generally you will pay a bit more from a used computer dealer than from a private party, but you may have the advantage of at least *some* kind of warranty, even if it is only a 3-day exchange privilege or a 30-day repair warranty.

Checking out a used computer

Without question, this should be done to the best of your ability. The best and simplest test is working with it, preferably using your own software and your own data, for as long as the seller will let you. If you try out all the stuff you can think of to do, and it performs satisfactorily, then you probably have a good one. Computers, unlike cars, are much more likely to be "all or nothing." There is not a whole lot of in-between: either it works well, or it doesn't work at all.

If you are uncertain, you could take it to a repair shop for a check-up. There are diagnostic disks for most hardware, which put it through its paces, exercising every component of the system, and reporting on its condition. Just as a four-engine jet can fly on three or even two engines, some computers can do a lot of impressive things, even if something is wrong with them, because the parts that have gone bad don't happen to be in use. The diagnostic tests should go a long way toward finding the inactive bad parts.

Can it be upgraded? Can it be lived with?

Not too many people trade in their Rolls-Royces because the ashtrays are full. But more than a few will trade in their old computer rather

than modernizing it with the addition of various bells and whistles. As a result, some real bargains can be found on the used market.

For instance, the Macintosh 512KE computer is genuinely obsolete. Never mind that it was state-of-the-art, and a wonder of the ages, all the way back when Mr. Reagan was our president. But now you can pick one up for a few hundred dollars. Would you want to? For most people, the answer is no, but for those in the following two categories, it could be a resounding yes:

Those who can live with it. If your main, or sole computer need is something really simple, then a simple old machine might suffice. If all you wish to do is learn to type, or play games, or run a modest accounting program, or monitor the lights and alarm systems in your home, or indeed just sort of learn to mess around with a computer in general, a Macintosh 512, or something comparable from the IBM world, may do. Your main problem will be ignoring the supercilious sneers of your higher-tech friends.

Those who choose to upgrade it. The computer "aftermarket" has come up with a wide range of clever products designed to make obsolete computers behave in a less senile manner. Often these are in the form of new internal parts, mostly chips, that either replace those that came with the machine, or snap onto them in piggyback fashion. (One company calls its product a "daughterboard" that snaps onto the computers own "motherboard.")

Such behaviors are usually economical if you do the work yourself. A dealer might charge you $100 or more to install a $50 chip. But mere mortals, with little or no experience, are often capable of doing the work themselves, especially when the add-on parts are bought from an enlightened supplier who provides detailed, illustrated instructions or even, in some cases, videotapes on how the work is to be done.

Even then, the economics of this approach are not spectacular. You might, for instance, buy a $300 machine, spend $500 to upgrade it, and end up with the equivalent of a new $1,000 machine.

What about parts and service for old or obsolete machines?

This is only a minor concern with popular brand names, or with more obscure machines that were, nonetheless, built with standard components. Even if the authorized dealers no longer "support" the older models, as is the case with the earlier Macintoshes and IBMs, there are a great many independent bureaus that will deal with them, including service by mail. (This is covered in the section on repairs, page 194).

It could be a major concern, however, with obscure brands built from nonstandard parts. During the heady years of the mid-80s, everybody and his brother was building hardware in the garage, using bits and pieces from electronic supply catalogues, not to mention gears scavenged from Hungarian food processors[25] and belts made from canning jar liners. I have seen people despondently walking the aisles of used computer shows (I think there are more held in northern California than the rest of the world combined, but they do happen from time to time in most larger cities), questing for the winding reel for their

One of the new computers in the billing department had gone berserk, possibly from the strain of replacing five elderly bookkeepers, and a hundred thousand dollars' worth credit had been erroneously issued to delinquent charge-account customers before anyone caught it.

—Lois Gold, *Necessary Objects*

---

[25] No one would ever believe the true story I was told in this regard, but if it ever comes to a court defense, I have the evidence.

Atahualpa Marco IV computer from Inca-Tech Industries (a 44-mile-long piece of knotted string). Or whatever.

Free consultations

It should be mentioned that one of the often significant advantages of buying used hardware or software, especially from an individual, is that you are more than likely to get a good deal of help in making things work. Don't expect a four-hour lesson in using the software, but you can expect to get a quick overview of how it works, and how you might use it.

The Shameful Warranty Situation

There are discoverable limits to the amount of change that the human organism can absorb.
—Alvin Toffler, *Future Shock*

Most computer warranties are absolutely shameful, and there's not much you can do about it.

Consider this scenario: You buy a cigarette lighter for 79 cents at the drugstore. Because of a manufacturing defect, one that is well known to the manufacturer, who has decided not to correct it or publicize it or to recall the product, the lighter explodes, causing your $250,000 house to burn to the ground. The manufacturer thereupon informs you, "Not only are we not going to pay for your house, we're not even going to refund the 79 cents you paid for the lighter."

Could anyone really try to get away with that behavior in this day and age? And would the buying public just sit there and accept this? The surprising answer is that this is precisely what is done throughout the computer industry. A munificent warranty, ranging from 12.8 weeks on up[26] followed by *no responsibility for anything,* even if the equipment they *knew* was defective destroys your business.

Very few people to whom I've talked have actually read or thought about the small type that appears in the literature with almost all computer stuff, hard and soft, that you buy. To counteract all those years of their putting these words in small discreet type, here is a typical warranty in large, hard-to-avoid type:

LIMITED WARRANTY

Manufacturer makes no warranties, either expressed or implied, with respect to this product, its quality, performance, merchantability, or fitness for any particular purpose, nor with respect to the manual describing the product. The product is sold "as is." The entire risk as to its quality and performance is with the buyer. Should the product prove defective, the buyer (and not the manufacturer, distributor, or retailer) assumes the entire cost of all necessary servicing, repair, or correction, and any incidental or consequential damages. In no event will the manufacturer be liable for direct, indirect, incidental, or consequential damages resulting from any defect in the product, even if the manufacturer has been advised of the possibility of such damages.

[26] For many years, the standard warranty was 90 days. Finally, in the last few years, some bold companies extended this to a year, and others followed suit, but there are still more than a few 90-day warranties out there.

I'm not a lawyer, but I've read enough to know that this kind of warranty is very rare in the consumer world. Product liability extends well beyond the cost of the product itself. If a headache pill kills someone because it had the wrong stuff in it, the manufacturer's liability goes well beyond refunding the ten-cent cost of the pill. If a six-dollar bolt causes the collapse of a hotel lobby bridge, killing scores, the liability goes well beyond six dollars.

Slowly and steadily, consumerists and consumer law will be devoting more time to the multibillion-dollar small computer world. That's why the 90-day warranty is fading away. Some hard disk drives even come with three- or five-year warranties now. But until everyone sees the light, there are really only five alternatives to consider with regard to warranties.

1. *Double them yourself.* Following the lead of American Express, other credit card companies are also offering the deal whereby you double the warranty of any product, up to one additional year, when you pay for it with that card. Since there is no added cost for this, it makes excellent sense to take advantage of the offer when buying hardware and even some software.

2. *Buy an extended warranty.* Some extended warranties simply extend, without alterations, the same warranty that was in effect for the first 90 or 365 days. Others toss in additional conditions rarely (remarkably enough) to the consumer's benefit. These might include adding a $50 or $100 deductible, or excluding certain parts or kinds of problems.

Like all insurance, you are gambling. Let's say you bought a $5,000 complete system, for which an extended warranty costs $500 a year. Let us also say that you knew for certain that out of every ten people in your position, two would have a $1,000 repair, and eight would have no repairs at all. Is it worth $500 a year to protect you from a 20% chance of a $1,000 repair? That's what insurance gambling is all about.

3. *Negotiate your own warranty.* This is a real possibility, either when you buy a complete small system from a single source, or a large system from the manufacturer. Not easy, but it *is* done.

4. *Take whatever they dish out.*

5. *Fight back.* A few lessons in Computer Consumer Karate are given on page 200.

The delayed warranty scam

A man who works in a retail computer store once told me that if he could induce a customer to fill out the warranty registration card before leaving the store, he would be paid a $150 bonus on a $2,000 sale. This seemed baffling to me, until I put two facts together.

INTRODUCING THE NEW

Chevrolet

* ★ Full 90-Day Limited Warranty
* ★ Six Convenient Repair Depots Nationwide
* ★ Learn To Drive It In Only 6 Months
* ★ Service Contract Available – Only $1500/Year

THIS WEEK'S SPECIALS AT
SAM'S RECORD STORE

LENA HORNE:
GREATEST HITS

33⅓ RPM Record

DEVO
BURNT CIRCUITS

42½ RPM Record

PAVAROTTI
sings
GERSHWIN

A 33⅓ RPM disk that plays only counter clockwise

SPECIAL ADAPTER

Lets your 47¾ horizontal turntable play 33⅓ records vertically at 35½ RPM

(Almost as good as the original.)

THE BEE GEES
AT EPCOT CENTER

PLAYS ON
29¼ RPM VERTICAL
TURNTABLE ONLY!

LIKE COMPUTER PRODUCTS . . .

THE NEW SHREDDING BLADE

for your

CUISINART

Comes complete with 578-page technical & instructional manual

---

SHARPEN PENCILS
WITH YOUR TOASTER

The Cosmotron
Mark III
bolts onto
any standard
household
toaster . . . !

PERFORMANCE YOU NEVER
DREAMED OF from your TOASTER

Installs in hours . . . a lifetime of pleasure.

CAUTION: installation may void your toaster warranty and/or cause hives to break out on your neck.

One is that it obviously costs the manufacturer money to make in-warranty repairs, and equally obviously, they do not lose money on out-of-warranty repairs.

The other is that many buyers simply don't send in their warranty registration until something actually goes wrong, whether that is two months or twenty months after their purchase. There would seem to be no law that *makes* you send in a warranty card promptly. Indeed, if you buy a Christmas present computer on sale in September, and send in the card, the warranty may well expire before the gift is opened.

So one manufacturer, at least, did its cost accounting, and figured out that they will save more than $150 if they can start the warranty clock ticking before you leave the store. Is this ethical? Is the customer's delayed registration behavior ethical? This is not a book on moral philosophy; I just thought you should know what some people are doing, and why you may be asked to leave your signed warranty registration behind in the store.

PART VII

BUYING SOFTWARE AND SUPPLIES

Let's start by considering what it really costs to buy a razor. About two bucks for my Gillette. Then, a new blade (say 50 cents each) every three or four days. Shaving cream, after-shave lotion, Band-Aids, etc. Over the anticipated five-year life of this particular $2 razor, my total cost will be more than $300.

Now if drugstores sold only "total shaving systems" (all the supplies needed for five years of shaving) for a mere $279.95, I suspect that beards would suddenly become more popular.

Business textbooks actually refer to the "razor and blade" school of marketing. You can give away the razor and your fortune will be made on the blades—because people buy them one at a time, and never think about the total real cost.

Razors = hardware. Blades = software. And if the general populace ever contemplated their actual software and additional hardware expenditures over five years, many people would be inclined to return to counting on their fingers and doing word processing with a ballpoint pen. Nintendo and the other game people would be in big trouble. Millions of people seem willing to buy a $100 or $200 game playing unit, and *then* buy $500 worth of individual game cartridges over the next few years. But very few would spend $500 to $700 all at once for the complete game system.

There are two reasons computer manufacturers don't give away their computers and then make zillions of dollars on the software.

One is that by and large, unlike razors and blades, the same companies that make the hardware no longer make the software. They used to. Much of the early IBM and Macintosh software came from the IBM and Apple companies; indeed it was often given away free with the computer. Then they started selling it. And then they spun off software manufacture into a separate company.

The other reason is that there are thousands of software developers and manufacturers out there. Software may be the only legal product in the history of marketing in which a lone entrepreneur can create something at home, manufacture it on the kitchen table for 50 cents a unit, and then sell it for hundreds of dollars. So even if the computer companies had their own software, they would be in hot and heavy competition with dozens or even hundreds of other companies, whose products might well be better than their own.

General Considerations in Choosing Software

Software is harder to choose than hardware for these six reasons:

1. There is so much more of it. While there are "only" hundreds of computer manufacturers, there are many thousands of software manufacturers, ranging from huge corporations to one-person cottage industries.

2. Some software companies sell only by mail, and some advertise sparsely, if at all.

3. It is not easy to browse through software the way you can browse through a museum gallery and gravitate toward those things you wish to inspect more closely. It can take anywhere from a few minutes to a few hours to determine whether any given software is even worth considering.

4. Because of the much smaller profit margin in selling most software, salespeople in computer stores are less enthusiastic about spending a lot of time with a customer shopping for software.

5. And even if they *are* willing, any one person is unlikely to be familiar with all the features of all the major (much less the minor) programs available in any given category.

6. Any given software seller, whether a retail store or a mail-order house, is unlikely to have all the major (much less the minor) programs available in any given category. If you know exactly what you want, you may have to shop around for it. If you don't know exactly what you want, you may have to settle for whatever is in stock.

Here are eight things you can do to make the software choosing experience more satisfactory:

1. *Read.* There are a dozen or more major computer magazines, and they all have articles and reviews of available software. Often, the reviews are comparative: the reviewer will cover two or five or twenty different word processing programs for the IBM, or six leading accounting programs for the Macintosh. Some magazines use a rating system, similar to the way *Consumer Reports* rates cars and toothpaste.

In addition to the magazines, there are books about software (only helpful if quite new), and annual summaries that provide capsule descriptions of hundreds or even thousands of software programs.

One major drawback of reviews is that they cannot possibly mention, much less evaluate, all the features of any given program. The one thing you especially want may not even be mentioned.

2. *Decide what features you need or want.* Each individual software program is like all others in its class in some ways, like some others in some ways, and unique in some ways. Once you learn about all the different things a given category of software *can* do, you should make your own priorities for what you must have, would like to have, and can do without.

For example, when my wife was writing her doctoral dissertation, she determined that all writing (word processing) software lets you type words, delete words, and move them around. Nearly all the programs had spelling checkers, but some do not let you add new words to the dictionary. Some programs had the option of entering footnotes (essential to her), but few gave the choice of putting the footnotes either at the bottom of the page, the end of a chapter, or the end of the entire manuscript. One did automatic indexing: she could create an index as she typed in the main text. Another, clearly going after the academic market, offered the option of automatically changing the bibliography from one academic style to another. Some checked grammar as well as spelling. Some could handle alternative alphabets (bjørn, and glaçé, and Symbols). None did everything she might have wanted, but her needs were not that unusual, and she determined that any one of three or four popular programs would serve her purpose.

If your needs *are* unusual, you will just have to do more diligent research. One man who wrote to me wondered if he might be the first person in history to want to calculate boomerang trajectories with his computer. No. Turned out that an Australian exchange student in California had already modified some existing statistical software for exactly that purpose.

3. *Users' groups.* Many users' groups subscribe to the philosophy expressed by the motto of the Berkeley Macintosh Users' Group, one of the largest in the country: "Our business is giving away free information." Some are very small; some are huge. Some dispense wisdom by phone; others ask that you write, or come to meetings. Most computer users seem to enjoy helping others, especially when it comes to offering opinions, pro and con, on the software they are using. So don't overlook this often free, and often immensely helpful service. (See page 191.)

4. *Determine if a demonstration version exists.* Oftentimes, purveyors of more expensive software (several hundred dollars and up) produce demo copies, some of which have all the features of the regular software, except for one or two key items which have been disabled (for instance, a word processing program that will not print, or a database program where you can only enter a few dozen records).

Demo disks typically sell for $5 to $10; sometimes they are free for the asking. No harm in asking.

5. *Try shareware.* The very concept of shareware helps restore one's faith in humanity. Then again, the way many people deal with shareware sort of chips away at that faith. Shareware is software that the creators or developers give away for free, with the expectation that if you like it, after giving it a fair test, you will send them some money. As you might expect, most shareware distributors are either individuals or very small companies. And as noble as the concept may seem, the reality is that only a tiny percentage of people who use shareware actually pay for it, even though the costs are usually amazingly low: often in the range of $5 to $20. You always know when you are using shareware, since the opening screen on the computer will tell you so, and will also tell you how much money to send if you end up using the program. (Since some shareware programs have been kicking around for years, some people feel it is prudent to write first to see if the creator is still there or has, perhaps, gone off to college.)

While a few shareware programs are full-fledged software in their own right (e.g., a sophisticated telecommunications program), others may be "add-ons" to existing software: for instance, a program that converts the numbers in an accounting program from dollars to other currencies; a Russian spelling checker for a word processing program; and the aforementioned boomerang trajectory calculator for a mathematics program.

Where do you find shareware? The four main sources are users' groups, computer stores, bulletin board services (you download the programs over your telephone line), and also some commercial services that accumulate dozens of shareware programs from many sources on a single disk, and sell those disks for $3 to $5 each (but you still must pay your shareware fee for each program you keep and use).

6. *Rent software.* They may be on the way out, due to pressure from many directions, but there are companies that rent software, typically charging about 10% of the retail cost for two to four weeks' usage. I have very mixed feelings about this. On one hand, it provides an opportunity to conduct a meaningful test, on your own computer and your own time. On the other hand, it provides an easy opportunity to make and keep an illegal copy before you return the original, and that, I am persuaded, is what all too many people do. My feelings about software piracy are made clear on page 220. You wouldn't steal a $200 tape recorder from the local department store (would you?). Why even think about stealing a $200 program from a computer software company?

7. *Borrow software.* Same logic for doing it, and for not doing it, as in the above paragraph. If you know someone who is using software in which you have interest, and if you can persuade him or her that

you will use a copy for a week or two, then erase it from your computer, I think you are on firm moral ground, even if you may technically be in violation of the copyright laws.

8. *Hire a consultant, professional or amateur.* Computer consultants are not necessarily people to whom you must pay thousands of dollars to spend weeks and weeks working on your problem. There are those who can tell you all you need to know in an hour or two, for less than a hundred bucks. You will find a listing for computer consultants in the Yellow Pages of many phone books. (You will also find a description of the service that the two principal authors of this book operate, on page 257.) Amateur consultants can be found at users' group meetings, or by making contact with the computer department or lab at a nearby college or high school. Since students are accustomed to working for starvation wages, you may well find a relevant expert who will tell you what you need, and perhaps even help install the software and tutor you in it, for a modest sum.

The Different Kinds of Software

Here is an overview of seven of the most popular categories of software, and a brief description of some other sorts as well.

Word processing

Word processing is a fancy term for writing. When you use the 10-cent word processor called a Number 2 Pencil, you enter data (write words on the paper), delete data (use the eraser), search and replace (you misspelled Aunt Esther's name somewhere in the letter; you look for it, find it, and correct it), and even cut and paste (scissors and glue).

On a computer, word processing does all the above things, and then some, electronically, on the screen. You don't print something out until it looks perfect on the screen. There are, of course, many kinds of writing: business reports, novels, scholarly papers with footnotes, nonfiction books with an index or two. Some people write screenplays or poems, requiring very specialized margins and indenting. Some require "mail merge": writing sales or fund-raising letters, where the same letter goes to many people, each with the person's name and other personalized information inserted at the proper places ("Just imagine, Sister Louisa, this brand-new Porsche parked outside Little Sisters of the Poor Convent. . . .")

All word processing programs can be used for writing and editing, including searching for certain words or phrases, and "search and replace" in which, for instance, all occurrences of "Dakota pigs" are automatically replaced with "Kadota figs."

Other word processing features include, but by no means are limited to the following:

- Spelling check, either as you type (it beeps, or flashes, when you type a word not in the dictionary), or all at once when you are done.

- Thesaurus, so when you are stumped, baffled, confused, bollixed, uncertain, thrown on beam-ends in a search for the right word, an array is provided for you.

- Mail merge, the business of inserting personalized features in the midst of a form letter.

- Footnotes, either at the bottom of a page, end of a chapter, or end of an entire manuscript.

"Did you hear about the lady who confused her food processor with her word processor?" "No, what did she get?" "Minced words."

- Graphic capabilities, where you can draw boxes around text, put horizontal or vertical lines on a page, have a multicolumn page (preferably with the option of columns of differing widths, a feature the popular program I am using this moment cannot do), paste pictures onto the page and make them larger or smaller; ability to make charts and tables, etc.

- Outlining, in which you can organize your thoughts in an outline form, then fill in the blank spaces.

- Macros, whereby you can designate certain keystrokes to print out much longer text, thus saving a good deal of time and increasing accuracy. For instance, I was once writing a report on German education, in which there were more than a few references to the famous Naturwissenschaftlicheshochschule (natural science high school). I set a macro, so each time I typed the control key and an L, "Naturwissenschaftlichehochschule" was entered in the text.

- Automatic production of tables of contents and indexes. You put an invisible code symbol next to words or phrases that then also go into the index or contents, complete with page numbers (which change, as you move the text around in a manuscript).

- Grammar and style checking. The software alerts you when you write wrong, as in "Give it to Malcolm and myself," or when you you repeat a word inadvertently. Some software tells you the average word and sentence length; some even calculates a readability score, which may tell you that the software manual you have written is at postdoctoral level. Bear in mind these are electronic opinions only. I tried a style checker on the Gettysburg Address (words too hard, sentences much too long), the Sermon on the Mount (too much unclear imagery), and Gertrude Stein's "a rose is a rose is a rose" poem (short simple words; easy to understand).

Spreadsheets

A spreadsheet does for numbers what word processing does for words: it permits you to enter numbers on a ledger sheet, and then manipulate them in a wide variety of ways. Each number you enter can be linked to other numbers by formulas. Imagine, for instance, a ledger sheet with three lines. Line one is "Cost of merchandise." Line two is "Sales tax." Line three is "Total cost." You can easily "tell" the software to take the number on line one, multiply it by the percentage figure on line two, add the result to the number on line one, and write the answer on line three.

Thus if you type in "$100" on line one, and "6.5%" on line two, the software will automatically write "$106.50" on line three.

Spreadsheets can be used for "what if" calculating or modeling. In the above complex example, you might wonder, "What if the sales tax

This is a blank disk
worth $.50

This is a sophisticated
accounting program
worth $300.00

rose to 7.25%; what would my total cost be then?" Replace the "6.5" with a "7.25" and you have your answer.

Of course in real life, most uses are far more complex. Spreadsheets are used to calculate and print out mortgage tables—and the "what if" function is invaluable when shopping for a mortgage and comparing different rates. They are used for keeping track of real data—anything for which you would use a pencil and ledger sheets—and manipulating that data. "If I get a 9.75% 5-year remodeling loan, and raise my tenants' rents by 4.5%, will I be better off than if I get a 12% 15-year loan and raise the rents by 3%—and how will various vacancy rates affect this?"

All spreadsheets allow you to enter numbers in an array of boxes formed by vertical columns and horizontal rows, and to set up formulas linking the various boxes. Spreadsheets vary in the following ways, among others:

• Number of rows and columns available. The range is from a few dozen to thousands.

• Amount of data you can enter in any one box. (Some people use spreadsheets as databases, and store entire names, addresses, and other text information in a given box.)

• Sophistication of the formulas that can link the various boxes, rows, and columns. Some are limited to basic mathematical operations; others can apply complex statistical techniques.

• Graphic capabilities. The matter of printing out charts and tables, with various typefaces, line widths, pictorial enhancements, etc. Also, some spreadsheets take designated numbers and produce pie charts, bar charts, graphs, and other pictorial forms of the data.

• Importing, exporting, and integrating. Some spreadsheets can inhale numbers directly from other programs (such as an accounting or bookkeeping program), and exhale them into still other programs, such as word processing. "Integrated" programs combine spreadsheets with, for instance, word processing. Thus you might have a word processed report that says, "Sales of weapons to Iran totaled [insert number from cell A-24 on spreadsheet], while secret aid to the Contras totaled [insert number from cell B-36 on spreadsheet] over the same time period." Thus your report would always be up-to-date.

Satisfying historical note: the electronic spreadsheet was invented by a Harvard graduate student named Dan Bricklin, whose professor deemed it to be mildly interesting, but of no real value. Bricklin marketed his idea under the name VisiCalc, and made many barrels of money, none of which he donated to the Harvard Home for Non-visionary Faculty.

Databases

A database is, quite simply, a place where information (data) is stored. A file cabinet is a database. So is a Rolodex, a little black book, and a metal box full of 3 × 5 cards. The data can be manipulated by moving files and cards around, erasing Rolodex slips, and shuffling your 3 × 5 cards into a different order.

A computerized database does all of these things electronically. One very common use is a mailing list. In a typical electronic database, you would decide on the names of a number of *fields* for each *record*. You might decide, for instance, that each record (each customer; each student; each employee; etc.) will have eight fields: first name, last name, address, city, state, postal code, home phone number, and favorite pasta sauce.

Once you have typed the information in once, it can be manipulated in a variety of ways, and need never be typed in again. You can sort your data alphabetically to print out a roster for the bowling team. You can sort it by city to find out how many customers you have in Duluth. You can create a page layout with just the name and address, configured to print out mailing labels. You can construct a *mail merge* letter that says, in effect, "Dear Mr. [Last name]. How's the weather out there in [city]?" And when you get your RSVPs to the Kiwanis Spaghetti Breakfast, you'll know how much Sauce Caruso and how much Sauce Napolitana and how much clam sauce to stock in.

All databases maintain records (equivalent to file folders in a filing cabinet), with the data in various fields (name, address, etc.) in each record. They all can manipulate the data in various ways, to print out labels, reports, etc. They vary in the following ways, among others:

- Number of total records it can hold. The range can be from a few hundred to infinite.
- Number of fields possible in each record.

- Size of each field. Commonly, a field will hold 255 characters, but some hold less and some more. (For a book that I write and regularly revise on earning college degrees through home study, I maintain information on more than 1,000 schools in a database, with fields for school name, address, degrees offered, fields of study, fax number, and 20 other things, including a detailed description of the school. Of necessity, I must have a database that permits more than 255 letters, about 50 words, per field.)

- Mail merge capability, in which selected data from the database can be sent, or exported, to other programs, such as word processing, to produce those personalized letters. (My favorite abuse this year is the publisher who sent a textbook sales letter to "Position Vacant, Chairman, Department of History. Dear Professor Vacant . . .")

- Spreadsheet capability. Some databases can also behave like spreadsheets. The fields can be linked together by formulas, just like the cells in a spreadsheet. For instance, in your fudge by mail business, you might keep your customer list in a database, with fields for name, address, etc., and also for number of pounds vanilla fudge bought, number of pounds chocolate fudge, total pounds bought, and total price. You can instruct the database to take the number in the "vanilla" field, add it to the number in the "chocolate" field, and put that number in the "total pounds" field. Next, it could take the "total pounds" figure, multiply it by the cost per pound, and enter that figure in the "total price field." You can then print out mailing labels, invoices, receipts, and other reports, all from the same data.

- Relational capability. A relational database links two independent files to each other. In the above fudge example, there was one file with the customer information. Now let's add a second file with pricing information: the price of chocolate fudge, of vanilla fudge, of roast beef fudge, etc. Instead of having to enter the prices in each customer's file, the customer file electronically links up with the price file, looks up the proper prices, and transfers them into the right fields. At the same time, based on the zip code in the customer file, the program could go to a separate file of all zip codes, and calculate the proper postage to send that much fudge to Ashtabula, or wherever.

Graphics

Trying to write about "graphics" in a small space is like writing about "transportation"—not just which car to buy, but considering the big picture: cars, boats, ice skates, piggyback rides, the Concorde, camels, etc. There are so many different ways to put images onto a screen (and ultimately onto a sheet of paper), entire books have been written about small parts of the graphics picture.

Graphic images (drawings, photographs, designs, and typography that has been manipulated into curves, shadows, etc.) come about in one of three ways: you can create them from scratch; you can buy disks full of already-prepared images (which you can use as is, or make changes to); and by scanning an already-printed or drawn image, transferring it electronically into the computer, to be used as is or further edited.

There is a wide range of software available for each of these purposes. Paint or Draw programs are used to create new illustrations or designs, or to edit existing ones. There are two very different technologies at work in painting and in drawing. Some software does one, some does the other, and a few do both.

When you *paint* on the screen, you are making a picture out of a great many tiny dots. A straight line one inch long might consist of 72 tiny dots, all in a row. A circle one inch in diameter would be made up of about 250 tiny dots, arrayed to look like a circle. You can edit these images by adding or removing dots. To make the one-inch line into a half-inch line, you would remove 36 of the 72 dots. Images made from dots, whether circles and lines or elaborate designs or photographs, are called *bitmapped* objects. Painting is fine when you require shadings of colors, or shades of gray, but when you print out a bitmapped image on a printer, you can still see all the tiny dots. That circle, observed closely, will be jaggly, rather than a smooth curve.

Drawing, on the other hand, consists of giving the computer a set of instructions to create a line drawing of a certain shape, whether it is a circle, a line, the letter Q, or an elaborate map or complicated line drawing of an armadillo fight. Because the drawing is a mathematical construct, it can be changed very simply by changing the mathematical instructions. The software does this for you; no mathematical knowledge is needed. If the letter Q is *painted* (made up of little dots) and you want to change it—enlarge, reduce, change the type font, rotate it, make it italic, etc.—the only way is by removing some dots and adding others. But when that Q is *drawn,* it can be changed—reduced, enlarged, italicized, rotated, the font changed, etc., keeping its identity—by changing the formula that created it. And when it is printed, it will look smooth and round, no matter how much it has been "edited."

Some software has a paint level and a draw level, sitting on top of one another, like a stack of two glass plates. You can, for instance, draw a circle on the draw level; it will have nice precise lines. Then you can go to the paint level, and fill in the circle with shading that goes from dark gray at the top to light gray or white at the bottom. When you print this, the two levels will print superimposed, and you will have a near-photographic image of your eight ball.

One specialized subset of the graphics world is CAD, or computer-assisted [or aided] design: software specifically designed for engineers,

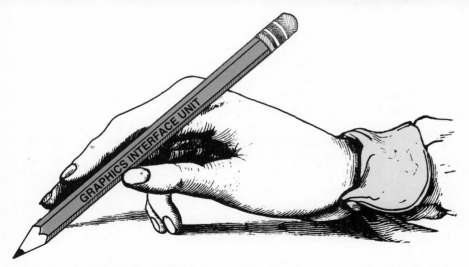

architects, draftsmen, and others who need to create detailed and sophisticated blueprints, schematic drawings, and electrical wiring plans. The available software is complex, expensive, and far more specialized than one short paragraph could ever hope to deal with.

Desktop publishing

"Desktop" simply refers to the location of your equipment; for some people it is tabletop, bookcasetop, or floortop. "Publishing" refers to creating pages full of words and/or pictures, which can then be printed on a printing press, photocopied, or used just as it emerges from the desktop printer. "Desktop publishing," then, is another way of saying "page layout and design software."

Most desktop publishing software starts you out with a large rectangle on the screen, representing a blank page (or two side-by-side blank pages): what Hemingway called "the great white bull"—the empty page, defying you to conquer it by filling it with brilliant prose, lovely graphics, or both.

With some software, you can actually write, draw, or paint directly on your blank white pages. But in almost all cases, you would create the text and the illustrations in other software, and then *import* them onto the page, where they can be moved around, enlarged, reduced, rotated, and otherwise manipulated (such as by having the text wrap around the irregular edges of an illustration). You may choose to add boxes around text, lines separating columns, borders around the edges of the pages, and other embellishments, while you are arranging the elements that will make up your page.

All desktop publishing programs will let you set the size of the page (from postage stamp to billboard size in some cases), the number of pages in the total publication (from one on up), and the configuration of the page (horizontal or vertical, one or more columns of text, etc.).

Nearly all allow you to edit text once it has been imported from a word processing program, and some also permit editing the illustrations.

The following features are those that will vary from one page layout or desktop publishing program to another:

• *Number of pages per document.* Some software allows you to create a document with an unlimited number of pages. Others have a limit, which can range from as little as 12 pages on up. Of course if you had a low limit and needed to produce a long report, you could create, for instance, four separate 12-page documents.

• *Size of page.* All software has a setting for "standard" (in the U.S.) 8½×11 inch pages. Most will also let you set the page size, with a range from postage stamp to legal paper (8½×14). Some have automatic settings for common sizes, including metric sizes, such as A3 and A4, used in most countries in the world. Some have a maximum page size as large as a full-size newspaper page; some even larger, permitting a 30-foot billboard-sized printout. (No, you don't need a printer that accepts 30-foot sheets of paper. These programs offer *tiling:* producing large sheets in the form of a mosaic, so that you must tape or glue individual printed sheets together to produce the big picture. A standard 30-foot billboard produced this way requires about 500 sheets of ordinary 8½×11 typing paper: a challenge, but not impossible.

• *Threading of text.* If you are creating a document longer than one page, you may wish to have a story that is "continued on page two" (or page 42, or whatever). And the continuation might, itself, be continued on a later page. Now, suppose you add a few sentences to the story on page one, making the story five lines longer. That will "push" five lines off the bottom of page one, and, with threading, they will appear automatically at the top of page two (or wherever the story is continued). If that means that five lines are pushed off the bottom of page 2, they will be threaded onto the next designated continuation location.

Virtually all page layout software offers threading in one form or another, some much more automatic and easy to use than others.

• *Kerning.* Kerning is the space between letters. For best visual effect, the spaces should not be equal for any two pairs of letters. For instance, when you have an uppercase "AW," especially in a large typeface, the letters should be much closer together than an "AR." When you have a "To," the "o" should ideally be sitting under the umbrella of the "T." Most page layout software has some automatic kerning built in, so that 50 or 100 or more pairs of letters will appear in what the designer of the program feels is optimum spacing. Some software permits you to increase or decrease the kerning between any two pairs of letters.

• *Text and graphic editing.* While desktop publishing software is not intended to be the place where new writing and graphic creation is done, some programs have word processing and/or design capabilities of their own, including spelling and grammar checkers. For some, this is a major convenience; for others, an unneeded frill.

- *Relational editing.* Let's say that you write a story using your word processing program, and then paste it into a page of a newsletter or report, using a page layout program, more than likely changing its appearance (new typeface, new column width, etc.). Later, if you go back and make some changes in the original word processed version, the changes will *not* appear automatically in the version produced with the page layout software. The same goes for numbers which you have produced with your spreadsheet and then transferred into the page layout, or illustrations created with a graphics program and pasted in. But there is relational page layout software, which maintains links with the original writing, numbers, or design, so that when the original is changed, so is the page layout.

Telecommunication

Telecommunication means using the telephone lines to communicate from your computer to other computers, either directly (computer to computer), or through the auspices of commercial or private bulletin board services. (Bulletin board services are discussed in more detail on page 139.)

To telecommunicate, you need both hardware (a modem; see page 77), and software that enables you to send and receive information through your modem over the telephone lines. There are simple telecommunication programs available through shareware for just a few dollars, and there are large and complex programs sold for many hundreds of dollars. All of them will enable you to send and receive information, but they do it differently. Here are some of the variables:

- *Navigation.* With the simplest software, if you want to learn the closing price for International Grommet and Sushi, you would type in the telephone number you are dialing. When the bulletin board computer answers, you would type in your name, and a password number; then a code that takes you to the business section, another code for the closing prices section, and finally the code number for IG and S. More sophisticated software can be set up to "navigate" you automatically through this maze by pressing a single key, which dials the number, enters your name and password, and makes the necessary code selections.

- *Flexibility.* If you were building a hotel, you could equip each room with 16 different kinds of electrical outlets, in all shapes, sizes, and voltages, so that each guest, no matter where they came from, could plug in their shavers, hair dryers, and electric British toast chillers.[27] Or you could offer "standard" wall plugs and let people worry

---

[27]This little-known appliance is widely used in England. It must be. Otherwise, how could the toast be so uniformly cold every morning?

SATORI GAMES PRESENTS

THAT'S WHERE THE MONEY IS

THE BANK ROBBERY GAME

FOR HOME VIDEO SYSTEMS

First choose the weapons you think you'll need – guns, gas masks, ropes, etc. Be careful you don't carry too much, or you'll move too slowly and get caught by Edgar the Guard. But if the randomized Tear Gas Spray hits you without a gas mask, its off to the Hoosegow! Watch out for rival gangs led by Big John D., Jesse and the Boys, and Patty and the Girls who want to rob the same bank! If you can Blow Up the Vault (you didn't forget the dynamite, did you?), if Edgar the Guard doesn't get you, and if you've positioned your Getaway Car in just the right place, you'll Escape with the Loot, and Meet your Moll in Miami Beach!

HOURS OF FUN FOR CHILDREN OF ALL AGES!

118

about finding their own adaptors. So it goes with telecommunication software. Some offer a wide range of variable settings, so you deal with whatever the computer you are calling dishes out. Others limit the range of things you can do, and/or the ease of doing them.

• *Ease of making changes.* Some telecommunication adjusts or resets itself automatically to the standards of the bulletin board being dealt with. Some can be set or reset by making simple changes on the screen. Some need to be set in advance, which assumes, of course, that you know the settings of the bulletin board you are calling (which often you don't). These "settings" are matters I neither understand nor have much wish to. If I am told that my software should be set to seven "data bits" (or eight), or even parity (or odd), or echo "on" (or "off"), I simply do what I am told, and the easier it is, the better.

Games

Games are one of the things computers do best, and yet some manufacturers and dealers foster the attitude that it is somehow undignified, unbusinesslike, and/or wrong to play them.

When my friend Harry bought himself an IBM PC, he announced in somber tones that it was for his business. Day after day, he sat in his study with the door closed, familiarizing himself with the equipment, and setting up his business records. Or so he told his wife and children.

But from time to time, decidedly unbusinesslike beep-beep-beeps came wafting under the door. They would stop quite suddenly when Pat would knock on the door and ask Harry what he was doing in there.

Harry, and many, many others, have somehow been intimidated into believing some of those *Wall Street Journal* ads with headlines like "This Computer Means Business," and "You Won't Be Using Your QX-44 to Play Games" and "Business, Not Monkey Business."

What nonsense. That's like selling a pencil and saying it's great for doing accounting, but you better not use it for writing poetry, drawing pictures of flowers, or solving crossword puzzles.

Here's why I say games are one of the things computers do best: an ideal program, whether for bookkeeping or for zapping aliens from Arcturus III, should have these four characteristics:

• comprehensible instructions
• easy to learn
• runs without flaws
• a positive experience for the user (not necessarily *fun* but at least satisfying)

With few exceptions, computer games meet all four criteria, and many nongame programs do not.

For those of us who love virtually *all* games, and will contentedly play "Button, button, who's got the button" for an hour with a three-year-old, it is difficult to remember that there actually are some people who do not enjoy games. My only message to these people is, don't reject them until you've given them a try. There's an awful lot more there than shoot-'em-up space games and the ultimately tedious Pac-Man. Some are actually designed to help the player (child or adult) learn more about geography, history, or psychology while playing the game. All of them help the user learn more about the computer. Some even feel they help develop hand-eye coordination.[28]

At first glance, computer games appear to be quite expensive. Many are in the $50 to $100 range. But with rare exceptions, I've gotten good value for money, based on the CPHOF (cost per hour of fun), as shown on the following CPHOF chart:

Event	Cost per hour of fun
Visit to a psychiatrist	$90+
Broadway musical	$30
Meal at a good restaurant	$25
Weekend at a fancy hotel	$5
First run movie	$3
Hardcover book	$2
Good computer game	$.50
Sunsets, parlor games, other home entertainments	$.00

Other software categories

There are many other categories of software, most of them very specific in function, and many of them rarely used by beginners.

Music

In an unprecedented moment of cooperation, the entire world's music industry agreed on a set of standards, whereby all music-producing hardware and software would be compatible with one another. MIDI, or the Musical Instrument Digital Interface, permits composers, performers, editors, producers, and home noodle-arounders to do wonderful things with music. For most situations, MIDI requires both hardware (typically a little black box connected to the computer) and software. There is a huge range of alternatives, so if this is your gig, you will want to read books on the subject, subscribe to magazines

---

[28] When I was a contestant on *Jeopardy*, I discovered that many of my fellow masochists had "trained" for the experience by playing video games, just for this eye-hand therapy.

PAC-MAN
SNAC-MAN
BLAC-MAN
FLAK-MAN
TRAC-MAN
ASTERO
YAK-MAN

ATARI

Some games have elaborate
sound effects.

like *Electronic Musician* and *Keyboard*, and hope there is a music
Special Interest Group (SIG) at your local computer users' group.

Presentations

Presentation software has always seemed to me to be an artificial category, created by software companies who identify a need you didn't
know you had, and for which only their software can help.[29] But the
stuff is apparently quite popular with people who put on public
speeches and presentations, involving slides or overhead projections
and other visuals. Essentially what it does is enable one to create a
series of visuals, composed of graphics and text, often against a col-
ored background, and then juggle them around, in case you decide
you want to talk about last year's sales figures before you talk about

---

[29] Over-the-counter patent medicine dealers have been known to do the same thing, since it is
much easier to create a new disease for an existing medication than to get government approval
for a new medication. "Sinus headache" is a good example. The ailment did not exist on its own
until the advertising agency for Dristan came up with the concept.

the landslide that swept the factory into the Waxahatchie River last week.

Project management

My challenge here is going to be to write this entire paragraph without once using the dreaded word "prioritize." Whether your project is starting a whole new company, buying a computer, or taking a trip to Schenectady, there are certain tasks that have to come before others. You have to buy the tickets before you get on the plane. You have to pour the concrete before you start building the walls. You have to design the brochure before you go to the printer. You have to run the help wanted ad a month before the new office opens.

If you already know all about PERT charts and Gantt charts and critical path management charts, then you should know that there is some very helpful computer software out there, to assist in preparing them. If you don't, you probably should not even consider the software until you have read more about what this technique can (and can't) do for needs like yours.

Multimedia

The National Buzzword Advisory Board has declared "multimedia" to be one of the most promising new buzzwords of the '90s. In the world of computers, it refers to the notion of a computer either controlling or itself *being* a variety of communication media: still pictures, moving images, sound, often used in some interactive fashion. The computer can *control* external devices, such as slide projectors, videocassette players, CD and laser disks, television cameras, stereo systems, music synthesizers, room lighting, vibrating chairs (think Disneyland, not Mistress Inga's House of Pain), window shades, and just about anything else including the kitchen sink. And the computer can produce its *own* still and moving images, sounds, music, and lighting effects. Computers with hot and cold running water have yet to appear on the scene, but there is a charming product called the Maquarium, which is a Macintosh case fitted out as an aquarium, with real fish swimming around where the screen used to be.

Virtual reality

There are some (especially those who have tried it) who believe that when we all have virtual reality computers, we will need nothing else in life, other than occasional new fluid added to our IV tube. In virtual reality, the computer creates an entire world, and "plays" it onto our eyelids via special goggles or into our brain, via electrodes. It is an interactive world. If the scene is a marketplace in Venice, when we move our eyeballs left, we "see" whatever is over there on the left. If we are wearing electric gloves hooked up to the computer, when we reach out to touch something (or someone), we have the actual sensation of having done so. At this writing, the field is in its infancy. Indeed, columnist Jon Carroll, having had the virtual reality experience, likened it to being at Kitty Hawk in 1903 to see the Wright brothers fly, while knowing that in less than one human lifespan, people would be walking on the moon. It is not unreasonable to hypothesize the availability of home virtual reality hardware and software. Travel and sex, among other things, may never be the same.

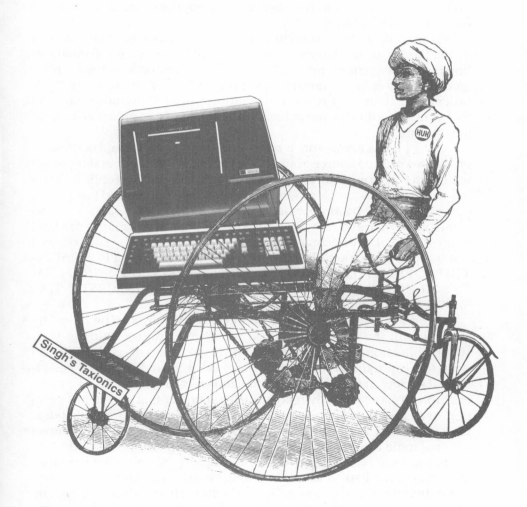

How to Learn about Unusual and Special Interest Software

You can come at it from two directions: from the computer world, or from the special interest world.

From the computer direction, the same sources that you can turn to for hardware information can also supply software information: books and magazines, annual compendia of available software for a given computer, users' groups, electronic bulletin board services, mail-order companies, and your local computer store. With thousands and thousands of software programs available, no one source will have all the information.

Once I had a need—no, a *wish*—for software that could make anagrams. No printed source could offer any leads, but a general message left on an electronic bulletin board brought four or five replies directing me to the Boston Computer Society, which had issued just such a program, called *Ars Magna* (itself an anagram of "anagrams"). It was available as shareware, with only $10 payable to its creator, Michael Morton (one of whose anagrams is "Mr. Machine Tool."). And so now I can happily go through life producing anagrams for "APPLE MACINTOSH" ("PHANTOM SPECIAL," or "A CHAMPION SLEPT"), "INTERNATIONAL BUSINESS MACHINES" ("NO MENACE—IS INSUBSTANTIAL SHRINE"), and anything else I wish.

Oftentimes, unusual or special interest software can be found by starting with the end users. If you want software to catalogue your stamp collection, look for ads and articles in stamp magazines. If you want to keep track of your family tree, ask a local or national genealogical society. If you require specialized software to run (to take three examples I have recently read about) a hair salon, a veterinary practice, or a taxidermy shop (no, I don't think the latter two are related; at least I hope not), you can ask local practitioners what they use, contact national trade associations in that field, or you can snoop around.

Some local businesses will be reluctant to tell you what they use; they may have had to conduct a long search, and why should they share their work with a potential competitor. This can be overcome by phoning comparable businesses in another town or city, and reassuring them that your coin-operated pony ride business will be conducted hundreds of miles away and will be no threat to them. It may also be overcome by stealing garbage. Now that the Supreme Court has ruled this is legal, a couple of people have reported that they learned what computer software a competitor was using (and a good deal more about their business) by bopping off with the garbage bags from behind the store, just ahead of the more traditional garbage collectors.

Buying Locally *versus* Buying by Mail

The advice given for buying hardware (page 83) is just as valid here: buy locally for service; buy mail-order for price. The main differences are:

• The profit on software is much less, so don't expect a great deal of service, at least without paying extra for it.

• Many retail stores will support (i.e., are familiar with) some of the major software they sell, but not most of it; there is just too much on the market. A mail-order seller, on the other hand, may have dozens, even hundreds of telephonists, who, among them, will have familiarity with most or all of the products they sell. On the third hand, the retail store may have locally related software that no mail-order house carries. In my local computer store, for instance, I have seen software designed specifically for real-estate agents in this state, to fill out the seven most commonly used forms in the practice of real estate here.

Buying Used
or Obsolete Software

Properly-used used software will have only been used once or twice, and could be a great bargain. "Properly used" means that the buyer immediately made copies of the disks and/or loaded them onto a hard disk, thereupon retiring the original disks, never to be used again, except in case of emergency.

Not everyone does this, of course. Some people use their original disks every day, and disks do wear down and eventually wear out, both electronically and mechanically.

The main reason used software comes onto the market is that the seller has gotten something newer and better (or at least different). The important factor becomes whether or not the software is upgradable, and, if so, whether or not it already has been upgraded.

For instance, I began my database (mailing list storage) odyssey with software called FileMaker 1. After a few years, the company improved the product, and came out with a brand new version, improbably called FileMaker 4. (Numbers 2 and 3 can be found only in a remote and distant land where the people fly around in Boeing 717s.) As a registered user (I had sent in my warranty card), I was offered the opportunity to buy the new version for quite a low price, and I did so. So then I had two versions: the older but entirely functional version 1, and the new version 4, each complete with manuals, storage box, etc.

I sold my version 1 to someone who didn't need all the improvements that version 4 offered—but it was essential to point out to that person that she could not get a cheap upgrade to version 4; the company will only do that once for each set of the originals. (Subsequently, it has been suggested to me that I may not have had the legal right to sell my own obsolete software.)

But on another occasion, I had an old version of a page layout program called, then, Ready, Set, Go. Newer versions had appeared, but since I had never enjoyed the one I had, I didn't bother to pay to get the newer stuff. So when I sold my old software, the new buyer was able to pay the upgrade fees and convert it into the latest model, at a price far lower than it would have cost to buy the latest one new.

Not all software is upgradable. Sometimes there is a time limit that has expired; sometimes the original company is out of business; sometimes there are no upgrades, and the latest most current version is also old and obsolete.

Get the original disks and manuals

Buying copies of disks and photocopies of manuals is like buying Rolex watches for $9 from that salesman in Times Square. The only two possibilities are that it is stolen or phony or perhaps both.

You must have the originals if you are going to upgrade, and you *should* have the originals to maintain your own sense of decency and fair play. Nuff said.

Buying Computer Supplies

Unless you are looking for after-purchase assistance in opening a box of disks or installing a new ribbon in your printer, the only two factors to consider in buying supplies are price and convenience.

To be sure, there are people who buy goods at "retail" price for the same reason they buy 67 cents worth of postage stamps for a dollar from one of those dreadful little vending machines: convenience and immediate need. But if you can plan even a day or two ahead, most of the time you will do better by mail. When a company in Texas sells a million disks a week, their selling price (under 50 cents each) is less than a local store can buy them for.

And there are some very enlightened mail-order sellers who have built their warehouses adjoining the "hubs" of various overnight delivery services, so that if you place an order by midnight (even 3 a.m. in one instance), you will have your order by 10:30 the same morning.

While most out-of-state mail-order houses will not charge you for sales tax (at least at this time), you do have the legal obligation to pay your state's use tax, and while they won't surround your house with a SWAT ("Say, What About Taxes?") team to collect a few bucks, it is increasingly likely they will go after you for major purchases.

PART VIII

USING COMPUTERS

The One Single Most Important Thing of All

This is a somewhat complex section, but believe me, it's worth the price of admission. If I were permitted one and only one thing to say to people who are contemplating a relationship with a computer, I would say the things in this section. These are the ideas that I desperately wish someone had not only *told* me when I got my first computer, but beat me over the head with, peered through the window to see that I heeded them, and put itching powder in my socks every day that I didn't.

The problem is that it is so easy to *say*—but so hard to convey the importance of it—especially since it won't *really* be important for perhaps half of the people reading this. Which half? Well, as John Wanamaker said about his advertising budget, "I know half my advertising dollars are wasted. The trouble is, I don't know which half."

Let us work into this with yet another automotive analogy. What if seat belts were even more uncomfortable than they are now, and so expensive that they added $3,000 to the cost of a new car. But they also would save over 100,000 lives a year, worldwide, if everybody wore one.

So if the King of the World decreed that everyone must install and wear seat belts, you could imagine the outrage. Opponents would point out, to begin with, that if there *were* no such thing as seat belts, 97% of us would never die in an auto accident anyway. Why penalize the vast majority for that unlucky 3%.

But then, the relatives and loved ones of the dead 3% (and the deceased themselves through spirit transmission) would be saying, with great vigor, "Why didn't you *tell* me? Why didn't you *make* us wear them?"

Well, there it is. It's that sort of thing. I am going to tell you, with as much conviction as I can. And you must promise that you will never, ever come up to me on the street and say, "Boy, have I had a terrible computer experience. Why didn't you warn me about that stuff you were discussing on page ___ of your book. I mean *really* warn me."

For half of you, then, here goes. And the other half better read it too.

Many individuals and businesses acquire a computer to take over some aspect of their lives or their activities. They "computerize" some-

thing. And as soon as the computer is up and running, they abandon—often irrevocably abandon—the old method for doing things.

Don't.

I believe that it is absolutely essential to continue using your old method, alongside the new, for at least two months, better three or four. And if you convert from one computer system to another, save your old disks; save your old software; even save your old computer, at least for a while.

This flies in the face of logic. As soon as the new computer is working well, there is an overwhelming, almost irresistible tendency to embrace it totally, and switch everything over to it as quickly as possible.

Untold grief has been experienced by businesses and individuals who have fallen into this trap. The new computer works wonderfully for a few hours, a few days, a few weeks.

So . . . out with the old horse-and-buggy methods and machinery.

Throw out the kerosene lamps when the electric power arrives (and break your leg falling in the dark, with the first power failure).

Put all your names and addresses and phone numbers into a record-keeping database program, and throw out that dog-eared address book. (Now it is Christmas, for some reason you can't access your main disk, and the backup disk was sitting too near your stereo and was erased by the magnets therein.)

Dispose of your wind-up watch when you buy an electric one (and miss an appointment in a distant city when your battery dies and you can't find a replacement).

Keeping the old and the new going side by side can be trivial in some cases (storing kerosene lamps; keeping a spare watch in your luggage, hanging onto the old address book) or it can be extremely complicated and quite expensive. Even in the latter instance, it is still well worth doing.

To paraphrase Pascal talking about belief in God, if you *do* keep the backup system going and never need it, you've spent a little extra time and money but haven't really suffered. But if you *don't* keep the old system going, and you *do* need it, you're in big, big trouble.

Few people disagree with this advice. Even fewer follow it. I know. I am one of those who has suffered more than once. When the new computer (or new program) works well the first time, there is a giddy feeling of well-being. Life is worth living. A feeling of infallibility. Invulnerability. So why take the time to write the numbers by hand into the old ledger book even once more. Senseless. Antiquated. And then . . .

. . . and then. Consider these case histories: one from my experience, and the rest selected from a goodly number conveyed to me by sadder and possibly wiser computer users.

Lost: $28,000 worth of names

Every morning, 50 to 100 letters would arrive in my mail-order business asking for product information. Names and addresses were typewritten onto 3 × 5 cards in an ancient spirit duplicator system. The cards were used to address envelopes, then filed away in shoe boxes.

When the computer arrived, a team of typists was engaged to work three shifts a day typing all 80,000 names into the database system. When the work was complete, following good computer practice, a copy of the master list was made and stored in a distant location. And the old-fashioned system, including all 80,000 recyclable cards, was donated to a large church.

And then . . . No one knows how it happened, but a few weeks later, we noticed that 4,000 names were missing from the original file. It may have been a flaw in the program, or something a not-properly-trained typist did. But we did not discover the loss when it happened, so the backup disk was copied from the now-flawed original: 4,000 names missing from each.

We got a new copy of the software, and we gave additional training to our typists, and the problem never occurred again. But those 4,000 names, which were worth $7 each to us, were gone forever. A $28,000 loss. The cost of continuing to use the old system alongside the new for three months would have been about $800.

Out to pasture too soon

It was one of the most modern stud farms in America. Thoroughbred horses worth millions of dollars were treated like visiting royalty.

Elaborate and extensive breeding and hereditary records were kept on every stallion and every client: data on tens of thousands of horses, going back eight to ten generations. All the record-keeping was in the charge of a Kentucky gentlewoman who had been keeper of the files for close to half a century. And then came the computer.

Software was acquired and modified to take care of all the duties previously handled by "Old Gillian." After a few weeks of rigorously testing the new system, "backwards and forwards, up and down, and twice sideways from Sunday," the computer was put in charge and Old Gillian was turned out to pasture.

Data entry (typing in names and numbers) was considered a low-level task and was given to two secretaries. The hardware and the software worked just fine, but the *instruction manual* contained several unclear points. They weren't unclear to the man who wrote the manual. And they didn't *seem* unclear to the two secretaries, because they never asked questions. They just blithely typed things in wrong.

In old movies of Africa, the natives either welcome the stranger as their savior and make him king, or they blame him for all their troubles and set him on the coals. So it is with the computer, which is crowned by some and cooked by others.

–Martin Greenburger

The errors were not discovered for more than three months, at which time it was too late to reconstruct the facts. Through lost business and loss of reputation, the owner of the farm reckons that his out-of-pocket loss exceeded $100,000. It would have cost less than a tenth of that to keep Old Gillian on for an additional three months, both duplicating and monitoring the computer's work in her old-fashioned reliable way.

The lost novel

John V. had fair success as a novelist, banging out a new one every couple of years on his old Smith-Corona portable. A slow typist and a meticulous editor, John was a perfect candidate for a word processing system, which he dutifully acquired and taught himself to use with aplomb.

Like many users of word processing, John felt no need to commit anything to paper. All his words were stored electronically on a disk, with a copy on another disk stored in a fireproof safe in the garage. Good computer housekeeping, as far as it went. And then disaster struck.

After a long and creative day at the keyboard, John had added several long chapters to his "original" file on the hard disk. Then, in the process of making a backup copy, he somehow confused the two files, and copied the *old* one onto the *new* one, instead of the other way around, thereby erasing 10 hours of hard work. This act was so demoralizing, so depressing, that John literally gave up work on that particular novel. He had not looked at it for three months at the time he communicated with me: his letter typed on a Smith-Corona typewriter.

Returns from downstate have been delayed

With much fanfare and publicity, the county went over to computerized vote counting. "No more 2 a.m. reports," they proclaimed. "With this high-speed system, the total count should be available within an hour of the closing of the polls."

Some places that computerize voting keep the old system in place for at least one election. The punched ballot cards are counted first by the high-speed computer, then again by slow-speed humans, simply to compare results. But this county did not feel the need. Budgets were tight, and if they could spare the pay for the usual 15 ballot counters, so much the better. Besides, the earnest young man from the computer company was so reassuring.

The polls closed on schedule at 8 p.m., at which time the absentee ballots were run through the computer. The results almost immediately appeared on the screen: 999,999,999 votes for one candidate, 0 votes for the other. This Albanian result was all the more surprising since only about a thousand absentee ballots had been cast.

The earnest young man worked frantically over his machine as the ballots came pouring in from the polling places. Four hours after the polls closed, an urgent call went out for the humans who had counted ballots in the past—but it was midnight, and most were unwilling to get out bed to lend a hand.

At 4 a.m., they gave up, and called the registrar of the nearest county that had similar equipment—a mere four-hour drive away. The ballots were loaded into two sheriff's cars, and by nine in the morning, they were ready to be run quickly through the high-speed vote-counting computer. The results were flashed back home a mere 14 hours after the polls closed.

The $250 saving in not keeping the old system going in parallel was greatly surpassed by the overtime salaries, gasoline, and other expenses accrued, not to mention depriving the electorate of the results of several crucial races for more than half a day.

The unkindest cut

When the big print shop got its brand-new computerized paper cutter, the only way to make room for it was to get rid of the old "guillotine" cutter, operated by the keen eye and strong arm of a shop worker.

The new machine was a wonder. All the coordinates of a series of cuts were typed into the computer, and then, with the push of a single button, the machine would go through its paces, moving great slabs of paper hither and yon, making precision cut after precision cut.

At least that's what it said in the advertisement. In practice, when the machine worked at all, it behaved more like Sweeney Todd, the crazed barber, making random cuts wherever it seemed to feel the need. But the old cutter had been sold to another shop hundreds of miles away. And a print shop without a paper cutter is like, well, a chef without a knife. Not too many customers want a 3-foot by 4-foot letterhead. So the printer went, hat in hand, to his chief competitor to beg (and ultimately pay handsomely for) use of the other man's old-fashioned cutter. It was three months before the computerized machine was back in service.

My files are full of tales like these: devastating problems involving inventory control systems, accounts receivable files, check-writing activities, typesetting, income tax records, and on and on.

In each case, precisely the same series of events occurred:

(1) Computer arrives.

(2) Old system abandoned too soon.

(3) Computer (or software or operator) problem occurs.

(4) Big problems.

The general rule is that the more dependent you are on anything, the more apt you are to become infuriated . . . when it doesn't work to perfection. . . . We have deluded ourselves into believing a machine can function perfectly, and when that delusion is exposed by failure, we become utterly enraged at the machinery. Of course, we are really angry at ourselves.

—Dr. Mel Mandel, (Psychiatrist)

In every case, the cost and bother of keeping the old system going in parallel with the new was far surpassed by the cost and bother of the computer problems.

As with most new machines and systems, many of the problems that ultimately will occur happen during the first few months.

Many people will read this and decide that:

(1) This is a trivial matter, or

(2) it can't or won't happen to me, or

(3) this is a risk I am willing to take, therefore I will do nothing.

Some of those who do nothing will have computers that run beautifully forever, and some will write me "I told you so" letters. Many, perhaps most, of those who *do* pay heed and run the old and the new together for a few months will *also* have perfect computers, and wonder why they bothered. This is the electronic equivalent of somehow being annoyed because you have been paying for fire insurance for all those years, and your building has never burned down, not even once.

If only one person—well, I'd actually prefer a dozen, or perhaps twenty-two thousand—follows this advice and is spared agony and expense when the system fails, I shall rest easier in Writer Heaven.

Bulletin Board Services

Used in a home or office, a computer is an appliance. It may do quite wonderful things for you, but it does little more than you could do on your own, albeit slower and less efficiently, with a typewriter, a calculator, a stack of 3 × 5 cards, a drafting table, and other obsolete but still functional devices.

One thing the small computer does that nothing else on earth can do for you is join you to the entire rest of world, in the most amazing ways, over that tiny little wire connecting your computer to a telephone jack, and the modem that turns your files (words, numbers, pictures) into signals that move along those wires at the speed of light.

I'm going to spend a bit of time on this subject, because of two factors: I really do believe this is the most interesting thing you can do with a computer; and the great majority of computer users have never tried it.

There are two ways to link yourself up to another computer: either directly (you dial the other computer's number, and there you are, ready to send or receive messages); or through somebody else's computer (often known as a bulletin board service or BBS). Some BBSes are completely free, some ask for donations, some charge (your credit card is billed) by the minute, some charge a flat fee per month. The big services range from $5 to $15 an hour, often with cheaper rates at night or on weekends.[30]

Some bulletin boards are gigantic international services, with tens, even hundreds of thousands of subscribers. They have names like CompuServe (the largest), GEnie, Prodigy, America Online, The Source, and The Well (Whole Earth 'Lectronic Link). Others may have ten or fifty participants who enjoy sending messages back and forth, and little more.

So what happens when you dial into a bulletin board, whether huge or tiny or in-between? You begin by making the phone call. Some of the big services have local numbers all over the U.S., which are "call forwarded" to the BBS in some distant city, but you only pay

---

[30]This is actually the only significant hazard of bulletin boards: since you are not billed until you get your phone and credit card invoice the next month, you can easily run up hundreds of dollars in fees, having a grand old time. Just as the casinos in Nevada have no clocks or windows, neither do many BBSes remind you how long you have been on, or how much it is costing you. (If one of your main purposes is sending long messages or reports, since you can send much faster than you can type, it often makes sense to write out your message in advance, and then "upload" it all at once, after you have made connection with the other computer.)

the local charges. Once you have typed in your name and either a password or a code number, you will see a menu of choices on the screen, which may include the following options, among many others:

• *E-mail*, or electronic mail, which is the private message service. Earlier this year, my wife went away for a couple of months to finish her dissertation in another state. Every day, one or both of us would call into a small local bulletin board, and leave E-mail messages for one another. After logging onto the BBS, the message appears on the screen, "You have mail in your mailbox," and there was the private message, which no one else could read.[31]

Some commercial BBS services also offer the option of paper or fax mail: you leave the message for your uncle in Omaha on the BBS computer; they print it out, put it in the mail, and it arrives in his real (not electronic) mailbox the next day—or over his fax machine.

• *News*. Large BBS services offer the option of reading the "wire" service reports from major newsgathering sources: Associated Press, the *Washington Post*, the *Wall Street Journal*, Reuters, and many other newspapers, magazines, and specialized newsletters. Some offer a "clipping service" so you do not have to scan through huge amounts of data. You can leave an instruction that you be notified whenever there is an article about Peruvian politics or solar energy or Pete Rose or whatever, and a list will be deposited automatically in your E-mail mailbox. You can also search by key words, to find, for instance, every article appearing in the *Wall Street Journal* in 1978 that was about cottonseed oil.

• *Research*. Big bulletin board services are like good-sized public libraries, available over your own computer. You can do research on thousands of companies; you can dip into U.S. census data; you can search through reference books, encyclopedias, chamber of commerce files, and much, much more.

• *Travel information*. On some BBSes, you can browse through the *Official Airline Guide,* other plane, train, and bus schedules, get information on what the weather is likely to be in Edinburgh in September, learn about the dining spots of Maracaibo, or the fleshpots of Bangor, Maine, and then actually make your reservations and buy your tickets over the computer.

• *Person to person interaction*. This is the real lure of BBSes for many of us. There can be several or dozens or even hundreds of "forums" available, in which people leave messages on topics of great interest to them: politics, sex, dining, relationships, specific hobbies, sports, whatever. These are public debates and discussions. All who call in can read all messages, and dive in with comments when they feel like it.

---

[31] Except the bulletin board system operator, known commonly as the SysOp, who has the ability, but rarely the wish, to read everything.

This is where people make fast friends (who can be 10,000 miles away; whom they will never meet in person). They buy and sell goods, make vacation house swaps, get into terrible arguments, and explore new cultures. (A few months ago, just to see what the experience would be like, I phoned a couple of BBSes in Hong Kong and in South Africa. For a phone expense less than the cost of one night at a hotel, I had a two-hour international experience of great interest.)

- *Technical advice.* Computer people are just amazingly helpful, especially when the help comes over the computer itself. Some of the big BBS services have forums where nothing goes on but people asking questions and sharing problems, and others, including representatives from some of the big companies, do their best to solve the problems. Indeed, one often finds, as part of the manual for a software or hardware product, an invitation to contact the company through its electronic mailbox on one of the national BBS services.

- *Shopping.* Some BBSes operate like an electronic mall, or a mail-order catalogue. You can browse through descriptions of products, and then place orders for books, electronic or computer gear, cookies, flowers, furniture, whatever, and it is shipped to you.

- *Software for the taking.* Some bulletin boards, including many of the free ones, specialize in offering a huge amount of software, which you can pluck from their giant hard disks, and download into your computer. A lot of this is free; some of it is shareware, for which you are expected to pay, on the honor system, if you decide to keep and use it. It may take 10, 15, 20 minutes or more to download a file from a bulletin board, so if you are paying by the minute, or for a toll call, this could become very expensive "free" software. Some BBSes have literally thousands of programs available, each indexed with a brief description of what it is and what it does, and stored in general categories, such as "games," "fonts," "word processing," and so on.

- *Highly specialized stuff.* Some entire bulletin boards, or sections of bulletin boards, are extremely narrowly specialized. Only a tiny fraction of BBS users would have interest, but boy, when a Mensan who is into witchcraft, or a left-handed dentist, or a one-legged woman,[32] or a Spanish-speaking orthodox Jew discovers there is a whole BBS just for others like her or him, these people are in fat city.

- *Terribly illegal stuff.* Yes, they are out there, and they are just as frightening as you may have read. Under a promise of maintaining anonymity, I was offered the opportunity to browse unhampered by security checks or code words through a so-called "ninja" bulletin board, and I came away rather shaken. There was detailed information on how to commit a hundred kinds of telephone fraud, how to make bombs, how to break into specific schools' computers and change

Shopping at home with your television and home computer is just as much fun as shopping at a Russian department store. The available merchandise is limited, and you can neither touch it nor examine it until after you have bought and paid for it.

—Arthur Elmont

---

[32]They use the BBS to trade the "other" shoe with one another. Aren't you glad you asked.

grades, how to get paychecks inflated at a major chain of department stores, long lists of passwords to break into military and large corporate computers. And somehow it was more scary than funny when my electronic "host" broke in at one point in my process to type, "Sorry, got to go; Mom is calling me to dinner."

About Programming

A program is the set of instructions that tells a computer what to do. I understand something of the philosophy of programming, although I have never actually written a program, and I probably never will.

It is easy enough to talk about programs in ordinary English. Here, for example, is a program:

1. Enter an amount of money, in dollars and cents.
2. Multiply the amount of money entered in Step 1 by .0416.
3. Add the number obtained in Step 2 to the number entered in Step 1.
4. Display the number obtained in Step 3 on the screen following the words, "The total amount of your purchase, including Hawaii sales tax, is:".

This clever little program might be called, "Program for Calculating Hawaii Sales Tax."

At this time, it is unnecessary and unimportant to know what actual keys are punched to tell the computer this. In fact, the specific words, numbers, and symbols will differ from one programming "language" to another. The simple fact is that it is possible to type in a series of logical steps that make the machine go through its paces. Within reason, everything that can be expressed in words can be rendered into programming instructions.

Expanding on the above example, let us say you have a Waikiki gift shop. With every purchase, you type in the buyer's name and address, the item(s) purchased, and price of each. The computer stores this information and calculates the sales tax and the total price. Let us then add two more steps to that program up there:

5. Take the amount calculated in Step 2 and store it away in a file called "Sales Tax."
6. On the first day of each month, take all the numbers stored in the file "Sales Tax," add them together, and print them after the words, "Total sales tax for the month just ended is:".

Once again, these are the sorts of things one says to a programmer, whose job it is to figure out how to communicate the instructions electronically to the computer.

For a final extension of this example, let us say you get in a special shipment of Elvis portraits on black velvet. You wish to notify your best customers of this important event. Let us say the code number for Elvis portraits on black velvet is 118.

They tell me computers are growing more "user friendly" — but you still have to wear goggles and get out in the mud and crank them.

—Marina Bear

Now you wish to have the computer search through its memory to find all customers who have the following specifications:

a. The product code of their last purchase is 118.

b. The amount of money entered in Step 1 is over $50 (you only want to write to the big spenders).

c. Their zip code is a number between 90000 and 92999 (you want to write only to people living in Southern California, the black velvet capital of the free world).

The programmer, then, is the person who takes the available data, the capabilities of the machine, and the desired result and figures out how to get from here to there. Not necessarily the best way, because there is rarely a single solution to any given programming need. Let's say I wish to have a program that will give me the sum of two numbers.

Simple elegant program:

1. Add the first number to the second number.

Less elegant program:

1. Multiply the first number by 8.
2. Multiply the second number by 6.
3. Divide the result of Step 1 by 4.
4. Divide the result of Step 2 by 3.
5. Add the result of Steps 3 and 4 together.
6. Divide the result of Step 5 by 2.

This inelegant program *will* do the job of adding two numbers together, and will take a computer only a few millionths of a second longer than the elegant one. The time difference hardly matters in many situations (it's hard to get a lot done in 3/1,000,000 of a second), but when a program requires thousands or even millions of separate calculations, the saving of a tiny fraction of a second thousands and thousands of times can be quite significant.

And anyway, it isn't just saving time, it is elegance. Programmers find it a challenge to seek an elegant solution. Here's a lovely example: When Carl Friedrich Gauss was a wee lad, his mathematics teacher gave the third grade class some busy work so he could attend to some personal business. "Add up all the numbers between 1 and 100. A prize to the student who finishes first with the correct answer." While the rest of the class was dutifully writing down 1 + 2 + 3 + 4, Gauss, in about 10 seconds, raised his hand with the correct answer. He instantly reasoned that 1 + 100 = 101; 2+ 99 = 101; 3 + 98 = 101. And so on, such that there would be 50 pairs, each totaling 101. And 50 × 101 = 5050. A mental programming feat befitting the lad who was to become the greatest mathematician of his time.

There is always a place for a bright young inventor.

FOR MONTHS, I HAD BEEN HEARING COMPUTER PROFESSIONALS EXCITEDLY DISCUSSING COMPUTER SYSTEMS THAT OPERATED WITH EUNUCHS.

I WAS AFRAID TO ASK.

TURNED OUT THEY WERE REFERRING TO A "HOT" NEW OPERATING SYSTEM, DEVELOPED BY THE BELL SYSTEM, CALLED "UNIX."

OH.

Stand up for your right not to be a programmer

Many programmers think that programming is so wonderful, so elegant, such fun, that anyone who does not want to become a programmer must be a few bricks shy of a load. This is roughly analogous to a happy stable cleaner failing to comprehend why *everyone* does not enjoy shoveling manure as much as he does.

Programming *can* be a challenging, creative, entertaining thing to do, and there are probably going to be more job openings for competent programmers than almost any other white-collar job over the next 20 years—especially those who can handle COBOL or dBASE applications for business. (The need will be especially acute in Japan.)

But you do not *need* to understand programming to use computers successfully any more than you need to understand enzyme action in order to enjoy a good meal. This is a fact that many people seem not to have grasped. Over and over again, I hear the lament, "I want to get into computers—but I don't see how I'll *ever* learn programming." The registrars at half a dozen colleges I surveyed told me the same thing: programming classes have high initial enrollment—*and* one of the highest dropout rates of any class offered.

Some people drop out because they can't understand what's going on. But the majority, I suspect, drop out because the more they learn about programming, the more they see that it is unnecessary to their goals.

People who really enjoy something immensely find it almost impossible to grasp the fact that I have no interest whatsoever. ("You don't want to go cross-country skiing even a *little* bit?" No. "You don't want to eat even a *little* of my squid soufflé?" No. "You don't want to learn a few of the *simplest* programming instructions?" No.)

I am delighted, I am thrilled, I am so impressed that legions of programmers are out there doing their thing, so that when I want to delete a file or change a word into italics or copy a chart into a report, I can do so with simple keyboard commands. These undoubtedly set off elaborate machinations involving instructions like GOTO, HIMEM, BLOAD, MID$, PARAMS, and POKE, but I don't have to know about it, any more than I need to know that in order to make my car go, I have to pump a little gasoline through a carburetor into a cylinder, compress it, and set fire to it 10 times a second. I just "step on the gas" and it all happens, just like magic.

Because of my programming chauvinism, over the years I have had more than a few angry letters, half anonymous, from programmers, saying, in effect, "You poor shlub. Don't you realize how important . . . " Of course I do. And I'll bet my backhand is better than theirs, and my vegetable soup tastier. Everybody doesn't have to do everything well. Or at all. Thank you.

The five levels of programming, and who will use them

If automation keeps up, man will atrophy all his limbs but the push-button finger.
  —Frank Lloyd Wright

Having just established that it is quite unnecessary for most of us, I shall now describe the five levels of programming that it is not necessary to learn. The reason is that there is an important distinction to make. People use the word "programming" in many ways, and there is confusion because they may be referring to different levels at different times. "By 1999, all college graduates will need to know programming." "Programming skill required for this job." "There is no need to learn programming." What is being talked about is quite different in each of those sentences. Different levels are being referred to.

Level 1: Machine language programming

At their most elemental, computers are, in effect, a series of off-on switches. The number "21," for instance, is represented by six consecutive switches in the off-on-off-on-off-on configuration. The number "9" consists of switches in the off-off-on-off-off-on order. How does one add "21" to "9"? There is an elaborate internal logic that "tells" the machine what to do with these two arrays of switches when separated by yet another array that corresponds to "+." *Somehow* (I neither know nor care how), the computer ends up with switches in an off-on-on-on-on-off pattern, which stands for a "30."

The machine language programmer is one who actually understands what goes on inside the machine itself. Only a tiny percentage of programmers can do this. Some people regard them as the elite of the field. Others regard it as a peculiar and largely unnecessary (if hard to acquire) skill, in the same direction as being able to recite Shakespeare while balancing a jug of water on your head.

Level 2: Programming with programming languages

The reason it is not necessary for most people in most situations to know anything about machine language is that the clever folks who have devised the various programming languages have done all the work needed to master the machine. For example, when you hit a "+" key on your $6.95 pocket calculator, the very act of hitting the "+" puts into action all those elaborate off-off-on-off switch manipulations needed to combine one set of switches (i.e., one number) with another. Because one person figured out how to do this wonderful shortcut once, and packed it all into the "+" key, no one ever has to do it again.

The people who developed the various programming languages have taken incredibly complex sets of machine behaviors, and combined all the dozens or hundreds or thousands of steps required to execute them into a single shorthand character or collection of a few letters. The programmer must understand what all these shorthand designations do, but has no need to understand *how* they do it.

There are dozens of programming languages in use. They all have the effect of making the computer do many internal maneuvers from a single keystroke (or two). The most popular programming languages have names like BASIC, Pascal, FORTRAN, and COBOL, which are acronyms for things neither you nor I need to remember.

When people talk about one programming language being more *powerful* than another, it means it can do more complex things with fewer keystrokes.

Some languages are designed to be most useful to certain categories of users: scientists, business people, engineers, beginners. But the *philosophy* of programming remains constant, so that a person who

There is no danger of machines running amok, unless, of course, they have been programmed to run amok.

–John Hargreaves

has become "fluent" in one programming language will find it easier to learn a second one than a person starting from scratch. ("Fluency," incidentally, is an apt term. Some universities that have foreign language requirements for its graduates will now accept fluency in FORTRAN or COBOL as meeting that requirement.)

Level 3: Program changing

Some people can edit another person's manuscript or correct another person's golf swing when they are incapable of writing or swinging on their own. Similarly, there are people who may not be able to create an elaborate program from scratch, but who have the skill to make creative changes in other people's programs.

To do this requires a knowledge of programming languages, and a good sense of the real world needs of users of the various programs. For example, a writer had a word processing program that was capable of putting footnotes at the bottom of a page. But the original programmer had not taken into account *really* long footnotes, which would have to lap over onto the next page. The writer found a program modifier who could delve into the original program, line by line, and make some minor adjustments to accommodate long footnotes.

The modifier told me she could *never* have written such a complex program from scratch, but she was able to do a bit of fine tuning on someone else's work.

Another example: many mailing list programs were originally designed for the five-digit zip code. Then the Postal Service announced the forthcoming change to nine digits. Some people had program modifiers go into their programs and expand the zip code capability to nine spaces . . . and soon after that, to program in the automatic hyphen required between numbers five and six.

Program modifying is a very tricky business. John Muir said that every time he moved a rock, he found it was tied to everything else in the universe. So it is with programming. People have found, to their dismay, that a minor change in Line 2740 can make a tiny change in six other lines which in turn are tied into 18 other lines. Several people used the Rubik's Cube analogy to describe how they got further and further in over their heads.

Level 4: Program adjusters

Some programs are designed to be changed by the customers. The method of making the changes is explained, sometimes even clearly, in the instructions. My word processing program is "set" for 8½×11 paper. I recently had occasion to write an article for an Australian publisher, who required "A4" metric spacing, slightly different in both dimensions. By going to the "Page Set Up" screen, I was able to

Programs can be altered manually (using pencil and paper) or electronically (directly on the computer).

change instantly to the alternative size. I was able to do it quickly because the original programmer had made it possible for me to do so.

Level 5: Program users

When you put a quarter in an arcade game, you are using a very clever and quite complex computer program—without giving a moment's thought to that fact. When you use your bank teller card, or a long distance telephone, or ask your travel agent to reserve you a room in Rarotonga,[33] you are tapping into elaborate computer systems that have been made to appear simple.

Someday, if all goes well, the great majority of programs will fit into the same category. Just as you give no thought now to the gears and pulleys that spring into action when you turn on your electric typewriter, so, one day, will you give no thought to the elaborate, sophisticated program that makes your word processor process words.

It is *that* kind of computer usage that will enlist legions of new participants in whatever kind of computer revolution we've got going today.

Whatever the total number of humans interacting with computers, my prediction is that participation in these five categories is likely to be roughly logarithmic in nature. By that, I mean that for each machine language programmer, there will be something like 10 programmers, 100 program modifiers, 1,000 program adjusters, and 10,000 program users.

I don't want to process words, I said. You will learn, she assured me. . . . We have the Hardwriter Program, the ImpossiCalc Program, (and) the Try-And-Index-It Program. . . .

—James Kilpatrick

---

[33] It was sheer magic. One week, our travel agent in California punched some keys on the shiny new computer in her office. The next week, the 747 landed on the South Pacific island of Rarotonga at three in the morning, and there at the airport waiting for us was a bleary-eyed old chap with our names scrawled on the back of an envelope. At the time, the island didn't even have telephone service. How could this have happened? No, don't tell me. I prefer magic.

How Do You Learn More?

"Computer literacy" has become a major catch phrase for our time. "Achieving computer literacy" is perceived as a worthy goal for all. "Computer illiteracy" is a sorry fate, to be avoided at all cost. And so on.

"Computer literacy" can have many meanings, just as plain old ordinary literacy does. Can you do nothing more than sign your name (check-signing literacy)? Can you talk to people well enough to buy a hat or locate the bathroom (conversational literacy)? Can you write a letter? an essay? a sonnet? a novel? Many different levels and kinds of literacy—every one of them either important or unimportant, depending on the circumstances. It is meaningless simply to say "Literacy is essential."[34]

The great majority of people on earth will live their lives and die without ever having laid fingers on a personal computer. Some people have already achieved great success in the computer world without having any technical or programming skills. (They do, however, have business skills or game-conceiving skills or other creative skills.) And most lie somewhere in between. It may be nice, or even desirable, to achieve some level of computer literacy—but somehow the world will go on if we don't.

Books

It is clear from the data on best-selling computer books, and from talks with bookstore clerks, that the prime customers for computer books are people who already have computers, and want to get more out of them. In one recent week, 18 of the top 20 best-selling computer books in a major chain were "How to" books linked to specific software: *Understanding Microsoft Word, Mastering Lotus 1-2-3, How to Use PageMaker 4.0.* Some of these books are superior in clarity or completeness to the manuals that come with software. Some simply offer a second opinion to uncertain users hoping to learn more.

---

[34] There is a wonderful story by Somerset Maugham about a church janitor, or sexton, who is fired when his boss, the minister learns he is illiterate. On the way home, heartbroken, he craves a cigarette, but cannot find a smoke shop in the neighborhood. He opens a tiny shop there to sell cigarettes, prospers, and after a few years he is the millionaire head of a national chain of smoke shops. He manages to hide his illiteracy for years, until one day a business associate finds out. "Good lord, man," the associate says, "as an illiterate, you have become one of the richest men in the country. What would you have been if you *could* read and write?" "Sexton of St. Anthony's Church!" the man replies.

The overlap in books is considerable. Not long ago, I sat down (at one of those enlightened bookstores that has chairs) with seven books devoted entirely to learning how to use Adobe Illustrator software. They were all of similar length, design, and content. As it happened, I had a couple of specific problems I had been wrestling with in trying to learn this rather complex program, and only two of the seven books covered them both. One was $17.95 and had a pretty cover. The other was $24.95 and didn't. My choice was made.

Magazines

An incredible magazine glut of the 1980s—during 1985, a new computer magazine was launched every three days!—has, thankfully, been reduced by attrition and overkill (and lack of interest) to a dozen or so major players, and another score of smaller special interest magazines. There are major monthly (and even weekly) magazines specific to IBM, Macintosh, Apple II, and Amiga, and there are some generic magazines like the venerable *Byte* and *InfoWorld*, that cover the entire computer industry.

Many computer users subscribe to one or two, and check out half a dozen others at the public library or the store each month, buying those with articles or advertisements that interest them. It is not uncommon for the major IBM and Macintosh magazines to run 300, 400, 500, or more pages each month. Both readers and advertisers seem insatiable in their desire to spend their money in this manner.

Computer courses

People who want to learn more about computers through formal coursework have many options available, as purveyors of academic materials have *also* discovered the extremely high level of interest (and willingness to spend money) in this field. Courses range from the very general and sometimes superficial ("What this electronic revolution is all about") to extremely technical ("Applications of FORTRAN in bridge design"), at prices ranging from free to thousands of dollars.

In all large cities, and many smaller towns, live courses are available through six different kinds of agencies: community and other colleges, proprietary schools, alternative learning centers, computer shows, users' groups, and private tutors. And courses are offered by mail to people living anywhere in the world.

Colleges

Nearly all colleges and universities now offer computer classes—often available evenings and weekends to the non-degree-seeking public. This is especially true of more than a thousand community or junior colleges, where courses are either free or very inexpensive, and often taught by working computer professionals doing this in their spare time. Some community colleges will design special courses to order for specific business applications, if enough students will take the course.

Proprietary schools

Proprietary (i.e., money-making) schools of all kinds offer computer courses to the public. Some of them are business colleges that have added computer divisions. Some are operated by large corporations, to train their own employees, but others are invited to pay and learn. Some have been newly established to ride the computer wave. Those that have been around for a year or so can be found in the Yellow Pages of the phone books.

Alternative learning centers

There are hundreds of them around the country, sometimes independently run, sometimes affiliated with churches or social agencies. In some centers, teachers can list any course they wish in the catalogue, ranging from divorce workshops to pickle making. If enough people turn up, the course goes on.

Users' groups

Local computer clubs, societies, and groups often have both formal and informal classes on computer use, ranging from those for absolute beginners to those looking for advanced training in specific sophisticated software. Any decent computer store should be up on the users' groups in the vicinity, and the major computer companies can supply information on groups devoted to their equipment.

Users' groups are often wonderful for providing immediate one-on-one training when you need it the most: when something terrible has happened, more than likely at 10 p.m. Friday evening at the start of a three-day weekend, and you know you can't reach the dealer until Tuesday morning, which seems impossibly far away. Salvation comes in the form of a help line you can call, and more often than not reach someone who has been there before, or, at the very least, when all else fails, can rush over with a bottle of Scotch, a carton of mint chip ice cream, and/or a new Disk Operating System to replace the one you destroyed when you fell off your chair when you got the electric shock from trying to adjust the cable that was making your monitor flicker, setting off an epileptic fit in the cat.

Private tutors

There are many situations in life, even some relevant to this book, where you can learn more from a knowledgeable person in two hours than in two months of struggling on your own. This is especially true at the start of a learning process. On more than one occasion, I have found that hiring a knowledgeable student (high school to doctoral) for a couple of hours to "jump start" my learning about a particular piece of software is far better than spending those two hours, or many more, trying to get a sense of what a particular program is all about.

If such people do not advertise locally, they can still be found with a phone call to the nearest high school or college computer department or lab. Your tutor may not be a great teacher, but he or she probably knows more about computers than you ever will, and once you overcome the curious feeling of being tutored by a mere child, your time will be well spent.

Courses by mail

Both public institutions and private companies offer computer courses by mail. More than 50 major universities offer courses by correspondence study to people living anywhere in the world. A typical course will cost anywhere from $100 to $400, and require anywhere from six weeks to a year to complete. There are usually no prerequisites; anyone can take any course. If you wish to earn college credit, you can take a locally-supervised exam, but this is not essential. You can, however, apply such credits to degrees that can be earned from accredited colleges and universities, entirely by mail.[35]

Just to get you started, here are three schools that offer a wide range of computer courses by correspondence study: University of California, Independent Study, Dept. NN, 2223 Fulton St., Berkeley, CA 94710; Oregon State System of Higher Education, Office of Independent Study, P. O. Box 1491, Portland, OR 97207; the Graduate School of the U.S. Department of Agriculture, Correspondence Study Program, 600 Maryland Ave. S.W., Room 133, Washington, DC 20024.

Those schools don't offer degrees by mail, but the following three accredited schools, among others, do: Regents College, University of the State of New York, Cultural Education Center, Albany, NY 12230; Thomas Edison State College, 101 W. State St., Trenton, NJ 02992; and Heriot-Watt University External MBA Degree Program, P. O. Box 7070, Berkeley, CA 94707.

Computer shows

Most shows are put on by independent entrepreneurs who rent a hall, then rent booth space to manufacturers, dealers, distributors, computer stores, users' groups, publishers, and others who have something to offer the computer-buying public. These can range from an afternoon in a small town shopping mall to a week in a big city convention center.

There are shows just for manufacturers and for distributors, but they are of far less interest to beginners than "end user" (that's us) shows. It is nice to know that the people who make the springs that push keyboard keys back up when you push them down have a place to exhibit their wares, but the audience is rather specialized. Still, if you want to attend a trade show, you will have to invest in a business

---

[35] And how do I learn more about *that?* I hear a few of you asking. Why, from a book entitled *College Degrees by Mail: 100 good schools offering Bachelor's, Master's, Doctorates and Law degrees through home study,* written by someone named John Bear, and available at your bookstore or from Ten Speed Press, the very same people who are bringing you this book.

card, either showing you as the president of Amazotronic Industries (or whatever), or simply as a computer consultant. Most times, no one will check.

End user shows are totally eclectic. There might be a large booth from IBM across the aisle from a tiny booth where a local entrepreneur is trying out a new bit of software. In addition to buying supplies and collecting souvenirs (pens, balloons, buttons, key chains, etc.), there are five kinds of reasons people go to shows. Most people I have talked to are generally satisfied in four of these areas, and usually frustrated in the fifth.

1. *What's new.* An opportunity to see more hardware and software in one place than any store or dealer is likely to have. Afterwards, shows can be rated by the number of shopping bags you managed to fill with free literature: a one-bag show, two-bags, etc.

2. *Hands-on experience.* Some booths offer the opportunity to try things out, either just for a few minutes of noodling around, or via a prepared 5- or 10- or 15-minute interactive demonstration.

3. *Educational events.* Many shows offer a series of lectures, seminars, or workshops on a range of topics as diverse as how to use Microsoft Excel to how to start a computer consulting business. Sometimes these lectures or classes are a part of the admission price; sometimes you pay separately. Most shows sell either tapes or transcripts of the classes at a lower price than you would have paid to take it in person.

4. *Networking.* Computer shows can be excellent places to meet people. I have seen informal users' groups spontaneously formed by two or three people standing around the Gizmotronix booth, who discover they have had similar problems, and have various ideas about how to solve them. Similar interactions occur at the snack bars while refueling on dreary expensive snacks, and in the "hospitality" lounges sometimes rented by larger companies in the hope of luring you to spend a little more time with their product.

5. *Talking to company people.* This is the area that sounds reasonable, but rarely works. People go to a show in hopes of talking to manufacturers' representatives, either to learn more about a product than the local computer store can offer, or to help resolve a problem or a complaint. One sees badges on people in booths indicating that they are vice-presidents or marketing directors or even the president of the company. I am quite convinced these badges have been pinned on dummies acquired from some local Rent-a-Booby service to impress the public with the importance of the booth. These *cannot* be the real officers, or the company would be down the tubes in a month.

I don't go as far as Kingsley Amis's Lucky Jim, who decided at an early age that there was no point acquiring new information because it pushed out an equivalent amount of information he already had, leaving him just where he started. As the new electronic marvels buzz away furiously, some of what they do will have value. But, as an inevitable accompaniment, they will preserve what ought to be torn up, discarded, cast aside, or should never have been born.

—Edwin Newman

You Are Smarter Than You May Have Thought (A Short Pep Talk)

I have talked to hundreds and hundreds of people, in person, by phone, and on talk shows, who were eager to report their computer experiences. The stories range from devastating to glorious. When people tell me mournfully that they don't think they are *ever* likely to get involved in computers—they just can't imagine how to begin—it has seemed appropriate to report this actual case history, as conveyed to me by the lady in Boston to whom it all happened.

The lady in question sort of thought she might like to find out what computers were all about. But she kept putting it off, because she felt intimidated before she even began her quest. Some of what she had read led her to believe that she lacked the manual dexterity to interact successfully with a computer.

(On the day she had that thought, she successfully and single-handedly took command of a 4,000-pound machine whose proper operation required her to coordinate and synchronize independent activities of her left hand, her right hand, her left foot, and her right foot, and to monitor, with eye and ear, various gauges and sounds, all of this while looking backwards over her left shoulder. She backed her car out of the garage.)

She had read just enough computer ads and articles to be able to fret about the apparently incomprehensible vocabulary of bits and bytes and modems not to mention peripherals and programming and other concepts that made "learning computers" sound like an academic enterprise beyond her mental abilities.

(On *that* day, she utilized the concepts of accounts payable and receivable, cash flow management, double entry bookkeeping, information storage and retrieval, mathematics, and inference. She balanced her checkbook. Then she performed an act which, amazingly, according to a Gallup survey, more than half the adults in America have never done: she voluntarily read a book other than the Bible.)

She tentatively set foot in a computer store, but felt uncomfortable and out of place in the sleek high-tech environment. She found it difficult to communicate with the young man on duty, who looked at her with a mixture of pity and disdain when she apparently failed his initial vocabulary test.

She left the computer store in confusion and mounting despair, but as she strolled down the aisle at the mall, her eye was caught by a window display at a Radio Shack store. Impulsively, she added a couple of hundred dollars to her credit card balance, and came home with a very basic IBM clone, read the manual, hooked it up, plugged it in, turned it on, started enjoying herself, bought a couple of books to supplement the manual, played games, started in on a home bookkeeping system, made a few tentative stabs at learning programming, found she enjoyed it, bought a book on programming, took a community college class on programming, bought a larger and more sophisticated computer, helped automate her husband's business, gave lectures on overcoming computer fear, taught classes in computerization, and finally opened her own computer service bureau in the storefront vacated by the bankruptcy of the computer store she had first visited.

Not everyone will take it this far, of course. But anyone who has enough smarts to read this book is beyond doubt capable of succeeding with computers, if he or she but wishes.

Computers certainly aren't for everyone. But the only way to find out is to dip your toe in the water. If the water is cold and uncomfortable, at least you'll have found out first hand, and not by hearsay, intimidation, or being warned off by inept lifeguards. It is far better to try now and discover you'd rather not, thank you, than to wait and wait, and then find out that way back in the 1990s, you had a chance to plunge into computers, but in the words of the Guinness Stout slogan, you "never tried it because you didn't like it."

PART IX

PROBLEMS WITH
COMPUTERS

The Inherent Fragility
of the Machinery

Long ago, back in the '70s, when nearly all computers were installed in special Computer Rooms, the main reason for doing this—philosophical and religious reason aside—was because computers were very delicate machines, highly susceptible to moisture, heat, dust, static electricity, and assorted other factors.

They still are.

However, the manufacturers are well aware that no one is going to buy a $200 Tandy, much less a $6,000 IBM, if they are told they must install it in a dust-free, temperature- and humidity-controlled room with raised antistatic flooring, a special electrical transformer, and possibly a lead-lined roof.

Computers are sensitive to temperature extremes.

To be sure, computers *do* work quite reliably on kitchen tables, laps, and even in smoke-filled rooms. But I am convinced that many of the problems that occur, and repairs that are required, could have been avoided if users had more appreciation for the delicate nature of the beast.

There are four general kinds of problems to worry about: environmental, "mysterious" forces, mechanical, and human beings.

The environment can cause problems

There are certain steps that can be taken to diminish the likelihood of problems caused by factors in the environment: dust, smoke, heat, moisture, dandruff, hair, etc.

Notice, however, that this section is not called "How to avoid . . . " or "How to solve . . . " The reason is that it just isn't worth it, either in cost or effort, to eliminate the problems entirely. If a $12 dustcover can reduce the number of dirt-related breakdowns from one every 50 days to one every 500 days, it is well worth the investment.[36]

The diagram on the next page reminds me of just how fragile my system really is. Daniel Leduc's terrifying analogy to disk head and disk is a jumbo jet flying at top speed over hilly terrain at an altitude of one foot.

Of course every grain of dust, particle of smoke, or flake of dandruff won't destroy your work. Thankfully, many of the times when a

---

[36]The value of a dustcover is greatly enhanced when it is used. Many are bought, but few are used regularly. Nailing it to the wall as a talisman against grime has little effect.

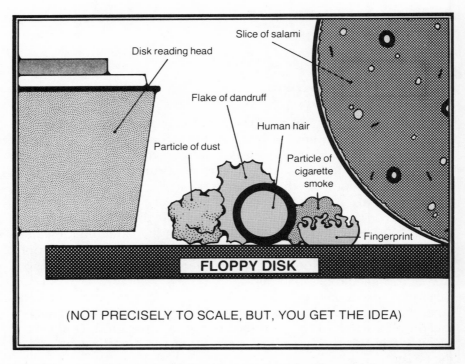

Disk reading head

Slice of salami

Flake of dandruff

Human hair

Particle of dust

Particle of cigarette smoke

Fingerprint

FLOPPY DISK

(NOT PRECISELY TO SCALE, BUT, YOU GET THE IDEA)

system error message is flashed, trying again will cause the operation to work because the offending particle has been pushed to the side the second time through.

The best way to minimize dust and dirt problems is by careful housekeeping and by following certain simple (but oh, so easy *not* to do) rituals:

• Always return your disks to a dust-free box when not in use. Your shirt pocket is *not* a dust-free box.

• Get a cover for the computer, the printer, the disk drive, and use it all the time. Be grateful that you do not have the problem I now have with (how shall I say this delicately?) gecko urine.

• Never smoke around the computer.

• Never touch the shiny parts of your disks.

• Vacuum the area around the computer regularly—but use extension wands, because the magnetic field generated by the vacuum cleaner can wreak havoc with your disks. Also, be careful not to stir up the dust.

• Pay attention to moisture and humidity. Unless you are inclined to carry your computer into the Turkish bath, there should be no major problems, but there can be minor ones or long-term ones. I live in quite a humid place, and when I had the case off my computer to add

Inanimate objects are classified scientifically into three major categories: those that don't work, those that break down, and those that get lost.

—Russell Baker

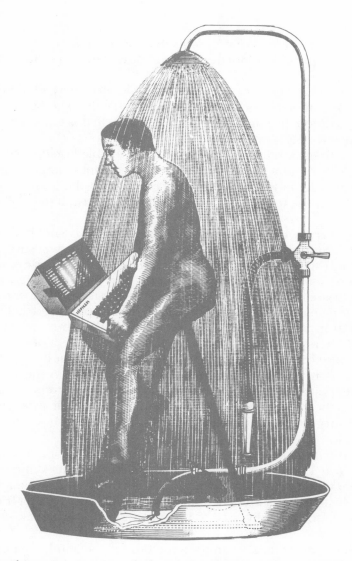

memory chips, I saw some little spots of rust and corrosion on the inside. The printout on the wall, as it were. It may be time to think about a dehumidifier.

"Mysterious" forces can cause problems

Many of the things that go wrong with computers and in computing can be traced to problems with electricity, magnetism, and other forces. It isn't necessary to understand the nature of the forces as long as you are aware of what they can do and, to the extent feasible, what can be done to guard against them.

Here are six kinds of problems that are most likely to occur. They can each range from minor nuisances to devastating system-destroying disasters.

1. *Too much power.* Normal household electricity in the U.S. and Canada is somewhere between 115 and 120 volts. The power companies try to keep the amount of electric current in this narrow range, but often they do not succeed.

As with the engine of your car, if the available horsepower rises or falls a little, there will be no problem. But a giant voltage surge is like strapping a jet engine on your rear bumper: at the least, this power surge will cause temporary loss of control; at most, it may destroy the machinery.

There are two important questions to which I do not believe there are yet definitive answers. One is how often large power surges occur. Is it every three days or every three decades? Some electric companies maintain there is no such thing as a giant power surge, unless perhaps if your home is struck by lightning. The other is whether or not surge protectors really work. Some people are quite convinced that the low-end ($10 to $50) surge protectors may actually do more harm than good. Others regard them as the electronic equivalent of a St. Christopher statue on the dashboard: it will probably never be needed, and when it is it may fail, but oh, the peace of mind in the meantime. (Greater peace of mind comes from those manufacturers of surge protectors who guarantee to replace your computer if it is fried by a power surge while their equipment is in use. But they don't pay to replace lost data.)

2. *Too little power.* This problem is more common, and harder to solve. You know the phenomenon of house lights dimming for a moment when a refrigerator motor comes on. That is because it takes more electricity to start up a motor than to run it, so for that fraction of a second, power is diverted to the motor from your lights—and your computer.

When power fails, even for a fraction of a second, whatever may have been in your temporary computer storage bins may be erased forever. A drop of 5 or 10 volts may not cause a problem, but 15 or 20 may be fatal to your data, although the computer itself will not be harmed.

The solution to power drops is a constant-voltage producer, called an uninterruptible power source, or UPS. These devices, which cost from $250 on up, take any line voltage and transform it into a nice steady 117 volts. And if the power goes off entirely, the built-in batteries will continue producing the 117 volts for the few minutes necessary to shut down the computers in a proper fashion.

3. *Static electricity.* This is the stuff that sometimes gives you a small shock when you touch a metal doorknob, and which enables

you to slide across a shag carpet in leather shoes and "stick" balloons or playing cards to the wall. (Look, if you want a book on physics, get a book on physics; that's all the explanation you're going to get from me.) Some consultants regard static electricity as a major problem. They suggest grounding yourself before touching the machine. Static electricity can effect the innards of your computer, even if you're not given to gliding across the floor and sticking balloons on your disk drive. A static voltage 1% of the size you could just barely feel is still enough to destroy a microchip. Some manufacturers recommend keeping computers in uncarpeted rooms, or using antistatic rug spray for existing carpets.

4. *Magnetism.* Magnetic waves kill computers. Let us say that you have taken 10 million little iron balls and spent a year arranging them on the floor to spell out the third act of King Lear. What happens if a strong magnet is passed over your creation? Well, exactly the same thing happens to all the little particles on the surface of your disk when it is exposed to a magnetic field, and, just as with the iron balls, the information is gone forever.

This can be a major problem, not because of fiends who sneak into people's houses and offices armed with giant electromagnets, but rather because there are hidden magnets at work all around you. Virtually all electric motors are magnetic to some extent—even the ones in your computer's disk drive and printer. It is a wise housekeeping practice never to leave disks out and about, especially near typewriters, office machines, telephones, fans, television sets, air conditioners, stereos (especially the loud speakers), vacuum cleaners, paper shredders, and other motorized stuff.

5. *X-rays.* People often ask whether they can pass their computers or disks through the X-ray devices at airports. Interestingly, the problem is not with the X-rays themselves, but with the huge magnet underneath the machine that churns out the X-rays. Better to carry disks and portable computers through the metal detector than have them pass through the luggage X-rayer. You may have to turn the portable on, to prove it is really a computer, and not a weapon. ("Take this plane to Havana, or I'll compute the value of pi to 400 places!")

6. *Gamma rays.* There is probably some top secret manual for computer repair people, in which they are told that when all else fails, they can always blame the problem on gamma rays. *Omni* magazine confirms, however, that if one of these rays, which regularly come wafting down from outer space, should pass through a computer, it is liable to wreak havoc in the most subtle ways, such as erasing just a tiny part of the information on a disk, perhaps a minus sign in an important calculation. Some big computer users shield their computer rooms with lead to ward off gamma rays and other particles that may be invented from time to time.

Actual path of a gamma ray through a typical home.

Unless you have run clean out of other things to worry about, it is not necessary to worry about gamma rays.

Mechanical problems

Even though many computers are advertised as having "only" seven moving parts, or something equally impressive, the fact is that they also have thousands of *nonmoving* parts. Many of these nonmoving parts are soldered or otherwise fastened to other nonmoving parts.

Anything that has been fastened to something else has the potential for coming undone. And of course anything that can potentially happen, probably will.

Soldered connections are especially fragile. Every time the computer is turned on, the circuits get a surge of power, thus heating and expanding them. When the computer is turned off, they cool down and shrink. The expand-contract cycle can create invisible flaws, which is why many people (but not all) recommend leaving your computer on all the time (with a screen saver installed, which causes the screen to go dark, thus keeping images from being permanently burned into it).

When computers are jostled, jarred, or shaken, not only can the soldered joints come loose, but so can electronic cards that have been snapped into the computer to add more memory, run a color video monitor, a fax machine, etc. Of course joints can be resoldered and cards can be resnapped, but while the repair itself might take half a minute and a nickel's worth of solder, it can take an $80-an-hour technician two hours to find the broken connection.

There is a whole separate set of things to worry about with hard disks, which are either built into computers or sit alongside them. Here you have this thing in a sealed box spinning at 60 revolutions per *second,* with a read-write head floating much less than a hair's width above it. It does not take much of a box jostle to cause a disaster.

ST. CHRISTOPHER
SURGE PREVENTION
UNIT

The watchword, then, is to treat your machinery as gently as possible, both while in use, and when moving it from place to place. When big computers have to be moved, they are carried in elaborate and expensive vans that are virtually giant self-propelled boxes full of foam rubber. The same care should be taken with small machinery—even, or perhaps especially, that which is supposed to be portable.

Human beings can cause problems

If it works, it's out of date.
—Stafford Beer

There are computer books and manuals for beginners that contain reassuring statements like, "No matter what you do, it is impossible to damage the computer itself because of programming or other minor errors on your part."

I don't want to alarm you unduly, but that isn't totally accurate. Several beginning programmers told me they managed to write a program that nearly destroyed their computer. Apparently what they did was, in effect, write a program that told the disk-reading head to "Go to point A" and when it got there, "Go to point B" and when it got there, "Go to point A" and so on, literally *ad infinitum,* except the mechanical parts will wear out or fall off long before infinity arrives, probably by next Wednesday.

Another common problem is that of removing or disconnecting cables while the computer is turned on. This can destroy the delicate circuitry that handles the data. Similarly, never turn off a computer, or remove a disk from a disk drive while the drive is still turning. This can have the same effect as removing a phonograph record from the turntable without lifting the tone arm. Most computers either have a red or green "drive in use" light, or software that gives you a message on the screen when it is safe to remove a disk.

I've saved the worst human problem for last: the problems caused by poor disk management. At least it is the most solvable problem of all.

Poor disk management

Let's say you have just finished a long session at the computer, typing in names and addresses, or writing a story, or entering medical data, or doing your income taxes. Of course you have been saving what you write—storing it on the disk every few minutes as you go along, so that if the power goes out, you will not have lost your work. When it is time to stop for the day, all your work is now stored on plastic, either on a hard disk or a floppy disk. What happens if that disk is lost, stolen, or destroyed by fire or magnetism? Clearly, it represents at least the loss of a vast amount of time and energy.

It can be far, far worse than that. Businesses that have lost their customer lists or accounts receivable records have gone bankrupt. Doctors who lost their patient records have prescribed medicine to which there was a fatal allergy.

The solution is so obvious, it is almost trivial: copy your disks and store the copies elsewhere.

It is, one might say, as obvious as the fact that wearing seat belts saves lives, and that smoking cigarettes causes lung cancer.

We humans are such peculiar creatures. Half of us don't wear seat belts, and tens of millions of us suck on tubes of burning vegetation. And vast legions of us don't take that extra minute at the end of a session with the computer to perform the simple acts that will prevent disaster.

The reason, of course, is that no one expects the disaster to be their own. It is safe to assume that most of the tens of thousands of

User-power alternative energy sources are available.

There are eight ways to put a disk into a drive—only one of them correct.

people whose lives would have been saved by seat belts last year did not plan to die in their cars. But they all did.

Oddly, the thing that many people, including yours truly, routinely do is to diligently make a copy of the data—and then store it on the shelf alongside the original. This isn't totally crazy; at least if one set is eaten by the computer, there will be a backup—*which should immediately itself be copied*. But it is just a little crazy, in the direction of keeping the key to your safe in your safe for safekeeping. Faced with the alternative of making a copy of my data, then transporting it all the way to the garage, where there is a fireproof file box[37] . . . well, there are always good reasons at the time. I'll try to do better. I really will. And so should you.

Both hardware and software suppliers are doing their best to make these tasks easier for us. There is excellent "backup" software, which takes you step-by-step through the necessary process, and even doesn't waste your time re-backing-up something that hasn't been changed since the last time. And there are tape backups, that look like (but are not made like) ordinary tape cassettes, and work on the same principle, holding many disks' worth of data.

The stone age may return on the gleaming wings of science.
—Winston Churchill

---

[37] Come to think of it, a fireproof box might not do wonders for the disks inside, during a fire. But it is better than most alternatives that come to mind.

The Dreaded 99% Factor

Is something that works 99% of the time good enough? It all depends. If your car worked 99% of the time, that means you'd have it for all but three or four days of the year, which isn't bad. If a baseball player got on base 99% of the time, they'd build a special wing for him at Cooperstown.

But suppose you had a pair of shoes that were comfortable 99% of the time—meaning that every hundredth step you took caused agonizing pains to shoot up your leg? And how about a game of Russian roulette in which you win 99% of the time. If there were a hundred guns on the table, and only one was loaded, what would it take to get you to pick one up at random and fire it at yourself? How useful would it be to close your front door 99% of the way when a maniac was coming up your front path with an axe?

Yup. There are indeed times and places when a 1% "error" rate isn't *nearly* good enough. And the world of computers is one of those places.

I have been in more than a few situations in which a computer expert has assured me that something or other could be done. "Piece of cake" is a phrase much favored by such people.[38] And then what happened was a 99% success rate, which turned out to be pretty much the same as total failure. Let me explain.

Recently, a colleague prepared a manuscript more than 500 pages long, typed on an IBM computer. I wished to have the data transferred to a Macintosh system, which meant converting the files. Could it be done? "Piece of cake," said the lady at the service bureau.

Well, for reasons still not fully understood, the conversion was about 99% accurate. But it wasn't just a matter of 1% of the letters coming out wrong.[39] The 99% factor really did us in with regard to special commands in the program. All characters are not created equal. Say you came to a fork in the road, and there you saw a sign like this:

It figures that if you can go out and buy a Julia Child cookbook, follow the directions and get a respectable souffle, there's no reason why you should settle for less from millions of dollars worth of machine.

—Suzanne Garment

---

[38] "Piece of cake" is the computer world's equivalent of "I'm from the government, and I'm here to help."

[39] That would be barely tolerable in our name and address program. If George Washington came out "George Sashington," no big deal. But if the S-for-W error occurred with George Whitman, we might have lost a customer and gained a lawsuit.

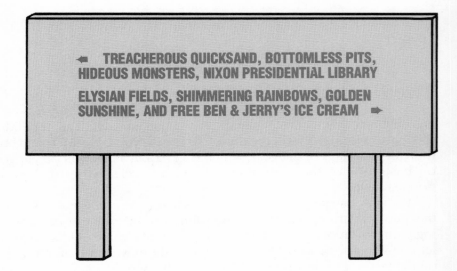

This sign has about a hundred characters. But they are not equal in importance. If the two O's fell off, the message "BTTMLESS PITS" is still pretty clear. But if the two arrows fell off, your afternoon hike would have a 50-50 chance of turning out to be less than wonderful.

It is the same in a program, when the 1% turns out to be a key command character, not an ordinary letter. For instance, in my colleague's manuscript, after the conversion, the command that stopped underlining failed to take hold. When the author intended to underline one word, the end result was a manuscript with 4,126 consecutive underlined words.

Of course it need not be exactly 99%. Whether it is 95% or 97% or even 99.999%, the principle is the same: a tiny error can be disastrous. As a professional musician who was attempting to use his personal computer to compose music put it to me, there are at least 50,000 separate pieces of information in the orchestral score to Tchaikovsky's *1812 Overture*. If the second oboe misses one command (note), no one will ever notice. But if the guy who fires the cannon at the end misses one command, the whole piece is ruined.

The man who was translating Jimmy Carter's speech into Polish in Warsaw may have been 99.9% accurate, but when he had Carter saying, "I want to make love[40] to the Polish people," instead of "I love the Polish people," that .01% of the speech was all anyone remembered.

A typing error, "He is not in London," instead of "He is now in London" caused an international incident. And there are those who believe that a "minor" translation error in a Japanese diplomatic communication led to the atomic bombing of Nagasaki.

There is no heavier burden than a great potential.

—Linus (Peanuts)

---

[40] Some accounts suggested a more graphic euphemism was used at this point.

Other Incompatibility Problems

There was a kid in our high school whose main claim to fame was that he had a small collection of 11" 27½ rpm phonograph records. In the late 1940s, when "long-playing" recording technology was just becoming available, there were no industry standards. Different manufacturers and inventors were experimenting with various sizes and speeds. Pat's father had reasoned that Americans were used to the 11" size (the height of ordinary typing paper), and to put precisely one hour of sound on an 11" disk (which *also* seemed logical) required a speed of 27½ rpm.

Thankfully for us, if not for Pat's father, all the record and phonograph manufacturers got together and agreed on a size and speed, which is why 12" 33⅓ rpm records can be played on virtually any machine.

Unfortunately, there have been few agreements among computer makers and software writers. In fact, if anything, for years they went in opposite directions. IBM software used to be compatible with nothing else on earth, the theory being that once you got all your data entered, you were an IBM captive for life. Apple urged software developers to follow a certain set of standards, so that the same keystrokes, for instance, would do the same thing, no matter what software was in use. Some followed these protocols precisely, others partly, some not at all.

So we are at a point where there are still a considerable range of options in hardware and software: 5¼"-disks, 3½"-disks, even 2"- and 8"-disks; single-, double-, and high-density disks; high- and low-density disk drives; and several different protocols or standards for the way data is stored on a disk.

Please understand, this does not refer to the *content* of the disk at all, but just the way it is structured. It is as if long-playing phonograph records were made in a dozen sizes and a dozen speeds. A 42⅝ rpm disk *might* play on a 47¼ rpm turntable, but if it did, it might sound a bit funny (99% sound compatibility).

Things are getting better, not so much because the software industry is being especially cooperative, but because:

• The hardware industry has come up with ingenious solutions, including disk drives that can read and write several formats and move data back and forth among them; and computers with two sizes of

Altering disk size is impractical.

disk drive built in, so you can put a 3½"-disk in one slot, a 5¼" in the other, and move stuff around.

● Data conversion services have arisen: clever experts who have figured out how to transfer data from one format or size or system to another. They can be found advertising in the classified sections of computer magazines. Typically they offer a 20 column by 20 row grid, with the names of all the different options across the top and down the left, with conversion prices where the rows and columns meet. Converting a disk from 5¼" IBM MS-DOS (MicroSoft Disk Operating System, one of two or three "standards" in the IBM world) to 3½" Apple Macintosh might cost as little as $5. Converting from an ancient (circa 1980) CP/M format on an 8"-disk to an Amiga DOS format might run $50 or more per disk.

Will there ever be a single industry-wide standard? Don't hold your breath. It's on the list, right after 27½ rpm 11" records.

Software Failure

I continue to be annoyed, but no longer surprised, by the number of errors in the software I use. The errors have ranged from relatively minor occasions in which columns of numbers did not line up evenly to more significant problems in which data were lost forever, or "error" messages marched across the screen.

As one more accustomed to books than electronic data, I knew that a publisher would never knowingly issue a book with chapters missing, an incorrect index, and a few pages printed upside down. How, then, could a software "publisher" sell a program with obvious (to me) errors?

One answer, I have learned, is that it is virtually impossible to test a software program in all the different ways that a customer is likely to use it. It's like some of the product recalls you read about. The doll company may have tested and "childproofed" its new Roseanne Arnold doll 17 ways from Sunday. Then some three-year-old discovers that the Stormin' Norman doll's combat boot is precisely the right size and shape to pry off Roseanne's head, swallows it, and precipitates years of lawsuits.

Once, for instance, I bought a FileMaker, a well-reviewed database program, to store information on schools for a book I write on earning nontraditional degrees. FileMaker is a wonderful program, clever, creative, intuitive, with an excellent manual. However, by the time my school file grew quite large, nearly two megabytes of data, FileMaker had slowed down to the pace of an arthritic snail. A simple search that had taken a few seconds was now taking three or four minutes. Even inserting one new word in the middle of a sentence was taking a minute or more. Totally unsatisfactory. A call to the company's help line was not too helpful. They had not tested files that large, and had nothing helpful at all to say to me. (My solution was to divide the big file into four smaller files, which is a real nuisance to work with, but at least I don't fall asleep waiting for the screen to respond.)

While I was writing this very book, which, as you may have noticed, has more than a few footnotes, I found that the extremely popular word processing program I was using, MacWrite, did not handle footnotes properly. Both numbering and spacing did not work correctly. I phoned the company (no toll-free line), and spent 15 minutes on hold. When I asked the technical support lady about this, she seemed skeptical, but then she was able to reproduce the problem on her own machine. "Well I'll be darned," she said, "You found an undocumented error. No one has reported this before." Even assuming this was not another case of the bedbug letter syndrome,[41] the end result was not helpful at all. If they corrected the problem, they would let me know, and, presumably, give me the opportunity to buy a new version of the software.

The important point here is that when something dreadful happens, many beginners immediately assume that *they* must somehow be at fault. Not necessarily so. And it isn't just the small low-priced software that is less than perfect. Apple, IBM, and some of the biggest software companies have had their major embarrassments. Microsoft Word, version 3.0.[42] Aldus PageMaker 2.0, which was on the market for about 20 minutes before the company rushed out version 3.0. Apple's System 6, which was about as near to a recall as the company would admit. The big companies are, at least, usually pretty good about correcting major errors, and then issuing free or (major irritant) low-cost ($5 or $10) replacements. Why should I have to pay for their mistakes? But at least they take some responsibility. When you have software from a company you have not heard of, and you telephone them, and the phone is answered, "Hello," you may be in trouble.

When all else fails, there is always Computer Consumer Karate (page 202).

---

[41] A railroad passenger once discovered bedbugs in his bed. He wrote an angry letter to the president of the railroad, who sent a long and abjectly apologetic reply, saying that in the hundred-year history of the railroad, such a thing had never been known to happen, but now they would institute new policies for hygiene and inspection. By mistake, the passenger's original letter was returned to him in the same envelope, and across the top, the railroad president had scrawled, "Send this jerk the bedbug letter."

[42] Each revised or updated version gets a new decimal number: 4.3, 4.4, 4.5. Then, when there is a major revision, it gets a new main number: 5.0. A high number doesn't necessarily mean that there have been many problems; it could mean that the manufacturer keeps improving it. The all-time bestselling shareware program, Red Ryder (a telecommunications program), reached version 10-point-something, because its author kept thinking of ways to make it better. It has been said of Red Ryder that you didn't *buy* it, you *subscribed* to it.

Don't Ask Why, Just Keep On Going

I have had literally hundreds of experiences in which the following sequence of events occurred:

1. Something undesirable happens. The printer doesn't print. The cursor freezes on the screen. The disk won't come out of the disk drive. The moon rocket crashes when it should have landed smoothly. Any one of scores of unwanted events.

2. I do many things. I check that everything is plugged in right. I repeat the procedure (and it still fails). I ask questions of friends or the ceiling, whichever is closer. I fret. I think evil thoughts. I even read the instructions. I try again, and suddenly, unexpectedly . . .

3. It all works perfectly. I haven't the remotest idea why. Was it something I did? Was it passage of time, allowing something to cool down (or warm up)? Had I made the same mistake several times in a row without noticing? Were my prayers answered?

At this point, there is a strong temptation to stop what you were originally doing, and try to find out what went wrong and why or how it was corrected. I strongly advise against this. To attempt to do so is almost always extremely time consuming, and worse, totally unproductive.

My father, who was an accountant in his early years, once worked for a boss who insisted that the books balance each month down to the last penny. If, after totaling thousands of complex transactions (without a computer!), the two sides of the ledger were off by three cents, dozens of hours of work were put in to find the discrepancy. Hundreds and hundreds of dollars to find a few pennies.

For some people this kind of perfection is a necessity—or at least a worthy goal. For many, it simply doesn't make sense.

So it is with trying to find out what went wrong with the computer *after* it is no longer wrong. (The exception, of course, is when the same thing happens over and over and over again, in which case it *is* important to know why.) But the great majority of computer mysteries are one-time-only events, so even if you *could* figure out why the screen went black or the paper jammed or you typed a "w" and got an "m" or why you lost the car keys or what happened to Amelia Earhart, it might be momentarily gratifying, but in the long run, as well as the medium and short run, it won't do you any good.

Evil People: The Problem of Computer Viruses

It isn't enough, we have to deal with everything from power surges to gamma rays. Now we have to deal with idiots, who sit in their sleazy homes and offices, thinking up ways to sabotage our computers. In the late 1980s, the concept of the computer virus burst upon the scene, and all our lives suddenly changed forever.

A computer virus is a program that enters computers secretly, either because it was hiding on a disk we insert, or because it came over the telephone lines while we were interacting with a distant computer. Once in our own computers, viruses typically multiply themselves and infect other programs on our disk. Then they lurk invisibly in the background, until something sets them off: a certain date, a passage of time, or something else happening in the computer. Then they go to work, carrying out the nefarious tasks they were designed to do. Sometimes this can be weeks, months, even years after they enter our machines.

Viruses can do something as benign as printing a silly message on the screen on Christmas day and then disappearing for good, or something as devastating as erasing the entire hard disk.

Dozens and dozens of viruses have been identified, but very few of the perpetrators have been identified, and when they have, the penalties have been, in general, far too mild for the financial and psychological damage they have caused.

There are ways to keep viruses out of your computer, and there are things you can do once you suspect you have one.

The only near certain way to keep your computer free of viruses is to practice the electronic equivalent of safe sex. Never interact over the phone lines with another computer. Never buy software from a private party. Never trade software with anyone. Unlike biological viruses, computer viruses do not float around in the air. The only way they can get into your computer is over the phone lines or from a disk.

I said "near certain" because there have been a few publicly reported instances in which major software companies inadvertently sent out disks that were already infected, probably by a disgruntled employee.

Thankfully, there have been people on the side of righteousness who have created some very clever and quite effective programs that both seek out and destroy viruses. These programs, with names like

Vaccine, Disinfectant, Gatekeeper, and a dozen others, will find almost all *known* viruses. But we are involved in a probably permanent cat-and-mouse game, in which the crackpots who enjoy foisting viruses on the world are hard at work to come up with new means of devastation that cannot be stopped by existing detective programs. As soon as a new virus is identified, the good guys go to work to come up with ways of combating it.

Some of the virus detection and eradication software is available free through users' groups, computer stores, bulletin boards, and a few enlightened computer companies. Some is sold as shareware, and some needs to be purchased at up to $100.

Some antivirus software works in the background, all the time, like a smoke detector or burglar alarm. It stands guard while you are doing other things with the computer. If something suspicious is found, it will flash a message on the screen: Virus such-and-such was discovered and destroyed. Other software must be activated to go on its search and attack mission, like letting loose a pack of Dobermans from time to time.

There are people who have grown quite paranoid about the matter of viruses. But it really isn't that bad, now that we know how to deal with them. If you interact regularly with other computers, whether over a network in your own office, or through a BBS in a distant city, you should definitely be alert to the possibility of viruses. But there is no need to abandon all electronic communication, and sit in a lead-lined basement room, electronic fly swatters in hand. If you take reasonable precautions, the probability of a devastating assault is very small indeed.

Actually, the psychological distress when I found my first virus was worse than the very minor damage done. I felt violated. I felt invaded. And I felt so powerless to do anything. It was as if some stranger had come into my house and used my toothbrush, read my private correspondence, and drooled into that casserole in the refrigerator, then retreated to a distant location, leaving not even a fingerprint behind.

Psychological Problems

The causes of anguish

Some people *want* to be told if they have terminal cancer. Others never want to know. Some people *want* to know if they are going to be surrounded by legions of child beggars on their trip to the Taj Mahal. Some people even open the brown envelope from Internal Revenue before the rest of their mail.

In other words, there are people who want to plan for the worst, well in advance, because it helps them deal with the problems if and when they come. For those people, I have some things to say about the four kinds of situations that have caused me the most distress, and how I dealt with them. Those who wish to fly blind may proceed at once to the chapter on sugarplum fairies, puppies, word games, paper-folding tricks, and chocolate chip cookies.[43]

Working with accurate but poor instructions

When I was very young, my grandfather bought me a book on how to play chess. It started out telling me that the king was the tallest figure, and the bishop had a slot in it, and that there were 32 black squares alternating with 32 white squares on the board. By about page three, it was discussing the merits of the *en passant* strategy that Capablanca used in Havana in 1927, as contrasted with Keres' use of mid-game center-board strategy.

I think the same author, or someone he has trained, is now busily engaged in writing computer instructions. I am no longer surprised, but I am regularly annoyed and often depressed by the poor quality of written materials that accompany computer-related products.

A whole industry has arisen because of this phenomenon: books that tell you what the manufacturer or supplier *should* have told you. Would anyone stand for it if you had to buy someone else's book on using your car or your refrigerator, because the owner's manual either was incomprehensible or incomplete or inaccurate or all three?

Working with inaccurate instructions

This is like working for days on a mammoth jigsaw puzzle, then discovering that the last three pieces are missing. The frustration of doing an immense amount of work in attempting to learn a complex new

---

[43] That section did not make it into this book. Watch for the forthcoming sequel, *101 Wholesome Activities to Occupy Your Time at the State Home for Former Computer Enthusiasts.*

procedure, and then coming upon a missing instruction or an incorrect instruction is highly distressing.

To *not* come upon it, and learn sometime later that the reason for continued failure had nothing to do with one's own inadequacies, but rather with the inadequacy of the instruction writer, is devastating. Sue them for the ulcers you will surely get.

Very recently, I purchased some memory chips to expand my computer's internal memory. I bought them from a major company, and they came with a wonderfully friendly and chatty manual. The only problem was that there were two glaring errors. No, actually only one *glared* (I was told at the end of the process to replace a certain part that I had not previously been told to remove). The other was so subtle, there was no way in the world I could have solved it on my own. Of course it was the weekend and the company was closed. So I left an SOS message on a couple of bulletin boards, and within an hour, some kind soul had told me just what to do.

Obvious equipment failure

The only thing more distressing to me than obvious equipment failure is the following:

Non-obvious equipment failure

This is the computer equivalent of walking around all day with your slip showing, or a huge crumb lodged in your beard.[44]

Although there are supposed to be "error messages" that flash on the screen to tell you when something is going wrong, this does not always happen—sometimes because the kind of error is one that does not have detectors, and sometimes because the error detection system itself is malfunctioning.

One man told me how his computer once deleted a whole bunch of sevens from his billing statements, so a customer who owed $179 would get a bill for $19. A novelist remembered the time her word processor, presumably with a poetic license of its own, duplicated a few paragraphs of her manuscript and inserted them in several other locations in the story. And there is the classic case, well known in psychological research circles, where a high school's computer printed students' locker numbers in the space where their I.Q. was supposed to go on the teachers' class lists. (The reason it is a classic case is that no one noticed the error at the time, but at the end of the year, the students with the highest locker numbers got the best grades.)

... 85% of the horse-drawn vehicle industry of the country is untouched by the automobile ... In 1906-1907, and coincident with an enormous demand for automobiles, the demand for buggies reached the highest tide in its history. The man who predicts the downfall of the automobile is a fool; the man who denies its great necessity . . . is a bigger fool; but the man who predicts the general annihilation of the horse and his vehicle is the greatest fool of all.

—Speech at the National Association of Carriage Builders, 1907

---

[44] If your slip is showing *and* you have a crumb in your beard, then you've *really* got problems.

Price shock syndrome

I may have been the first person in the entire world to buy a digital watch. As all gadget historians know, they went on sale in the summer of 1972 in selected stores. I got mine at Tiffany's in New York early in the morning of the first day. It was a Hamilton Pulsar. It cost $350. It displayed the time in red numbers when you pushed a button. It seemed to weigh half a ton. And it made me very, very happy.

Within a year, the price had fallen to under $200, and there were some models that also told the date. I looked at them wistfully, but without major regrets.

Within three years, the price was down to $79, including a stopwatch. With much sadness, I retired the Pulsar to a drawer where it reposes to this very day.[45] After all, I then thought, how much cheaper, and how much more complicated, could they possibly get.

The answer, of course, lies in the fact that there is an army of at least 40,000 creative engineers at the Casio factory alone, whose only role in life is to figure out how to cram more and more stuff into a watch, at a lower and lower price. My present watch, two years old and already obsolete, merely has a six-function calculator, an alarm, a stopwatch, a 100-record phone index, a 200-year calendar, and a datebook. It cost $29. But the newer ones have a five-language dictionary, a depth gauge, complex mathematical functions, and they monitor your heartbeat and play tunes. When that model includes a space invaders game and tells me when the salmon fishing is good off the coast, I'll probably have to buy it. That is, if it is under $14.95.

The point of all this is that prices are changing at a rate unprecedented in history. Seventy years ago, it cost the average worker about 200 days' salary to buy a Model T Ford. Today it costs the average worker about 200 days' salary to buy a Ford. In gold rush times, an ounce of gold bought you a good new suit. It still does. But 20 years after the first electronic four-function calculator went on sale for $800, you can walk into any drugstore or supermarket and buy, for under $10, a pocket device that can do more than the multimillion dollar "automatic brains" of the 1940s.

How do people respond to this sort of thing? Some with unbridled joy. Some with annoyance or anger.

Everybody knows someone whose great-grandfather traded half of Los Angeles for a half interest in a Chinese laundry, or made some other transaction that, in retrospect, was not a wonderful deal. I had an uncle who rejected a 50-50 partnership offered by an ambitious young chocolate salesman named Milton Snavely Hershey, and regretted it all his life. And of course there is the standard "I knew it. I just *knew* it"

---

[45] Attention museums of historical technology: I am open to an offer.

response when a certain stock goes up, or the roulette wheel stops on number 21.

Such people are prime candidates for developing ulcers and turning into crotchety old geezers. (My uncle did both)

It never makes sense to a person who is suffering miserably when someone says, "You'll get over it soon—no one ever died of a broken heart (or a common cold, or whatever)." I *do* remind myself of this whenever I see a new computer product that is vastly cheaper than what I paid. It doesn't stop me from being a little annoyed, but I can generally put it behind me with either or both of these two thoughts:

1. No one forced me to buy what I already have. The price must have been satisfactory at the time. The stuff is working pretty well. I don't sit and stew if my neighbor gets a car like mine at a better price. I don't fret that I didn't buy IBM stock when it was $10 a share. And I'm *certainly* not the sort of person who checks the sale ads in the newspaper after I've bought something, to see if I could have gotten it cheaper elsewhere.[46]

2. I have not signed any lifetime contracts. I am fully capable of junking, setting aside, or selling any or all of my computer hardware and software. And I have done so more than once.

The most debilitating form of price shock syndrome is to buy nothing, in the near certain knowledge that the price will be less in a month or a year. This topic is covered in detail on page 30, the "But wait!" syndrome. Sufferers never take into account the pleasure they would have gotten *during* that month or year, or even the money they might have saved by using that particular item for a longer time.

It is so simple to say, "If you want it, and if you can afford it, buy it now." But it is so much harder actually to *do*.

The "Gee Whiz" syndrome

Nothing I had done in this life prepared me for the feelings I experienced during my first hours at the COMDEX computer show in Las Vegas. Walking through the door into the world's largest computer show, I easily could have believed that I had died and gone to gadget heaven.

I knew that I was not immune to the "Gee Whiz" syndrome—the feeling that overcomes many small computer users when they are suddenly exposed to something that is much more desirable than anything they own. But here I was surrounded by more than 10,000 items, and every single one of them infinitely superior to the crud I was using back home.

---

[46] Unless, of course, I bought it at one of those companies that guarantees to beat any price you find within 30 days of purchase.

AN EXCLUSIVE OFFER
TO READERS OF THIS PUBLICATION

RECENT developments in microcomponent technology now permit us to make available an extraordinary precision device—the KL-1000. Weighing less than one ounce, it is no larger than a domestic olive, yet it performs all the photographic, data-processing, and informational-retrieval functions you yourself do—automatically.

The KL-1000 adjusts to available light, sets shutter speed and aperture, then calculates, displays, and prints out on plain paper tape the cube root of your Social Security number. This is photography made so automatic it leaves you completely "out of the picture." The KL-1000 not only flashes "SAY CHEESE" and "STOP MOVING AROUND" on its unique L.E.D. monitor screen, it also warns you that you're not taking enough photographs, advances the film after each exposure, then hot-wires your car to rush the completed roll to the drugstore for processing. Don't feel like capturing those personal moments of your life before forgetting them? Relax. It isn't up to you anymore.

A whole world of precision capability is out there, waiting to enter your home and your life with this fully integrated, so-much-more-than-a-camera device, so much more than a camera. Micro-fiche-and-chips technology makes it a computer, too—performing virtually all functions including logarithms, in Roman numerals. Its binaural jack accommodates two sets of featherweight headphones, so both you and a friend can rollerskate to Coast Guard channel-depth broadcasts. Its light-activated voice simulator tells you to balance the family budget, chart stocks and bonds, stop smoking, clean your room, and be considerate of others. You can talk back, too: the clip-on dynamic microphone instantly triggers a sustained, loud buzzing—enough to wake the soundest sleeper—if you say anything at all within a fifty-foot radius of the KL-1000.

Yet that is not all, because disc-and-data fineline crosshair-tronics has enabled us to program the KL-1000 to do *everything*—and more—automatically. Consider these exclusive features:

AT THE OFFICE. Thanks to mini-laser technopathy, the KL-1000 not only copies any-sized document, it actually vaporizes the original's byline without a trace, and substitutes your own name, sex, political affiliation, and yearly income. Its data-network-access function lets you be part of the grid, too, as it narrowcasts product inventory and your inflow-outflow figures directly to your digital watch. The KL-1000A word-processing attachment assures perfection every time—misspelled words or computational errors are immediately obliterated by its built-in document shredder, which also shorts out all electrical power to the entire building and releases a semi-toxic paralyzing gas. Just get it right the first time, and forget it!

WHILE TRAVELLING. Optional carry-strap lets you wear it on your belt, or leave it in your room—the strap extends to a full half mile, and retains enough water in even the lightest drizzles to provide nooselike snugness and hamper torso circulation. Or remain in the room yourself; the unit travels freely on its own, and will simulate your signature on major purchases of clothing, art, and real estate without your even knowing. In every major foreign city, the KL-1000 does it all: orders gourmet meals for twenty while you struggle with the menu, loudly contradicts you in museums, and forwards your souvenir purchases to General Delivery, Lima, Peru. All you do is pay freight and handling. And you need never again worry about destroyed traveller's checks, cancelled credit cards, and misplaced passports—the KL-1000 does all these, and more, while you sleep. In the morning, enjoy your own original compositions of up to twelve accordionlike notes in real music,

"the international language." The KL-1000 will record and transcribe these melodies automatically, then engrave the notes onto an attractive brass pendant, which it will offer for sale to friends and strangers. Do not worry about accidentally switching off the unit, either, because you can't—not even deliberately.

AT HOME. Self-contained forty-eight-hour timer lets it tell itself when forty-eight hours have elapsed, after which timer resets itself automatically. All you do is hide in a closet. Later, use the microwave transponder attachment to receive hitherto unavailable signals from turkeys, roasts, and hams. When no one is home, it plays both eight-track and cassette recordings, switches lights and appliances on and off, and displays random words in Italian on its high-resolution screen. The KL-1000 wards off burglars all night long by announcing, in a voice mathematically similar to you own, "We're awake . . . we're awake . . ." Then, in the morning, it counts your pushups, uses all the hot water, and ignores you at the table. Coffee? Of course. There's even some for you. And don't worry about getting dressed—it gets dressed for everyone, then dials ten frequently called telephone numbers and leaves a short inspirational message in your name. All you do is stay undressed, watch, and go back to bed.

Advances in macro-waferonics enable the KL-1000 to use 3-D graphic simulation to transfer black-and-white computerized likenesses of you and your family to T-shirts, dogs, and frozen foods. Switch from audio to visual read-out for its smoke-detection mode, and receive a hard-copy sheet reading "SMOKE" when your house burns down.

A DEVICE of state-of-the-art convenience, the KL-1000 has already projected your technological needs and, with funds transferred from your checking or savings account, has purchased itself. It has already expedited its own delivery.

Indeed, the KL-1000 is already in your home or office—over there, near that lamp. It is already on line, shredding potatoes and complaining about your posture, automatically. All you do is nothing. Just set it at "HIGH" and run away. You'll never have to do anything else for as long as it lives.

—ELLIS WEINER

The "Gee Whiz" phenomenon has little to do with price (which can cause psychological problems of its own, as just discussed). It is, I think, regression to the feeling that first occurred in early childhood when the kid next door got a better doll or bike or sled. I think I was seven when my best friend, Bobby Rosenblum, got an incredible toy garage set with a motorized elevator. I still remember it vividly, and I suspect that the seeds of our eventual estrangement were planted that day.[47]

As I walked up and down the more-than-three miles of aisles, eyes glazing, shopping bags filling, I began to reflect on the nature of the "Gee Whiz" syndrome I was experiencing. What makes it possible, of course, is the remarkable rate of progress in the computer field. Ten years after Duryea demonstrated the first practical automobile, cars were still primitive, underpowered, uncomfortable, and unreliable. Ten years after the Wright brothers' flight, airplanes were still a novelty, with no practical or commercial use. But ten years after the first primitive electronic adding machine came on the market at $800, it was possible to go into a drugstore and buy a far better one for 1% of that price.

The three ways people deal with "Gee Whiz" can be a major factor in whether or not they have a positive computer experience.

1. *I must have it right now, no matter what.* Reason flies away in the face of an irrational desire to have something right now. So many people have told me things like, "When I saw my first laser printer, I had to have it that very day." "They let me try out the painting program on the Macintosh, and before I knew what I was doing, I had my Visa card in my hand."

Some of these people sounded very much like confused defendants on the witness stand. "Gee, Your Honor, when I came to my senses, I was standing there with the computer in my hand, and there was my bank account lying dead on the floor . . . "

In one respect, there is really nothing wrong with this behavior in many cases. It is, at least, the ultimate answer to the "But wait!" syndrome. However, carried to excess, impulse buying can be debilitating, both to financial well-being and to harmonious computer life. It really *is* desirable to plan purchases in advance, to shop around for the best deal, I thought to myself earlier this week, just after opening a direct mail offer for an amazing new word processor, and finding my finger, entirely on its own, lurching for the phone and dialing the 800 toll-free number.

2. *I must have it, and I will have it, and because of that, I won't do anything else until I do have it.* I have witnessed more than a few

Electronic calculators can solve problems which the man who made them cannot solve; but no government-subsidized commission of engineers and physicists could create a worm.
—Joseph Wood Krutch

---

[47]Bobby: if you're reading this, I've gotten over it. We can be friends again. Unless you've got a NeXT computer and a color laser printer.

cases of this electronic equivalent of holding your breath until you turn blue. A recent example: a businessman who told me he had fallen quite irrationally in love with a full-color laser printer. But it is out of his price range, by at least one zero. Still, even though he has a computer, he is making do with a very primitive 9-dot printer and his business letters look like laundry lists. But he won't buy an interim decent printer, because it would be "wasted money" since the full-color job will be his one day.

3. *I admire it, but* . . . There is, thankfully, a wide gap between "Gee Whiz" and "I must have it." Most people in most situations have a quite healthy response to a terrific new product: something on the order of, "Oh, that is splendid. I am delighted to know there is a hard disk powered by chipmunks that plays the Hallelujah Chorus and bakes brownies as it accesses data. Someday I may need one, so I shall file the brochure away in my "Gee Whiz" file for further reference."

I left my first COMDEX show with, truly, 17 shopping bags full of literature, nearly all of it for the "Gee Whiz" file. It's fun to look at, and to use for amazing and amusing my friends. That was nearly nine years ago. I saved the "Gee Whizziest" of all literature in a little time capsule (paper bag on shelf), vowing to get it out after ten years, to see if any of the wonders of the early '80s had made it into the '90s. There will be a report.

Communication Problems: The Matter of "Technobabble"

The only course I came close to flunking in college was calculus. Then I happened upon a wonderful book called *Calculus Made Easy*.[48] The author begins with a splendid essay on how Vocabulary is the most precious weapon in the arsenal of the high priests of any scientific discipline. He goes on to give simple English definitions and explanations of all the concepts I was failing to comprehend. It was as if a veil had been lifted, and calculus was a breeze thereafter.

The high priests of the computer world—programmers, salespeople, writers, consultants—also guard their language. Some (by no means all, thankfully) not only refuse and disdain to use comprehensible English to describe the simple things they do, they grab things out of our simple, nontechnical world, and make them their own.

This fact becomes clear the moment you activate the exterior/interior interface module (door) and enter the computer sales parlor.

Elsewhere (page 245), I have endeavored to explain, in language that even *I* can understand, just what many of the most common computer-related words and phrases actually mean. You don't need to memorize them all, but it is not a terrible idea to know some of the basics. But that doesn't mean you have to put up with salespeople or technicians who will not speak to you in clear, intelligible English (or whatever language is spoken in your town).

It is essential to remember that it is (and always will be) a buyer's market. Over the years, a fair number of salespeople throughout northern California lost some sizable commissions because they could not or would not speak to me in English. "You can access three peripherals simultaneously through the SCSI port," one once said to me. No I can't, I thought, but I *can* utilize the interior/exterior interface module, and head for another store.

To make your job a little easier (perhaps even a little more fun), you might want to make photocopies of the following cards, for use in situations where technobabbling occurs.

---

[48] By Silvanus Thompson; republished by St. Martin's Press in 1965.

Does anyone here speak English?

I AM AN INTELLIGENT BEGINNER

The reason I have handed you this card is because I have not understood one (1) thing you have said for the last five (5) minutes. I am going home to read some John McPhee, Kurt Vonnegut, or William Buckley to reassure myself that the English language is alive and well. If you have personnel capable of communicating in intelligible English, you can reach me at the following telephone number:

PART X

SOLUTIONS TO
COMPUTER PROBLEMS

Finding a Support Group

Once, in a weak moment, I bought a do-it-yourself spiral staircase kit by mail from a company in England. What a disaster. The unintelligibility of the instructions was exceeded only by the difficulty of making the parts fit together properly. I remember vividly the feeling of utter aloneness as I fought this particular monster. In a moment of deep despair, I phoned the supplier in England, and while he couldn't or wouldn't answer my questions[49] he at least gave me the names of every other American buyer: all two of them.

So I telephoned the man in Pennsylvania and the man in Massachusetts, who had been having no more luck than I, and we formed a Users' Group. We gave each other encouragement. We shared our findings.[50] We kept each other from heading down fruitless paths. And eventually we all had reasonably satisfactory spiral staircases in our respective homes.

The same kind of thing can and does happen with computer owners.

One of the best things users' groups do is publish lists of people you can call, who are specialists in certain hardware and software. These are people who are just volunteering their time to help others, as they may well need help themselves at other times. There is almost never any cost involved. And even if you joined a helpful group in a distant location, it could still be worth it to make a long-distance call or two to help solve your problems.

Users' groups can be located by asking at local computer stores, asking the computer companies (larger ones maintain lists of groups), and finding lists on bulletin boards (electronic and cork), as well as in various computer publications, usually local or regional ones such as *Microtimes* and *Computer Currents*.

---

[49] He probably hadn't figured out how to build the damn thing himself.

[50] A major breakthrough was the discovery that the bolts dated from before World War II, and were of a reverse-threading, odd-spacing variety used only by one defunct motorcycle maker.

All About RYFMS

I was talking to the manager of a computer store when his assistant came over and interrupted us.

"You're wanted on the phone," she said to the manager.

"Who is it?"

"I'm afraid it's another ryfm."

The manager grimaced, and reached for the telephone whereupon, with seemingly exaggerated politeness, he proceeded to "talk a customer down" from some horrendous problem he or she was having.

Of course I had to ask. The manager blushed quite profusely, and informed me that "ryfm" was just a little joke of theirs.

Not quite so.

Diligent research has yielded the information that computer store personnel regularly refer to certain customers as "ryfms" (pronounced "riffims"). "Ryfm" stands for "Read your fucking manual." And so, of course, a ryfm is someone who calls up or comes in to buttonhole a store employee when the answer to his or her question is clearly stated in the instruction manual.

When not to be a ryfm

It really is a kindness to *try* to read the manual first. There is at least a chance that the answer can quickly and easily be found. There is also a chance that it cannot—but at least you've made the effort, and you can feel good about explaining to the expert that you *did* try.

When it's OK to be a ryfm

Most of the time, actually, if you're willing to stand up for your rights— particularly your right *not* to have to be a technical expert in order to use your computer.

Once I bought an electronic "card" to snap into my computer, so it could operate a certain printer. At least I thought I could just snap it in. No way. The card came with a 137-page manual, the cover of which warned me that if I did things wrong, I might permanently damage my computer. That was the last thing I understood for sure. By page 6, we were on baud rates, hardware handshakes, parity bits, and ETX-ACK/XON-XOF switch settings. I glanced ahead. On page 62, I found "C7AB:BD B8 05 129 PASTATUS2 IDA STSBYTE,X ;GET ERROR FLAGS."

That did it. I decided I had no intention of R-ing my F-ing M. In high dudgeon, I marched back to the store with hardware in hand and said, "Make this work for me." Within half an hour they did. I have never read the manual. I am waiting for the made-for-television mini-serial.

Computer Repair

When the software people say, "It's a hardware problem," and the hardware people say, "It's a software problem."

When something goes wrong, it is desirable (but not always possible) to figure out, first, whether the problem is with the hardware or the software. This is *not* always possible. More than once, I have been in situations where the software company insisted the problem was with the hardware, and the hardware company insisted the problem was with the software.

How can such a problem happen?

Imagine, if you will, that you are stranded on a little desert island with nothing but a good stereo set and a single tape cassette. (The island, conveniently, has an electrical outlet.) After years of contentedly listening to your cassette, one day you push "Play" and the sound comes out all garbled.

What has gone wrong? Has something happened to the cassette, or to the tape deck? If you had a second cassette, you could play that, and if it sounded good, you'd know the problem was with the first cassette. If you had a second tape deck, you could play your cassette in that. But you have only one of each, and if two repairmen should happen to float ashore, there could well be a situation in which one says, "It's a hardware (i.e., the tape player) problem," and the other says, "It's a software (i.e., the tape cassette) problem."

"Frustration."

With computers, the problem is compounded by the fact that improperly-working hardware can actually destroy, or worse still, subtly alter the software, so that even if you have an identical machine on which to try your disks, they may not work, leading you to think it is a software problem, when in fact it is not. Your defective hardware has damaged your software.

What does the person in the middle (you) do when the experts disagree? Now is the time for your users' group or support group, that's for sure. But there have been satisfactory resolutions if the two disagreeing repair people will talk to one another. Repairers are generally not only honest and helpful, but also tenacious when it comes to tracking down the source of trouble. Once when my printer went awry, and the printer repairman insisted the fault lay with my label-printing program sending bad information to the printer, I paid for a long distance phone call between the repairman and the software company, and between them the problem was isolated and solved. Turned out to be a 30-cent chip that took hours to find and minutes to replace.

It is a lot easier to discuss means of avoiding the situation in the first place, or at least minimizing its likelihood.

• Buy your hardware and at least your major software from the same source, with an understanding that they are responsible not just for the separate parts, but for the system working as a whole. Many stores offer to assemble "turnkey" systems, which will be up and running in your very home or office. Of course you pay more in money, but what do you save in time and anguish?

• Buy things for which you will have access to duplicates, to avoid the desert island stereo problem.

Repair philosophy

Every few years, some magazine does a car repair survey, in which they create some minor problem, like disconnecting one spark plug wire, and then take the car to a great many repair shops, where the results always range from those who say, "Oops. Loose wire. There you go. No charge," to those who adopt a tragic expression and start intoning about the need for an immediate $750 repair job.

Giving up is an entirely valid alternative.

I can hardly wait for someone to do this with computer repairers. One thing they will certainly discover is that many so-called repair shops are not in the repair business at all, they are in the replacement business. It is much easier to train someone to replace an entire major element of a computer, rather than finding out which component (or part of a component) was defective.

Last year, the screen suddenly went black (with a thin vertical white line) on one of our office computers. We phoned the local dealer's repairman (or, as it turned out, replaceman) who said, "Oh, yes, that's the logic board. I can install a new one for $300." We phoned another place, and they said, "Oh, yes, that's the logic board. It has nine major components on it. We can replace all nine for $115." Then a third place. Same diagnosis, then "It has to be one of three components. We can replace those three for $65, or just the bad one for $30."

We ended up replacing all nine. It's the New York Subway Bulb Theory. In the New York subways, they used to send people out to replace burned out light bulbs. The labor cost generally exceeded the cost of the bulbs. And so someone, probably a cost accountant, figured out that if they replaced *all* the bulbs in one station, whether they were burned out or not, there would be a considerable cost saving.

If you have a choice of repair shops, and especially if your computer is out of warranty, you may wish to ask if they subscribe to the replace or the repair philosophy.

Local repairs

There are factory-authorized repairers (who are, more often than not, replacers), and there are independents (who may be repairers or replacers or both). Some are truly expert at fixing things. Some are also good at calming you down and helping determine what happened, but many are not so wonderful at human interaction. They may be terrific at changing a 48-pin chip blindfolded, but when it comes to dealing with a distraught customer, sometimes I think they ought to be chained in the back room. Some are simply weird. I once carried an ailing computer to a well-recommended man who did repairs in his home. "I'm having trouble with this computer," I said. "Well," he growled, "What did you expect with Mercury in retrograde?"

At the other end of that scale, once, when a repair shop had tried and failed three times to fix the same problem, they sent for the manufacturer's roving troubleshooter. At the appointed moment, a very large man in black leather roared up on his Harley. He strode into the shop, removed a few tools from his backpack, and in less than 10 minutes, everything was working perfectly. As he packed his tools, I expressed my profound gratitude. "No big deal," he said as he remounted his beast. "If I'd thought it would take more than 10 minutes, I would have put more than a nickel in the parking meter." And off he roared.

While repair people may differ significantly in both repair and communication skills, there are two things you can do to improve the chances of a successful interaction:

1. *Document all your actions.* If the problem is a subtle one, possibly involving some interaction of the hardware and the software, it could be very important for the repairer to know just what you tried, and what happened when you tried it. Write down what buttons you pushed, what if anything you saw on the screen, and what happened next.

If the problem is not one that is repeatable, or if the whole system has died, it is *still* important to recall and write down as much as possible of what you did just before the failure occurred. Be sure to write it down at the time, rather than try to reminisce in the presence of the repairer. ("Well, I think the blue smoke came *after* I closed the disk drive door; no, wait, the monitor exploded *before* the smoke, and then the cat died *during* the fire, or was it *after* . . . ")

2. *Bring everything in.* Even if you are confident that the problem is in one piece of equipment, or in a particular disk, bring your entire

IF AT FIRST YOU DON'T SUCCEED TRY AGAIN THEN QUIT. NO SENSE BEING A DAMN FOOL ABOUT IT.

There is a real need for an all-night repair service.

system to the repair depot (unless they have specifically advised you not to). It is important to be able to test each element separately with a system known to be working. Problems can occur in unexpected places.

One man whose printer was double-spacing when it should have been single-spacing was certain the problem had to be in the software or in the internal logic of the computer. He didn't even bring the printer to the repair shop. But everything else checked out. Turned out (Alert: squeamish people turn the page right NOW) that a banana slug had crawled into the printer and died in a hideous manner, short circuiting part of the inner workings. For perhaps the first time, the classic mechanic's lament—"I've been working on these babies for 20 years, and I never saw nuttin' like *that*"—really was true.

Another powerful reason to bring everything in is that you can see it working before your eyes, when you come to pick it up. If a car is going kah-chunk kah-chunk and flames are shooting out of the cigarette lighter hole, it will be pretty obvious if the problem has been fixed when you come to pick it up. Computer problems can be much more subtle or at least more complex. But if you bring in your own software, and see everything working on the repairer's workbench, you're probably in good shape.

The other thing to shop for, besides philosophy and price, is turn-around time. Most repairs, and all replacements, are really very fast. A few hours at best. Yet some places have huge backlogs, so that even a 15-minute chip replacement can take several weeks.

Mail-order repairs

In these days of relatively-inexpensive overnight delivery services, it has become feasible to run a repair service where all your customers ship stuff in. Even warranty repair for some products is done this way, rather than having any authorized dealers. With low overhead, and the ability to set up shop in places where pay scales are lower, often these services can be considerable cheaper, and often just as fast, as local repairs. While I was writing this book, my full-page display unit fizzled. I sent it back to Minnesota on a Monday, and it was back in my hands on Thursday, three days later. I was impressed.

Some mail-order repair services advertise in the classified sections in the back of computer magazines. It definitely makes sense to write or, better still, telephone first, both to discuss your problem, and to get a feel for the personality of the company.

Telephone repairs

Most software companies, and many hardware companies, have their own technical support assistance available by telephone. Some of

them even try to talk you through the repair, once the diagnosis has been made. (I have done this. I always feel like the person in that story the *Reader's Digest* runs almost every month: "We were at 16,000 feet when my husband died, and I managed to land it myself. . . . " But it is a very satisfying feeling when you are done, especially if the darned thing works.)

The various companies vary along these lines, among others, with regard to telephone repair or consulting policy:

1. *Charges.* Sometimes they charge you, sometimes they don't. Some require you to pay for the call (even for things under warranty). Others provide toll-free phone lines, and some have you-pay-by-the-minute telephone repair service. Some offer a choice: you can pay so much a year for a fixed number of minutes of you-pay-for-the-call service; a somewhat larger amount for an unlimited amount of toll-free calls; or the option of a 900 number with an automatic flat fee ($15, perhaps) charged to your phone bill.

2. *Availability.* Some companies have hundreds of tech people available. Others may put you on hold until your hair turns even grayer. Some are there 24 hours a day (such as the support staff for the Amiga 500); others seem to have people occasionally there, perhaps between staff volleyball games, but there will be an answering machine onto which you can cry.

3. *And then what?* Suppose your telephone counselor determines that a replacement part is needed, or the whole unit must be sent in. Policies vary considerably. Amiga (again) delivers replacement parts by overnight express. IBM promises 48-hour turnaround for spare parts for its PS/1. After 11 years, I'm still waiting for a replacement disk drive from Micromation, perhaps because the company failed soon after I placed my order, although not, I think, as a direct result.

Do-it-yourself repairs

Since computer repairs can be expensive, time-consuming, and even unreliable, there is a strong temptation to consider doing your own. Sometimes this is a good idea. Sometimes it is not. The real dilemma is knowing when to try.

The best rule of thumb is, if you feel comfortable trying, *and* if you have a really good book, video, or set of instructions that describe this repair, it is worth a shot. This is especially true of mechanical, as opposed to electronic repairs. The beauty of mechanical problems is that they are often visible to the naked eye. A bad chip looks exactly the same as a good chip. But if white smoke is rising from your disk drive, that is probably where the problem lies (unless your disk drive has just elected the new Pope).

When the prospect of doing your own repairs comes along, be sure to take into account the three hazards:

1. *Killing your warranty.* Most warranties are automatically voided if it is clear to the manufacturer that you have tampered with the equipment in any way. Some companies actually go as far as placing a non-removable-without-tearing seal over the door to the inner works. Broken seal, no warranty.

This can cause knotty problems. One man I spoke to had a disk drive fail. He removed the outer casing (a simple task involving removal of four screws), discovered that a rubber belt had come off its pulley, replaced the belt, replaced the casing, and had a disk drive that worked—for about an hour. When it failed again, he could find nothing wrong, but the fact of his first successful repair (and the seal he broke) voided his warranty, and the manufacturer wouldn't fix the second (and, as it turned out, totally unrelated) problem until he agreed to pay their usual fees for so doing.

2. *Killing your computer.* One reason manufacturers *do* worry about untrained people plowing around in the works, is that there is ample opportunity to wreak much greater havoc in the act of curing a simple problem. There are many things the untrained or careless do-it-yourselfer can do, but the main danger is static. A charge much smaller than any human could feel can fry a chip, and fried chips are a dreadful problem because they cause random-appearing or intermittent failures, that grow worse with time, and are devilish to try to diagnose properly.

3. *Killing yourself.* The real danger is that even when the power supply is off in many IBMs and Macintoshes, there is still voltage sup-

plied to some components. Also, in some popular computers, the neck of the cathode-ray ("television") tube retains full voltage, even when the computer is turned off and unplugged, and the 30,000-volt shock it can deliver would most emphatically be hazardous to your health.

In summary, there are really much better reasons for *not* tinkering with your computer, than for trying to solve problems yourself. Faced with a long delay and/or a huge repair bill, the temptation to give it a try can be strong. But repairs are rarely intuitive. The chances are you will remove the case and won't see anything obviously wrong. A good book (or even video) on repair is highly recommended.

What if you don't repair

Something is wrong, but not devastating. A funny noise; an occasional system error message; a screen image that flickers or wobbles. Do you really need to do anything about it?

The answer is an overwhelming "Maybe." There is a precise analogy with a toothache.

Maybe it is something temporary that will pass.

Maybe it is something minor that will never get any worse.

Maybe it is something that is now minor but will get worse and worse with time.

Maybe it is a sign that something awful has already happened.

Maybe you'll never know unless you see an expert.

The Last Resort:
Computer Consumer
Karate

This section is designed for people who are having trouble with their *own* computer hardware and software—but many of the techniques have relevance for people who are being harassed by *other people's computers*. Consider, for instance, the Case of the Two John Bears.

Long ago, when we lived in Chicago, I used an American Oil credit card. After dutifully and promptly paying bills that ranged between $20 and $30 a month (I *said* this was long ago), one month I got a bill for over $300. For the first time, I inspected the individual receipts, and discovered about half of them were signed "John Bear" but not in my handwriting, and that the someone-else had just bought five new tires.

I found another John Bear in the phone book, and when he checked his Amoco receipts, he found I had signed half of them. The company computer, unable to comprehend the fact of two John Bears, had given us the same credit card number, and randomly distributed charges between us for over two years. He had been paying some of my bills and I had been paying some of his.

I dutifully went through the succession of procedures that are generally recommended for gaining satisfaction in such cases:

1. Polite letter (or two) to the company.
2. Less polite letter (or two) to the company.
3. Letter to newspaper "consumer action" line.
4. Withholding payment, with letters explaining why.
5. Letter to the president of the company.
6. Attempts to telephone the company, first collect, then prepaid.
7. Letters to regulatory and consumer protection agencies.

All of the above failed. The only response from Amoco was computer-printed threats to pay up or else.

That was when I invented (or perhaps discovered) the approach that ranks in the top four consumer karate techniques.[51]

---

[51] I can say this with authority, because I later wrote the first Ph.D. dissertation ever on how corporations are influenced by customers.

Consumer Karate Method #1
THE SHOTGUN TECHNIQUE

Business executives love to get listed in various "Who's Who" directories, from *Who's Who in America* to *Who's Who in the Petroleum Industry*. Significantly, most listings include family information and a home address.

From the *Standard and Poor* and *Dun and Bradstreet* directories, I learned the names of two dozen top Amoco executives, their law firms, and their advertising agents. Then, from other directories, I secured the home address and wife's name of most of them.

Next I wrote personal letters to the wives of all of these blokes, *at their home,* begging for action: "Your husband's company is driving me crazy. He doesn't answer my letters. *Please* see if you can get him to help me."

Three things happened.

1. The computer problem was cleared up within three days.

2. For the next three *months,* I was getting letters from various Amoco executives (and a few wives) assuring me that matters would be taken care of soon, not to worry.

3. I received a "corrected" bill for $119.07, which I have no doubt was indeed correct. I wrote out an invoice to Amoco for my time and expenses in fighting them. Remarkably, it came to $119.05. I mailed them my check for $.02 with a copy of their bill marked "Paid in full" and I never heard from them again.

Consumer Karate Method #2
SEND IT BACK

Most manufacturers of electronic goods expect their customers to behave in certain well-established ways. One of these expectations is that when a customer has an unsatisfactory product, he or she will deal with the retail outlet or a factory-approved repair facility.

When customers break the mold, companies large and small are often at a loss as to how to respond.

One simple example. I bought a small tape recorder at Sears. After four months, it stopped working. The warranty had expired, and the local Sears repair depot said it would cost more to fix it than to buy a new one, so I should junk it.

I went through the initial complaint letter stages just described. I *did* receive a few patient and friendly explanations of why I was not going to get satisfaction. But it wasn't worth pursuing the "shotgun approach" over a $30 machine.

So I looked up the name of the president of Sears in the *World Almanac* and I mailed him (certified) the tape recorder, with a brief

> Automation: a phenomenon which causes long lines to form at unemployment offices, the unions to rant, pink slips to rain—all for the good of the country.
>
> —Irwin Van Grove

note asking him to fix it and return it to me. Now letters are small and ignorable or throw-outable, but here's this actual *object* sitting on his (or someone's) desk. It can't easily be tossed in the trash. ("Please *do* something with that *object*," I imagined the president of Sears saying.)

Anyway, I received a working tape recorder back in about two weeks.

It is permitted to dispose of an unfriendly computer.

A few years later, I did the same thing with a software accounting program called MacOneWrite. When this large box arrived on the president's desk, she called me to apologize, and sent me not only an immediate replacement, but a significant amount of other software as well, to repay me for my anguish.

Consumer Karate Method #3
USE INFLUENCE

If you were having trouble with your Rosenkrantz Mark IV computer—*and* having trouble getting them to deal with your trouble—and if you could write to them thus: "My uncle, Sam Rosenkrantz, largest investor in your company, hopes that you'll deal with my problem really soon"—the probability is high that they would deal with your problem really soon.

But what if you don't know any officers or investors in the company? No problem. You don't even have to lie. Just imply. Simply get a name—an officer as listed in one of the business directories, or better still, a major shareholder (check with a stockbroker who may have filings from any public offerings the company may have made). Let's say you learn there is a major stockholder named James R. Hardesty, Jr.

Your letter, probably to a vice president (the president is more likely to know Mr. Hardesty personally), might say, "Before I take this relatively minor problem to Jim Hardesty, I thought I would try one last time to see if we can get it cleared up without bothering him."

Unless good ol' Jim died last week or is now in prison, the probability is good that they will go ahead and try to satisfy you without checking on the nature of the implied relationship.

I used this method on a NorthStar computer, when the factory outlet told me it would take 30 days for a repair. With a magic name invoked, they actually fixed it while I waited.

Consumer Karate Method #4
PUBLIC EMBARRASSMENT

More than once, I have seen people outside computer shows, or even dealers' showrooms, passing out leaflets saying, in effect, "Please don't buy [such and such]" with an explanation of how that particular product turned out to be defective, and the dealer or manufacturer did not satisfy them.

Informational picketing is a tried and true technique of consumer action groups. It has been used successfully at automobile dealerships, appliance stores, and computer retailers, with anywhere from one person to dozens of people marching back and forth with signs or leaflets.

One of the main reasons this works is that they don't know, can't know, how far you are willing to go. Will you be there all day? All week? For the rest of your life? With a dozen friends? With your entire battalion? Better far, in most cases, to make peace and stop this embarrassment, which could do far more harm than the modest request being made by the demonstrators.

Mail-order purchase? No problem. Either actual or threat of an embarrassing action may do the trick. I sent my daughter's tape player back to the manufacturer for repairs. A month passed, two months. They weren't going to fix it because we couldn't prove it was under warranty. Using the power of desktop publishing, I wrote out and printed a heartrending press release on how my desperately ill, bedridden daughter (well, she did have a slight cold) was pining away, because she didn't have her tape player. Every day she would open her rheumy eyes and through swollen lips whisper, "Is my music back yet?" I sent a copy to the top officers of the tape recorder company, with a suggestion that I would be sending out carloads of these tear-jerkers any day now. A brand-new tape player came to us, virtually by return mail, and the repaired original one followed a few days later.

There are, of course, other methods, some of them quite drastic indeed. Someday I shall make public how I single-handedly (I like to think) drove the British Leyland Motor Company into bankruptcy, because of what they did to my Land Rover. But that's enough for now. I hope you won't stoop to considering petty and irrelevant revenge, like having 40 tons of manure dumped on the company president's lawn, or putting sleazy sex books randomly on the public library shelves in the president's home town, with bookplates saying "Gift of (president's name)" in them. Such acts may be temporarily satisfying, but they are unlikely to get your *own* problem solved.

Two more points.

Every time I talk about these consumer karate methods to people, someone is sure to say, "But what if *everybody* did these things?" The only suitable answer is the one Yossarian gave to that question in *Catch-22:* "Then I'd be crazy not to."

Finally, what about the *company's* side of things, I hear some people saying. The customer is most emphatically *not* always right. True enough. But they *usually* are. I have run both retail and mail-order businesses, and I learned early on that it is far better to treat all complaints sensibly (and perhaps be nice to a phony or two who didn't deserve it) than to mistrust everyone and investigate and contest virtually every complaint, and irritate practically everybody.

PART XI

THE DARK UNDERBELLY OF THE COMPUTER WORLD

1,000,000 Mistakes Per Second: The Problems of Being Fast, Dumb, and Big

Let's say you're driving down a suburban street at five miles an hour. Suddenly the entire Rotary Club steps out in front of your car. At that speed, you have no problem gently braking to a stop. But what if you had been traveling a hundred miles an hour? No matter how good a driver you are, the very *fact* of the high speed means that when you do make a mistake, it's going to be a doozy.

The worst shortstop in baseball history once made five errors in one inning. A really bad accountant might, if left unchecked, make a few dozen blunders a day. But even a small computer is fully capable of making one million mistakes per second.

Dreadful computer problems will happen because computers are faster, dumber, and/or bigger than most human beings. Let's look briefly at each factor.

1. *Faster.* Because computers are *so* fast, many people find it hard to adapt their slow lives to the lightning output. As *The New York Times* reported, "a business can become so dependent on them for billing and accounting that a faulty computer could bankrupt a firm before its human officers realized that anything was wrong."

This has, in fact, happened—very likely, many, many times. For example, an insurance company called Triangle Industries claimed, in its suit against a computer company, that the business' cash flow was destroyed when the computer paid money out, but did not bill clients. By the time humans got wind of this, the $20 million business was forced into liquidation.

The Wheeling Heating Company of West Virginia had accounting software that "constantly spewed forth incorrect invoices and payroll checks." After sales had fallen by half, the company president "pulled the plug. We went back to pencil and paper, and we're doing much better," he said.

Not all disasters caused by computer speed are quite so devastating. My label-printing program once jammed, and before anyone noticed, it had printed out 4,000 labels for the same person. Quite possibly if I *also* had a computerized mail room, I might have mailed 4,000

One of the new computers in the billing department had gone berserk, possibly from the strain of replacing five elderly bookkeepers, and a hundred thousand dollars' worth of credit had been erroneously issued to delinquent charge-account customers before anyone caught it.

—Lois Gold, *Necessary Objects*

books to that poor lady in New Hampshire. Fortunately, a human instantly noticed what had happened and destroyed 3,999 labels. Not so lucky was a national magazine that *did* in fact once send 30,000 copies of the same issue to one subscriber.

2. *Dumber.* Computer people are fond of saying that computers are really just big dumb adding machines; it is the *programmers* who are smart. The problem is that it is often either impossible or not worth the bother to anticipate and deal with all the errors that might occur.

One community decided to use their computer to match census-type data with school data, to locate any children over six who were not in school. The programmer left two columns to record the ages of people. And that's why a 107-year-old lady whose age was recorded as "07" received a visit from the truant officer.

The same sort of thing happens often in those "personal" bulk mail letters, sometimes programmed to print, in effect, "Dear [Title] [Last name]," leading to the "Dept. of Acctg" getting letters addressed, "Dear Mr. Acctg." One of my two all-time favorites[52] was a medical school's Department of Gynecology being offered the rare opportunity to purchase "the Gynecology family crest."

As annoying or amusing as this stuff may be, the fact is that many businesses *are* making money with such such approaches. But they would *not* make money if they had to hire humans to go through their mailings and extract all the errors. It is cheaper to send out a mailing knowing that 2% to 5% are either silly or wrong.

Problems often arise when human beings defer to the "wisdom" of the computer. If the computer says so, it must be true. Critic Rex Reed wrote about the time he was arrested by store detectives for using a "stolen" credit card (which was his own). When Reed finally convinced them of his identity, they still tore up his credit card. Why? "Our computer has been told that you are dead, and we cannot change that."

3. *Bigger.* The more parts something has, the greater the likelihood that at least some of them will fail. A small computer has thousands of times as many parts as a simple calculator (if we consider each of the microscopically small components of a chip as a part). A small calculator has vastly more parts than an abacus, and an abacus has about 10 times the number of parts as the typical human has digital counting wands (fingers).

Computer philosophers argue over whether increasing the size of a system increases the likelihood of errors *arithmetically* or *geometrically*. In other words, if I have one item (a computer) and add a second item (a hard disk), will I have twice as many errors or four times

---
[52] The other is described on page 113.

Let us assume that the computer is a faster working, more compact library. But just as today's students don't know how to use the library, tomorrow's will be helpless when confronting their tiny, inexpensive, speedy computers with their tiny, underexercised, hopelessly sluggish minds.

—John Simon

What is possible for technology to do, technology will have done . . . Regardless, regardless of anything.

—Archiblad MacLeish

as many errors? When I add a printer, is it going to be *three* times as many or *eight* times as many?

A good argument can be made for the geometrical theory. Not only does each expansion offer the opportunity for more errors in that unit itself, but since it will interact with each other unit, the opportunities for failure may be multiplied. Certainly there is evidence that one of the biggest computers of all has also been one of the most failure-prone of all. As *The Washington Monthly* put it, "What if the Pentagon spent $10 billion on the computer that is the nerve center of the entire U.S. military apparatus, and then botched up the job so completely that the system didn't work at all almost 70% of the time and was pitifully inadequate the other 30%? . . . Well, it's happened." They go on to explain how the "WIMEX" (Worldwide Military Command and Control System) failed in 85% (247 of 290) of its tests. Interestingly, this is just about the published failure rate for the much-vaunted "smart bombs" that were supposed to go precisely to military targets during the 1991 Gulf War.

What can we do?

Worry. Healthy concern offers the best hope of avoiding or forestalling small problems in the home and office, and even massive problems on a global scale. If only everyone who deals with computers would remember, always and everywhere, that they *are* in fact big, dumb, fast machines that do not dispense Holy Writ (unless, of course, they have been programmed to do so).

Published accounts of computer-related disasters, from the recipe program that said "two cups Tabasco sauce" instead of "two drops," to Chernobyl and Three Mile Island, are replete with "If only . . . " and "We should have . . . " and "Next time we'll know that . . . "

Something to keep in mind. Whether you are barreling along at a hundred miles an hour or a million calculations a second, the potential for disaster is immense. There is nothing inherently *wrong* with those speeds. You just want to stay extra alert and keep your seat belt—physical or electronic—buckled.

"Maybe I Could Just Die Early:" Fear of Computers

It was a 51-year-old vice president of a medium-sized company who voiced the plaintive lament. He had been informed that his department was being "computerized." He tried to cope. He bought (but could not read) computer books. He hung around computer stores, but could not confess his fear. Finally, in desperation, he went to the counselor that his company had sensibly provided during the transition. Too young to retire, too old to start over, he wailed, "Maybe I could just die early."

How widespread is this kind of fear?

Very. A major management consulting firm conducted a national survey which determined that about one-third of all professionals are initially "not receptive" to the idea of computers, but with training and counseling, about 90% eventually "come around."

Even if that 90% figure, which I suspect may be quite high, is accurate, that *still* means there are millions of people out there who may *never "come around."*

As one would logically predict, the level of fear is greatest among older people, but it is quite prevalent among people in their 20s and 30s as well. Of course as computer literate children move into the workplace, the percentages will decline, but it is clear that "computerphobia" is a problem that will be with us for many years to come.

What is the nature of the fear?

I have identified eight different reasons people are afraid of computers. Some people may have one; some may have them all.

1. *Fear of losing job.* As *Business Week* put it, "You can resist it, or you can embrace it. You can submit to its discipline or you can bend it to your own ends. And how you respond is likely to affect your career, not to mention your peace of mind." Fear-of-computers counselor Richard Byrne reports, "I experience a lot of executives who are nervous about 17-year-old kids taking their jobs away from them. . . ."

2. *Loss of status.* A Harvard Business School professor says that the more foolproof computers become, the more people using them begin

There is no more need to learn computer terminology to use a computer than there is to learn the names of your digestive enzymes in order to enjoy a good meal.

–Michael Rothenberg

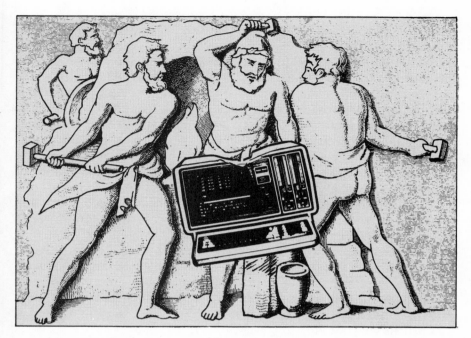

to feel "insignificant and overwhelmed." Morale and motivation plummet.

Time magazine put it this way: "Having built careers on intangibles like personality and leadership, executives may fear that a computer, with its unshakable command of facts and figures, will erode their authority." And a *Wall Street Journal* editor writes, "Computer enthusiasts overlook . . . emotional snarls. As a result, managerial egos are bruised and minor matters bloom into major stumbling blocks." The *Journal* also reports that women executives who can skillfully type into their office computers are "constantly needled by other managers asking if they 'take dictation too.'"

3. *Can't type.* It is surprising how common a fear this is. Typing is something secretaries and clerks do, not higher-ups. A vice president of a big chemical company who resisted computers "wondered if it is an efficient use of . . . time searching for 'p' on the keyboard."

4. *Fear of math.* Seymour Papert, an expert in teaching programming to children, says that "most people who are not mathematicians view the computer field as incomprehensible, even threatening. This 'mathophobia' . . . will inhibit large segments of society from achieving fluency in a computerized world."

5. *Fear of instant rebuke.* Much of society is built on a certain level of courtesy and gentility in dealing with others' errors: "Say, Jenkins, don't you think it might have been better if . . . " The computer is intol-

erant, and comes back with an instant "ERROR" message, which some find most unsettling.

6. *Too late to start.* While some people aren't sure the revolution has started, others fear that it is over and all the booty has been shared. But it is abundantly clear that it is never too late to begin. Three members of the "development team" for this book came to computers in their 70s. Tom Whiteside came to computers in his 80s, years after retiring as a bank chairman. At 90, he is at work on his fifth book. (And if you're a geezer of 55 or more, check out SeniorNet, the National Community of Computer-Using Seniors, c/o the School of Education, University of San Francisco, San Francisco CA 94117.)

7. *Fear of becoming too dependent on it.* Some people worry that they will grow to like their computer *too* much—and then they will live in fear of power outages and breakdowns.

8. *Fear of never being good enough.* This is mine. I never learned to play bridge because my father was a Grand Master and I knew I'd never have the time to get that good. Same for me with programming. I'd rather not start than be a duffer. As *Business Week* put it, computers "are like pianos—you can become a virtuoso, or you can play 'Chopsticks' all your life."

What do people do about computer fear?

Typically, they either fight the fear or fight the computer.

1. *Fighting the fear.* Some enlightened companies offer counseling, advice, and hands-on experience—often with small computers that can be borrowed and taken home, or used after-hours or on weekends, to make a friend of the perceived foe. In my small office, we invested in a series of hands-on teaching videos, so that new employees and old can learn the basics on their own.

There are organizations, large and small, that offer short courses addressing computer fear. The American Management Association has offered a three-day *Computer Phobia* seminar, whose brochure says, "Register today and leave your computer phobia behind you." You'll also leave $800 behind you. Another company offers a weekend course designed "to help people jump into the deep end of the computer revolution, enjoy the ride, and come out surfing the third wave." Cowabunga, indeed (but how do I get the salt water out of my disk drive?).

2. *Fighting the computer.* Some people enjoy computer breakdowns, and may even contribute to them. As Shoshannah Zuboff of the Harvard Business School put it, "The resulting fear of impotence and concomitant loss of status leads sometimes to retaliation."

Although computer sabotage is definitely a problem (see page 225), most people don't go as far as putting sugar in the computer's gas tank. They are more subtle. For instance, a major bank installed, at great expense, an "executive information system" to send memos and other information back and forth. Top management couldn't see the benefit of using it, since their secretaries did all the work anyway. And lower executives saw it as losing control. They could no longer avoid messages, claiming they had never received them. In an attempt to make the system more acceptable, the bank added an "executive daily calendar." Each employee could inspect each others' calendar electronically to learn where he or she was, and when they would be available for appointments. But nobody wanted to admit to a sparse calendar. So, to regain control of their lives, many employees spontaneously began filling their electronic calendars with fictitious appointments. Eventually the system was discontinued. But, significantly, the computers remained in place. They almost always do.

Health Hazards
of Computers

In the 1930s and 1940s, there was a great vogue for watches with dials that glowed in the dark. What made them glow was a radioactive radium compound, applied by hand to the numbers on the watch face. The unfortunate souls who painted the numbers used to lick their brushes to get a fine point. Many of them later contracted cancer and died.

In our eagerness to adopt new technologies, we are prone to rush ahead and buy or use the latest thing—only to discover, years or decades later, that we should have left well enough alone. When I was a child, shoe stores used to use a fluoroscope to show mommas how nicely the bones of the foot fit into the shoe. Then came the realization that the X-rays used were also liable to *destroy* those cute little bones. Away with those particular machines.

An essential issue to acknowledge, and perhaps to worry about with regard to computers, is whether or not there is something about them that, like asbestos, nuclear waste, and radium dials, will come back to haunt us years from now. Are there any "If only I had known . . ." situations that can actually be known now?

Perhaps. There are people who worry about three different kinds of problems that small computers may be causing—both now and for our future: the physical, the psychological, and the spiritual.

1. Physical problems

Historians may find it curious, perhaps incomprehensible, that in the latter years of the 20th century, millions of people chose to sit virtually still (except for their fingers and eyeballs), hour after hour, in an uncomfortable chair, staring at little letters and numbers on a flickering screen, 18 inches from their nose. In the late '80s and early '90s, awareness of the potential problems entered the public consciousness.

Suffolk County, New York enacted America's first public ordinance protecting users of office computers (Canada, and other countries, had already done such things). It was overturned by a state court, and is on appeal. San Francisco checked in next, with a comprehensive city law regulating the number of hours a person can sit in front of a screen, and mandating adjustable chairs, glare-free screens, and good lighting.

The measure, strongly opposed by the Chamber of Commerce, was passed by a bitterly divided Board of Supervisors.

Health factors that some (or many) people worry about include:

1. *Electromagnetic radiation from the computer monitor.* No one denies that computer monitors produce magnetic fields, especially strong within two feet of the screen. The question is: what effect, if any, do such fields have on humans? Those who are alarmed point to studies showing increased cancer rates for people regularly exposed to such radiation, such as families living beneath high-voltage power lines and telephone cable splicers. Others suggest an increased rate of miscarriages for regular computer users.[53]

The availability of monitors that shield the cathode-ray tube can go far to ameliorate this problem. Such monitors are available at a premium of 20% to 200% more than the radiation-producing sorts.

2. *Headaches, dizziness, eyestrain, and blurred vision.* The problems are caused by glare, by subtly flickering screens (which some feel have the potential to bring on an epileptic fit), and by unclear (dusty and smudged) screens. Proper lighting, antiglare screens or screen-covers, and antistatic glass cleaners have all been suggested as ways of reducing the problem.

3. *Repetitive stress injury, or RSI.* Doing the same thing over and over and over again can have a damaging effect on various parts of the body, as in the back pain resulting from sitting endlessly, even in a well-designed chair. (The San Francisco law mandates 15-minute stand-up-and-walk-around breaks every two hours.) One of the most common, and often devastating problems is caused in the hands, arms, and wrists, by working at the keyboard for hours on end. Carpal Tunnel Syndrome and other painful and debilitating ailments can often be prevented or alleviated, many feel, by use of arm or wrist rests: a narrow strip of padded material placed just in front of the keyboard.

2. Psychological problems

Some of the psychological problems that can be caused by computers have been discussed earlier, but there may be more to it than simple anguish and fear. *Omni* magazine reports that "Computer scientists at the Massachusetts Institute of Technology have given an alarming analysis of the computer threat to human society. . . . [They] stated that computers were engulfing almost all functions of human society." According to Dr. Joseph Weizenbaum, "We are rapidly losing, have perhaps already lost, physical and mental control of our society."

---

[53] The darkest picture is painted by Paul Brodeur in his book *Currents of Death: Power lines, computer terminals, and the attempt to cover up their threat to your health.* More hope is offered in Steven Sauter's book, *Improving VDT Work: Causes and control of health in VDT use.* (VDT means Video Display Terminal, the computer's screen.)

The concern is that computers are perceived as so powerful, they destroy people's self-image and the urge to be creative. Just as a lady we knew who joined Jehovah's Witnesses said, "Why bother to diet; the world is going to end very soon anyway, and I will get a perfect body in the next world," so, presumably, are people saying, or thinking, "Why bother to learn new skills and try to solve problems; the computers will always be able to do it better and faster."

The point is not whether these people are right, but whether enough people will come to this point of view to have a noticeable negative effect on productivity and creativity in our society.

3. Spiritual problems

This is a much harder area to get a handle on, but there are certainly a lot of persuasive people who are worried about computers simply because they are somehow *wrong,* or inappropriate, for this day and age.

For one thing, there is the matter of positive ions. Computer systems give off positively charged particles. Some people believe that when there are too many positive ions in an area, humans suffer. They develop a feeling of being ill at ease without knowing exactly why. They grow irritable and crotchety. When the ion balance is restored, either through a negative ion generating device, or by breathing fresh air, matters improve.

This is not an all-or-nothing, black or white situation. It is a matter of tiny degrees. When there are too many positive ions, the quality of life may be just not quite as satisfactory.

Even more esoteric is the notion of geomancy, or the Chinese practice of *feng shui:* the study of how people live on the earth in relation to natural lines of force, gravity, magnetic poles, and so forth. In one common manifestation, there are people who believe it is important to sleep positioned in a north-south direction. Some geomancers have gone further, and suggest that computers do not fit into the natural harmony of the earth; that where there are computers, there will inevitably be increased unrest, turmoil, and distress, both among individual users, and in society as a whole.

These matters interest and concern me, but not enough to dispose of my computers in order to please Mother Earth. I tend to think of it like this:

Suppose in the year 1900, someone had said: "I have a terrific new invention. It will enable you to get from one place to another 20 times faster than you can walk, and four times faster than your horse. Its only drawback is that by the 1990s, it will be killing 150,000 people a year in accidents, and untold more from respiratory disease because of

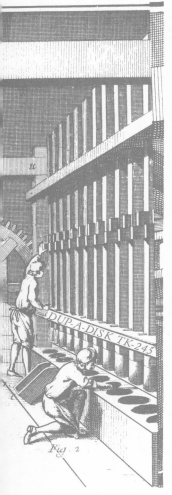

DUP-A-DISK TK-245

Fig. 2

the way it will pollute the atmosphere. Shall I go forth and produce it, or shall I destroy the plans forever?"

When put that way, most citizens probably would have voted to outlaw the automobile.

Now, suppose in the 1990s, someone said, "I have a terrific new invention. It will enable you to calculate your income taxes and write reports four times faster than before. It will play wonderful games with you, and enable the military to design amazing new weapons. Its only drawback is that because of electromagnetic radiation, positive ions, and other factors, it will cause the deaths of at least 150,000 people a year by the year 2080. Shall I go forth, or shall I destroy the plans forever?"

Without benefit of such foresight, we are plowing madly onward. We can only hope that we are all not the radium watch dial painters of today.

The real danger is not that computers will begin to think like men, but that men will begin to think like computers.

—Sydney J. Harris

Modern man is the victim of the very instruments he values most. Every gain in power, every mastery of natural forces, every scientific addition to knowledge has proved potentially dangerous, because it has not been accompanied by equal gains in self understanding and self discipline.

—Lewis Mumford

Piracy: Dealing with the Decision Whether or Not to be a Pirate

The ethics class will now convene. Attendance is mandatory. Take your seat over there. Let us say that someone came along and offered you a machine that could make absolutely perfect copies of a $100 bill. You put a $100 bill in the slot, and out came two $100 bills. You were told that using this machine was illegal, and if you were caught using it, you would be jailed. But at the same time, you know that millions of people are already using it, and no one has ever been arrested. Would you use the machine?

Let's carry this one step further. What if you were *also* told that every time you used the machine to make a $100 bill, $20 was deducted from the bank account of a total stranger who lived a thousand miles away, and who would never know that it was you who had subtracted money from his account. Now do you use the machine?

It is the case that most computer programs can be quickly, cheaply, and easily copied, using the computer itself. This is an extremely desirable feature, because if a disk is damaged or lost, you will have a replacement, or backup copy available.

It is also the case that most software is copyrighted, and making copies, other than for your own personal use as a spare, is strictly forbidden.

Look at it this way. The word processing program I am using right now sells for about $150 at the discount houses. Physically it consists of three disks (about $1.50), an instruction manual (maybe $3 more), and a box. *And* it consists of at least $145 worth of skill and creativity and cleverness on the part of the person or people who devised the program, and who deserve to be rewarded for their abilities.

So let's say that a close friend who has the same model computer wants to get into word processing. Why should he buy $1.50 worth of disks for $150 when I can whip off a copy for him in less than two minutes? No alarms will go off at the manufacturer's offices when an illegal copy is being made.[54] Sure, the disk package has a stern warn-

---

[54] Until the late 1980s, most software was made electronically uncopyable (except by people who bought other software that enabled them to make copies of uncopyable software). But there was such customer distress, over the inability to make backup copies, or to move software from one computer to another, that virtually all the companies removed copy protection from all but the least expensive game programs.

ing on it ("Unauthorized copying is a violation of Federal Law, and may carry a fine of up to $50,000 or imprisonment or both"). But we all know that no individual user is ever going to be prosecuted for this, any more than for illegally taping music off the radio.

As a person who earns my living from royalties, I am extremely sympathetic to those people who earn a pittance every time a box of their software is sold, and who, if we can believe some alarmed industry spokespeople, are losing 90% of their income, since, they claim, there are nine illegal copies of many popular programs for every legal one in use.

Indeed, if the technology suddenly arose to make an instant copy of one of my books for 50 cents, I'm sure I would be more than just bothered by piracy; I would be on the barricades.

Well, what are we to do when we have people who would never think of stealing a $150 typewriter from a stationery store or taking a nickel out of a blind man's cup, blithely stealing $150 software right and left.

Oh, I know. Let's completely reform human nature. Yes, that's it.

And failing that, let's keep harping on the issue every time someone writes a computer book, or makes a computer speech. At least the 55-mile-an-hour speed limit *did* reduce the average speed on the interstate highways from 75 to 70.

Stealing Computers and Computer Time

It hadn't occurred to me that people actually steal computers until mine was stolen. And it hadn't occurred to me that people steal time on other people's small computers until I saw all the protective gadgets sold at computer shows.

Theft prevention

At thief school,[55] I imagine one of the things they teach is to pay attention to the price/weight ratio of stealable goods. Better to steal 10 diamond rings worth $1,000 each than a grand piano worth $10,000. Here is how computers rank in a rather arbitrary price-per-pound list:

Stamp collection	$10,000/lb
Gold	$5,000/lb
Macintosh SE30 computer	$130/lb
Steinway grand piano	$20/lb
Latest Stephen King bestseller	$5/lb
Hide-a-bed sofa	$3/lb
Chicken	$1/lb

In other words, computers rank fairly high on the desirability index for thieves, and indeed a good many small computers *are* stolen.

In addition to all the standard things people do to protect their premises (locks on doors, remembering to use locks on doors, guard dogs, alarm systems, land mines, etc.), there are two kinds of gadgets sold specifically to keep people from stealing small computers.

One category includes devices that fasten permanently (with super glue or one-way screws[56]) to your desk or table, and to which the computer can be locked. Either the computer is glued to a plate which locks to the plate you have glued to your desk, or a cable passes through a hole in the computer (some computers have one just for this purpose), and a hole in the desk plate. This is said to discourage all but the most persistent thieves, or furniture thieves who will inadvertently take your computer along when they steal your table.

---

[55] The question logically arises of what else goes on in the electronics department at thief school. An insider, Mr. M.Y., reports an amazing electronic breakthrough to counterattack those antitheft barking dog tapes: a tape recording of meat.

[56] This is a hardware term, not what you thought. You can buy screws that have slots designed so they can be screwed in, but never removed.

The other category is alarm devices, which fasten to a wall plug, and into which you plug the computer. When someone unplugs it, either because they are stealing it, or because they are moving it so they can vacuum behind your desk, a shrill alarm goes off, deafening the thief (or the maid), and perhaps causing either to drop the computer to the floor and run.

The value of either category depends, of course, on your own personal situation. Your homeowner's or business insurance policy may cover computers now, or may require a special rider, and may provide just as much peace of mind.

Preventing theft of computer time

This can be a major problem with large computers that are on most of the time, and that have telephone line connections. The literature of computer anecdotes is full of stories of teenagers from Iowa City (or somewhere) who use their school or home computer to double the size of payroll checks of a company in Tennessee, to send 10,000 Mailgrams to their favorite teacher, or to launch a missile attack against Ecuador.[57]

This is of little relevance to the small computer user, whose main concern may be that unauthorized business colleagues, fellow students, family members, or pets may use his or her machine after hours. Presumably this is something of a problem, because products exist to keep it from happening. They take the form of plastic covers for the keys, or the entire computer, which lock into place, or key-controlled off-on switches.

---

[57] *The Cuckoo's Egg* by Cliff Stoll is a charming but alarming account of how a spy in Germany penetrated a computer at the University of California and, through the Berkeley computer, broke into "top security" computers all over the country.

The Sledgehammers
of the Night:
Computer Sabotage

A newspaper reporter from Colorado once called my "therapy line" and told me, almost enthusiastically, how easy it was to write and edit on the computer terminals that had been installed at his paper a few years earlier. He really didn't miss his old Remington Standard type-writer much at all.

So why was he calling? Well, it turned out he did have a problem or two. Or 20. Just yesterday, in fact, a major story, written under pressure of a tight deadline, was totally lost somewhere in the bowels of the computer system. And there is no carbon copy, as on the old Remington. This wasn't the first time. And there's the flickering green screen which gave him regular headaches.

Now his voice took on a conspiratorial tone. He asked for (and got) assurance that I would not mention his name or city.

"You know what I'd do," he said, "if the doctor told me I had incurable cancer, and had only six months to live? I'd go to the hard-ware store and buy the biggest sledgehammer they had. Then I'd go to the newspaper office in the middle of the night and I'd smash every one of the 30 computer terminals there into smithereens. *That's* what I would do."

He probably would, too.

And not everyone waits for a terminal cancer diagnosis, either. Computer sabotage is a significant problem in the nation's offices and factories. Even the home computer is not safe, although the problem there is more often an impulsive act, rather than planned mayhem.

Leaving out, as irrelevant to this book, cases in which people sabo-tage computers in order to get revenge on their employer, their com-pany, or the world, we are left with two kinds of situations in our casebook: people who want to kill their computer because it doesn't work properly, and people who want to kill their computer because they believe it is trying to kill them.

Sabotaging a poorly working machine

The literature and lore of computers are replete with tales of people getting so fed up with malfunctioning machinery that they try to put it

out of its misery. Here are a few of the stories I discovered from some newspaper research in the library:

- A man in Washington murdered his home computer with a shotgun. Two blasts, right between the disk drives. "I had taken all I was gonna take from the little bastard," he told the sheriff.
- A woman in Illinois set her Apple carefully in her driveway and drove back and forth over it half a dozen times.
- A bureaucrat in Texas threw a Tandy computer from a sixth-floor office window to the street below.
- An architectural firm in Massachusetts held a funeral for its computer system, then buried it beneath six feet of dirt.

Since these, and many more like them, are stories that actually made the newspapers, we must wonder how many more tales there are, either secretly carried out, or simply not deemed sufficiently newsworthy for the major papers.

And not all destructive fantasies happen. A disgruntled computer user who is also a private pilot told me of his wish to drop his computer onto the offices of the company that made it, from a height of five thousand feet. He said that the only reason he hasn't is because he could not be sure that it would land on the office of the person who designed the disk drives.

Killing the machine before it kills you

I begin to believe that the computer is not the great god we have been led to believe, but a hollow idol, manipulated by crafty priests.

–Bernard Levin

Physical and psychological hazards involved in using a computer are discussed on page 216. Most victims (or people who feel victimized) deal with perceived problems in what might be called a socially acceptable manner: they take what is dished out; they try to make changes; or they sue the pants off their employers or the computer company.

But some people perceive a great evil in the machine, and feel they are doing mankind a favor by eliminating it from the face of the earth. Also from newspaper files:

- A New York woman who believed she was losing her eyesight from watching a computer screen for years, sprayed black paint on the screen, the insides of the computer, and her desk as well.[58]
- A man who came to believe that his programs were being altered just a little bit every night, set fire to 50 floppy disks in the company restroom.
- A Canadian wife who felt that her husband's home computer was breaking up their marriage weighted it (the computer, not the husband) with rocks and drowned it in a nearby lake.

---

[58] This is a tragic situation, but it does bring to mind one of the few ethnic slur computer jokes: How can you identify a [insert nationality to be slurred]'s computer? It has white-out fluid on the screen.

- And when virtually all the employees of a carpet warehouse threatened to quit soon after a new computer system was installed, claiming it was destroying the quality of life there, the management not only removed the offending system, but called in a priest to exorcise the evil electronic spirits that might remain.

Dealing with the urge to kill

Unless one has irrefutable evidence that one's computer is trying to kill someone (e.g. HAL[59] in the movie *2001*), it is probably much healthier (and generally more economical) not to murder your computer. However, there are indisputably times when *something* has to be done for your own mental health.

My daughter Mariah once found considerable satisfaction in destroying just one floppy disk—one that had been causing her problems. Disks burn quite nicely, with a multicolored flame, and little flaming "buzz bombs" of particles that whiz to the ground. Of course this is environmentally unsound, and must be done carefully to avoid setting your carpet ablaze. I have burned only two disks in my many years with small computers. Since the same one dollar expenditure would have bought me less than one minute with a psychiatrist, I consider it an excellent investment in mental health.

---

[59] Has everyone by now noticed what you get when you take the next letter in the alphabet after each of these three letters?

Computer Crime

This is not the place for a definitive survey of computer crime. Thomas Whiteside[60] has already done that in his splendid book, *Computer Capers: Tales of Electronic Thievery, Embezzlement, and Fraud*. Nor is it the place for a "how to" manual, either on perpetrating or detecting computer crime. But I think it is important to point out how easy the former is, and how difficult the latter is.

We are *all* victims of computer crimes, if only in that we pay higher fees for bank, credit card, insurance, and other services, because *some-one* has to pay back the more-than-$5 billion that is stolen through computer crime each year.

Some industry spokespeople deny the figure is even one-tenth this high, but others believe it could be a great deal higher. The reason for this huge difference of opinion is that by its very nature, computer crime is almost impossible to detect.

If a robber points a gun at a bank teller, fills a sack, and roars off, no one will dispute that the bank has been robbed. But when a computer criminal makes a minor adjustment in the bank's computer and transfers one dollar from each of a million accounts to his own account, it may be years, if ever, before anyone notices.

With telephone computer links, such crimes can be committed without ever setting foot in the bank. There are hundreds of published accounts of people—often teenagers using their home or school computer—who tap into someone else's computer and wreak havoc. Sometimes they just leave amusing messages; sometimes they do a great deal more. For instance, four 13-year-olds at a fancy New York private school penetrated the computer of several banks and corporations, juggling accounts and erasing millions of bits of information.

Why computer crime goes undetected

I fear none of the existing machines; what I fear is the extraordinary rapidity with which they are becoming something very different to what they are at present . . . Should not that movement be jealously watched and checked while we can still check it?

—Samuel Butler, 1872

If you left a $20 bill on your dresser at night and it was gone in the morning, you would begin to suspect a crime. But let's say you left *three* $20 bills out: one on your dresser at home, one on the seat of your car, and one on your desk in the office. Along comes a thief who breaks into your house and steals the $20 bill from your dresser, and spends it on a swell dinner at the diner. But then, just before you awaken, he steals the $20 from your car and leaves it on your dresser.

---

[60] Not the same Thomas Whiteside mentioned on page 214.

Just before you go to your car, he steals the $20 from your office and puts it in your car. Before you arrive at the office, he has gone back and stolen the $20 from your dresser and put it in your office. Since you can only be in one place at a time, you believe you have three $20 bills, but in fact you only have two. The thief has stolen one-third of your assets.

Using this strategy, computer thieves have set up incredibly elaborate electronic systems to cover up their crimes. They rig a bank's computer to take money out of many accounts, but to transfer it back in from other people's accounts just before the auditor comes through.

I visited one of the most successful computer criminals of all time at a California state prison in Vacaville, where he was serving a two-year sentence for stealing millions from a large bank.[61] He told me that he was aware of dozens and dozens of crimes currently being committed—some of them in progress for several years—and most of which, he predicted, would never be detected because of ingenious track-covering programs.

A penny here, a penny there, it adds up

Many computer crimes are as close to victimless as any crime can be. This doesn't make them OK, but it may help explain why penalties are usually so mild. While a typical armed bank robber nets $2,500 and serves 11 years if caught and convicted, the typical computer bank robber nets over $100,000 and serves less than three years. Here are three of the common techniques:

• Once, when bank interest rates were 5⅓%, a programmer for a bank noticed that the bank was paying 5.333% to two account-holders and, randomly, 5.334% to the third, so it would all come out even. He rigged things so *all* customers got 5.333%, and *he* got the remaining .001% added into his account. That's only a penny a year per thousand dollars. But with ten billion in accounts, that tiny percentage was netting him $100,000 a year.

• A man rigged the computer at a dog racing track to figure the payoffs on one race per day as if there had been three additional winners. So each of the thousands of real winners would get a dollar or two less, and this chap, with his winning tickets issued by an accomplice *after* the race, was netting several thousand dollars a day.

• An employee at a large insurance company adjusted a program that added a dollar a year to each customer's annual billing. For months, no one noticed, and over a million dollars a month was skimmed off, ending up (electronically, of course) in a Swiss bank.

---

[61] And I'd love to get in touch with him again, so if you're reading this, B.K.G., please write or call me at the address given on page 257.

Other popular forms of computer crime

- *Stealing information.* One company taps into another company's computer to learning about their sales, pricing changes, and other trade secrets.

- *Changing information.* Students enter their school's computer and change their grades. This is almost impossible to discover. A major university issues over a million grades a year, and to cross-check each one with the professors' grade cards would cost a fortune. (And more and more schools are switching over to systems where faculty record grades directly into the school computer over touch-tone telephones. There is no paper track at all.)

Recently, I attended the national convention of college and university registrars. There were several very popular sessions on the matter of computer fraud. Registrars shared case histories in which students attempted to change grades, add units, and even record that degrees were awarded when they were not. When I asked the FBI white-collar crime specialist in attendance if he thought these discovered cases were the tip of a huge iceberg, he solemnly nodded "Yes."

- *Stealing merchandise.* A college student worked at a telephone company warehouse during the summer, and learned that branches would order merchandise by tapping in the information on touch-tone phones. Over the next few years, he ordered over a million dollars in parts, which he then sold through his "cover" company, Creative Telephone.

- *Creating people.* If a computer says someone is real, they are real. The billion-dollar Equity Funding scandal involved inventing thousands of nonexistent people, giving them life insurance policies, and then selling those policies at a discount to other companies. That's the grand scale. There are many cases where companies bought nonexistent goods from nonexistent suppliers with real money, added phantom people to the payroll, and even set up an entire nonexistent branch office for which real desks, computers, and cars were purchased (and then sold).

What can be done?

Not a whole lot. Awareness is part of it, of course. One computer detective says that most companies protect the change in their soft drink machine more carefully than access to their computers. Most banks spend more on video cameras and armed guards than on seeking out electronic fraud. Yet it seems clear that whatever system an honest expert can invent, a dishonest expert can solve and defeat.

An enlightened public offers faint hope. A crook who was swiping 15 cents from each customer by adding that amount to the bank's monthly service charge was caught because one bank customer fought through the bank's supercilious "We can't be wrong" attitude, and finally got through to someone willing to check out a 15 cent discrepancy. The international spy caper finally uncloaked and described in *The Cuckoo's Egg* was discovered because one intrepid computer hobbyist wouldn't rest until he had tracked down the source of a 75 cent error in a computer usage bill. But these are rare events. It seems clear that the computer boom will grow hand in hand (or, more accurately, hand in pocket) with the electronic crime boom.

The Jangling Can: Computers and Invasion of Privacy

A friend recently opened an elegant dress shop for large-sized women. In order to publicize her store, she was able to go to one company and rent a list of names and addresses of all the overweight women living in the area. How can this be? Because many states sell driver's license application information to the highest bidder, and all the computer had to do was search the lists for females living in certain zip-code areas whose weight was disproportionate to their height. From another company, she could buy up to two million names of people who had bought "queen-size" panty hose by mail.

Every time you use your name in public (and some private) places, whether to get a driver's license, buy a product by mail, check into a hotel or motel, give to a charity, write your congressperson, enter a hospital, rent a car, or join a union, you end up in someone's computer, and your name and address and other information about you (like your weight, number of children, political affiliation, and religion) become a salable commodity. Right now, unless you are someone really special (multimillionaire, known sucker for get rich quick schemes, etc.), your name and address are worth about seven to ten cents on the open market.

How much do computers really know about us? Do you want a list of Jewish dentists who drive Volvos? A man in Ohio got such a list by using computers to cross-check computerized lists of Jews, dentists, and Volvo owners, all of which are readily available.

It gets even scarier as ingenious marketers start looking at our lifestyle patterns, and selling our names based on, for instance, the kinds of purchases we make with our credit cards (backpacking equipment, erotic videos, gourmet candies, whatever); the magazines we subscribe to; the charities we support; and the books we choose from a book club.

As Joel Chaseman, speaking as president of Post-Newsweek Stations, put it, what will happen "when the computers of cable companies and charge card companies speak to AT&T's computer, and together discuss what you've watched, where you've gone, what you've read, the source and size of your income, and what calls you have made. The computers know and they will tell, unless Congress decides they should not . . . "

And the worst may be yet to come. Every president since Dwight Eisenhower has been intrigued with the idea of a National Data Bank. If all the information the government has collected at various times on each individual were combined into a single giant computer, would there not be wonderful benefits (to the government)?

By matching census data with draft data, all unregistered people over 18 could be identified. By matching driver's licenses with people who get aid to the blind, frauds could be uncovered. By comparing income tax returns with real estate filings, people who failed to declare real estate profits could be uncovered.

There are only two problems with all of this: errors and Hitlers.

1. *Errors.* Computers do make mistakes. If the government attempted to cross-check and correlate a dozen factors for a quarter of a billion Americans, and if the machinery operated at 99.999% accuracy, then there would only be a few *billion* errors made. When author Charles Reich testified before the U.S. Congress in opposition to the National Data Bank idea, he likened such errors to a jangling can. "All the rest of his life, wherever he (the innocent victim) went, he would have a tin can jangling along behind him."

2. *Hitlers.* Civil libertarians point out that if Germany had had a National Data Bank in 1939, Hitler's extermination of the Jews would have happened much faster and more efficiently. It seems amazing to me that the same people who oppose gun registration (because then the Commies would know where to come and get their guns) generally support the National Data Bank idea. How do they know that the next Hitler to come down the pike won't have it in for Catholics or old people or Masons or veterans or truck drivers or Jewish dentists who drive Volvos?

What can we do?

Oppose the National Data Bank. More than three-fourths of Americans do, according to one major nationwide poll.

Support the American Civil Liberties Union's battle against the National Data Bank.

Reflect on the Swedish approach, where the Data Inspection Board regulates every computer data bank in the country that keeps personal records. They license data keepers, check out security systems, and investigate and prosecute violations.

If you use your small computer in business or any public-related way, use it responsibly.

Track the computerization of your own life by using different names or middle initials in harmless public situations. We once took out a magazine subscription in the name of my daughter's pet rat, Sean Lord Derryberry. If that rat had a mailbox, it would never be empty. Offers, catalogues, Easter seals, charity requests, and inevitably the opportunity to buy his family's coat of arms.

Most of the larger mail order businesses (including magazine subscription departments) offer the option of having your name removed from their list, and the Direct Mail Association in New York offers the service whereby your name can, if you request it, be removed from the lists of all their member companies. But of course it may have been rented 17 times to 17 other organizations before it is deleted, and each of those 17 will use it and can rent it to still others, and the tin can goes jangling along.

PART XII

WHERE, THEN, ARE THINGS GOING

Spanish Ladies on Bicycles:
Computers and the Economy

"Electronic Brain to Replace Million Workers," screamed the headline in a 1953 science magazine. Throughout the 1950s, many philosophers devoted much time and many square inches of text to the matter of how computers would affect the economy.

Remarkably, well into the fourth decade of the computer age, we are still not entirely sure what the effect has been, or what it will be. As Jon Stewart once wrote in *Saturday Review,* "The United States government is notable for its lack of initiative in calculating the job impact of the new technology . . . "

It seems easier for critics to investigate and to point with alarm (or pride) at individual cases, than at society as a whole. For example:

• Business A "hires" a computer and fires two bookkeepers and an accountant as a result.

• Factory B installs computers along its assembly line and lets seven hourly workers and one foreman go.

• Newspaper C proposes computerizing its pressroom, whereupon the union announces this will eliminate 64 jobs, and calls a strike.

It may appear that some of the early "electronic brain" fears were correct. And yet, when we look more closely at individual cases, we often see that things are far more complex than they may have appeared on the surface.

• Business A may have fired two pencil pushers and a bean counter, but they had to hire a higher-salaried programmer, take out an expensive service contract, and retrain other employees. Things got shuffled around, the profits didn't improve at all.

• Factory B has so many problems getting their computers up and running, and learning to live with them, that they actually *lost* money for the first two years of their computer era, but are hoping to show a profit for the third.

• Newspaper C negotiated an arrangement with the union whereby no one will be fired, but the work force will be reduced by attrition over the years. So five people are paid to operate the addressing and labeling department, even though two people and the computer could do it just as well.

One thing that seems clear to most pundits is that a great many "traditional" jobs are being lost. A report on the effect of computerizing French industry was so devastating, the reigning government suppressed it until after a forthcoming election. (It predicted that nearly a third of the people in labor-intensive industries—banking, insurance, etc.—would lose their jobs within 10 years.)

In America, the Service Employees International Union (which used to represent elevator operators and bowling alley pin spotters, so they *know* what automation can do) has expressed similar concerns about American office workers.

But as jobs are lost, others are gained. In the world of computers, there are two main categories—well, three if we include Spanish women on bicycles.

1. *Programmers.* The smallest category is computer programmers. In the next decade or so, we will need from one to five million (depending on whose predictions you read). Some people believe the boom is out there, just over the horizon. Others are saying that programmers may be the space scientists of the next decade: all trained up and no place to go.

2. *Attendants.* Computers require a great deal of attention, from when a business first considers one (planners, salespeople, etc.) to installations (architects, designers, movers, electricians, heating and ventilation people, etc.) to its operation (data entry clerks, paper movers) to its upkeep (repairers, cleaners, adjusters, etc.).

3. *Spanish women on bicycles.* Sometimes totally new and unexpected jobs are created by computerization. Robert Hutchins told the story of a huge bakery in Germany that computerized its operations. Dozens of highly trained bakers were dismissed. The computerized ovens had error-detection systems which turned on a little red light when something was going wrong. To monitor the red lights, the bakery hired a platoon of Spanish women (the cheapest available labor) to ride up and down the aisles on bicycles. When they saw a red light, they reported it to a foreman who sent out a technician.

In the same vein, a large refrigerated packing plant installed computer-controlled thermostats to replace the old mechanical ones. The old ones clicked off or on every 10 to 15 minutes, and turned the air conditioning on or off as a result. The new ones monitored the temperature 60 times a second, and turned the compressors on and off so often that two people had to be hired just to repair or replace switches, relays, and wiring that wore out. Their salaries nearly equaled the savings from the more precisely controlled atmosphere.

There are many who think the main impact of computers on the economy so far is a major reshuffling of jobs—away from the middle, with some to a higher end, and most to a lower. As Peter Drucker puts it, "The main impact of the computer has been the providing of unlimited jobs for clerks."

Computers are undoubtedly having a significant effect on the way much of the world operates—but whether they are good, bad, or indifferent for the economy is still a matter of speculation and dispute.

The Future:
How Computers Might
Really Change Things

For most people in most situations, machinery (including computers) has made it possible to do things faster (going shopping by car versus horse and wagon) or better (reading a book by light bulb versus reading by candle) or cheaper (buying an expensive mass-produced toy versus a one-of-a-kind handmade one), but not all that differently.

As Jeff Angus writes, "Studies indicate that trained people take every bit as long to produce a page on a computer as they did on a typewriter, without improving communication. Why? Because people are spending more time with sophisticated word processors trying to make their documents look more 'professional.' The information they present is no more accurate or useful . . . ; it's just prettier."

Computers (especially the kind we never think about, because they have disappeared into things) hold the promise of assisting human beings in doing things in totally new ways, not just faster, better, and/or cheaper ways. In a park in Saint Louis last year, I saw a man sitting on a bench in a lovely setting, with a cellular telephone, a battery-powered fax machine, and a portable computer. For all I know, he may have been sending or receiving a dreary sales report on grommets and wing nuts, but it hardly mattered. He was sitting there doing business in a way that would not have been possible a short time earlier. Indeed, with those three artifacts, he did not need (and perhaps did not have) an office. And a cellular computer with a fax modem built in, reduces the machinery to a single five-pound case.

Checkless, cashless, paperless home banking? Ho hum. It's still banking, maybe a little faster, maybe a little easier. A new kind of storage device that can hold a thousand times as much data? Big deal. What's in it for me? Ah, but consider the prospect of designing your own morning newspaper—what categories of news, which features, which comics, what level of crossword puzzle, what kind of advertising—and having it printed on your home printer just before you get up in the morning. That's the sort of thing that keeps me looking forward to tomorrow. Nah, it'll never be done by tomorrow, but wait!

My Computer Autobiography

The title of this book could have been, "How I went from a $35,000 Digital computer to a $15,000 Micromation computer to a $10,000 NorthStar computer to a $3,000 Apple computer to a $2,000 Epson computer to a $1,000 Macintosh computer and found something approaching true happiness."

A little hard to remember, albeit reasonably accurate.

The purpose of this section, then, is to establish my credentials for writing a book of this sort. There is nothing wrong with those many people who spend a few months with a certain computer and then write the "definitive text" on What It All Means. However a certain perspective, gained only through having a wide range of experience, is missing. People have actually written articles and even guidebooks to faraway lands based on a three-week trip. Their sweeping generalizations ("It almost always rains in Macho Grande, and the women do not take kindly to strangers") are not utterly reliable.

I bought my first computer in 1975. My mail order business had about 80,000 names and addresses on an antiquated mechanical system. My then-partner and I decided we would get the best computer we could afford. We went to the then-largest manufacturer of small ("small" in 1975 meant under $100,000) computers, Digital Equipment Corporation, and, with software, accessories, and all, paid about $35,000. Four 8" double-sided double-density disk drives. (There were no hard disks in those days.)

It never worked well. The manufacturer claimed it was delivered and installed improperly by the dealer, and that the specially written software (there was no off-the-shelf software in those days) had major flaws. The software company always claimed it was a hardware problem, and that their programs were perfect. However, from delivery day to the day we sent it away, more than four hundred hours of repair and service time were logged. (After 18 months, we actually moved our business 150 miles, primarily to be nearer to a DEC repairman.)

When my partner and I split up, he kept the DEC. I got two chairs, a table, and the fire extinguisher.

Computer number two was a Micromation, bought largely because it was one of the very few machines that came with a one-year, not a 90-day warranty. Two 8" drives, a Texas Instruments printer, and a lot of software, some off the shelf, some specially written, and a total bill around $15,000.

The first major lesson learned was that a one-year warranty saves some money, but if the machine has to be hand-carried in to the company, including up a long flight of stairs, and the company is 150 miles away, there is a certain lessening of the convenience factor, especially since major repairs were required every few months.

Having rapidly developed the axiom, "Never buy anything you can't lift," when an opportunity arose to trade the Micromation system even-Steven for a smaller NorthStar Horizon (two 5¼" double-sided double-density drives), a system then selling for around $10,000, I leaped at it.

The first need was to convert all the records from the 8" to the smaller disks. While theoretically this is no more complex than converting your record collection to cassette tapes, in practice it was my first awareness of the dreaded 99% factor. If you lose 1% of your notes when converting Beethoven, no one will ever know. If you lose 1% of your data, you're in big trouble.

There were many problems with the NorthStar, but the company was reasonably helpful, and just as a glimmer of light appeared at the end of the tunnel, thieves turned off the light. The NorthStar was stolen over the New Year's weekend of 1981. Talk about mixed emotions. . . .

When the insurance check finally came, I bought the *only* computer that was then locally sold, serviced and, allegedly, supported: an Apple II+ with two single-sided 5¼" drives. It served me long and faithfully, but I lost my heart to another, when Epson announced its QX-10, a machine of magnificent creativity (for the time) albeit less than wonderful execution and miserable support. If Epson headquarters had ever returned a phone call (mine or, from what many people told me, anyone else's) the QX-10 might well have evolved into the standard for personal computers today.

As it happened, in 1984, I was on a nationwide talk show tour, talking about computers. The question was always asked, "What do you use, yourself?" And one day in 1985, Albert Chu, an executive with Apple Computer, called me up and said, in effect, "If we were to give you one of our new Macintoshes, would you consider using it? You may find it has much of what the Epson offered, and a good deal more." Without much coaxing, I propelled myself promptly to Cupertino, California, spent a day swapping ideas with some of the assembled heads of Apple's foreign subsidiaries, and went home with a 128K Macintosh and a printer in hand.

As you have doubtless deduced, I have been in the Macintosh camp ever since, and I am a generally happy camper. That 128K has been upgraded so many times, it is starting to show its face-lift and tummy-tuck scars. It now runs a Mirror Technologies full-page display, and is still in use every day. If they come out with the Cray upgrade for the 128, I'll probably go for that as well.

It has been joined by my wife's SE and by a Classic, both paid for with real money. Someday there will be a need for color, I guess, but it has not come along yet.

What of the IBM world? I carry a Toshiba MS-DOS portable, because it cost a quarter as much as a Macintosh portable, and with LapLink software, files can be readily transported from the IBM side to the Mac side and back. But I see no more reason to delve deeply into IBM than I would to learn to speak fluent Japanese just because I might visit that country one day.

This is not an anti-IBM statement; indeed, if they had ever offered me a free one, I might be using one today, and making nasty little asides about the cute little underpowered small-screen black and white Mac. It is more a statement about the lack of necessity (for most people in most situations) to achieve a high level of facility and literacy in two quite different systems.

And anyway, my coauthor and business partner, Dave Pozerycki, *is* one of those people who knows nearly everything about both the Mac and the IBM world.

Is this the end, then? Goodness, no. I am still sitting here waiting for the following:

- a 10-pound-or-less battery-powered computer with
- a large hard disk drive or read-write CD disk drive built in,
- a full-page color screen,
- 50-hour batteries, with spare lightweight battery cartridges I can carry around,
- a backlighted, nonglare, nonradiating screen,
- a 5-pound snap-on battery-powered letter-quality printer with full graphics capability,
- 100% compatibility with Macintosh and IBM and with all my software and all my files, and
- a price under $2,000.

Well let's see. The "Calculate Your Life Expectancy" feature of *Andrew Tobias' Managing Your Money* tells me that as I write these words, I have 33 years to go (not guaranteed). Since 33 years ago I was using a slide rule, and the smallest cheapest computer anyone could buy cost in the millions and filled a large room, I figure my chances look pretty good.

Glossary

There are computer dictionaries on the market with thousands and thousands of definitions. The few definitions that follow are those that are most likely to be helpful to the intelligent beginner. It is useful to know the words "hardware" and "software." Beyond that, nothing is essential. There will be no quiz at the end.

alphanumeric
Characters including both letters and numbers (and usually punctuation marks and other symbols). Printers are alphanumeric; most calculators numeric only.

application
A program that causes the computer to do certain things. "I have a new word processing application."

ASCII
Pronounced "ass-key," it is an industry standard for electronically describing all letters, numbers, and symbols that a computer produces. Virtually all computers use ASCII code, which is the only reason one computer can usually "read" things produced on another computer, even with a different operating system, and with different software.

assembly language
A programming language permitting advanced programmers to write complex or sophisticated programs. No one who understands assembly language will be reading this book.

backup
A copy of important files. One should always make backup copies of programs, data, and other records. Sensible people store the backup in another location.

BASIC
One of the most common and simplest programming languages, developed for beginners at Dartmouth many years ago.

baud rate
The rate at which data are sent, or transmitted, from one place to another. One baud (rhymes with "flawed") is one bit per second. Com-

IMPORTANT RULE:

Beware of any computer book using

just as you should beware of any Chinese restaurant using

THIS TYPE FACE

puters communicate at rates from 300 baud up to 9,600 or more. Humans talk to each other at about 10 baud.

bay
A place to put hard and floppy drives inside the main computer box.

binary
The number system all computers use; all numbers are expressed through a combination of 1s and 0s (equivalent to switches being on or off).

bit
The basic unit of information or data used by computers. A bit is represented by a 1 or a 0, corresponding to a switch being on or off. A string of eight bits makes one byte.

boot up
The act of electronically transferring a program from a disk into the temporary memory (RAM) of a computer, so that it can be used. "Why don't you boot up that disk, and we'll see what we've got."

byte
A string of eight bits, equivalent to a single character: a letter, number, or other symbol.

cache
Also cache memory. A bank of memory which acts very fast, where the computer stores often-used commands for faster access. This can speed up operations by over half.

CD-ROM
Information stored on a compact disk in "read only" memory; you can read it but you can't change or edit it.

character
Generally the same as byte: a single letter, number, or symbol. The word "byte" was probably invented because a "512 kilo-character computer" sounds funny.

chip
A tiny (fingernail-sized or a bit larger) hunk of silicon on which are etched thousands of tiny electronic circuits. One chip can hold as much stuff as a roomful of 1960 machinery.

compatible
Two things that can work with each other are compatible: a computer and a certain software program; a computer and a printer; etc.

compiler
A special program that takes instructions written in programming language and translates them into the machine language the computer understands. Sort of the equivalent of the waitress who hears, "Two poached eggs on toast" (input) and shouts to the chef, "Adam and Eve on a raft" (output).

computer
An extremely fast and complex adding machine.

configuration
The layout or design of a computer system, often used as a verb: "We'll configure a system to meet your needs."

controller
A circuit that the hard and floppy disks attach to. Speedier ones are more expensive.

coprocessor
A special chip that can be added to a computer to speed numerical computation. Helpful for statistics, math, and graphics but not necessary.

CPU
The central processing unit, or CPU, is the actual core of a computer: the logic and circuits where data are processed.

CRT
Cathode-ray tube: the "picture tube" in a television monitor or computer terminal. Computer descriptions might refer, for instance, to a 9" CRT.

database
A collection of data, and the software that manipulates it. "The school had the names of all its students in its database, and used its database software to sort them alphabetically, and store grade information."

diagnostics
Tests used to determine whether a computer, printer, or other hardware is working properly. Some hardware has built-in diagnostics: push a button, and it tells you, in effect, how it is doing.

disk
Some purists insist that a disk is the big metal thing used in big computers, while the small plastic things used in small computers are "diskettes." Most people who use diskettes call them "disks" or "floppies" (from "floppy disk" because they are flexible inside their shells).

Information is stored magnetically on disks in the same way it is stored on audio or video tapes. Floppy disks come in sizes from 2" to 8" in diameter, but 3½" and 5¼" are the most common.

disk drive
A unit, either built into a computer or freestanding, which "plays" a disk in much the same way a cassette deck plays a cassette.

diskette
See disk.

dot matrix
A printing system in which each letter is formed from an array or matrix of tiny dots.

double-density
A disk and disk drive that squeezes twice as much information into the same space as a now-obsolete single-density system. Also called "dual-density."

double-sided
A disk and disk drive system in which information can be stored on and extracted from both sides of the disk. Virtually all disks and disk drives are double-sided, but single-sided can still be found in older systems.

downtime
The time a computer is out of service, or "down." People used to talk about the "downtime record" of a computer. Now they talk about MTBF: mean time between failures.

DPI
Dots Per Inch: a measure of the quality of printer output. Ink jet and laser printers typically produce 300 dots per inch or more; phototype-setters 1,200 or more.

8-bit processor
A computer that can "swallow" 8 bits, or 1 byte at a time. This is the smallest size in common use, and is about one-fourth as fast as a 16-bit and one-sixteenth as fast as a 32-bit.

end user
Computer companies and dealers refer to the customer—you and me—as the end user.

export

Sending data to another program or location. "I will export my customer list from my main database to my label printing program."

file

A collection of specific information stored in a given place in a computer's memory, not unlike a file stored in a filing cabinet. The things in a file are often called "records."

floppy disk

See disk.

gigabyte

One million bytes, or one thousand megabytes, or 1,000K.

GIGO

Garbage In, Garbage Out. In other words, a computer is no better than what you put into it. (In some circles, however, this is known as "Garbage In, Gospel Out." In other words, whatever a computer says must be right.)

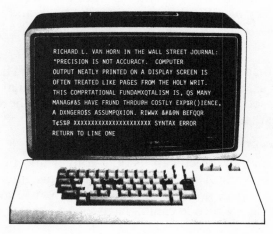

RICHARD L. VAN HORN IN THE WALL STREET JOURNAL:
"PRECISION IS NOT ACCURACY. COMPUTER
OUTPUT NEATLY PRINTED ON A DISPLAY SCREEN IS
OFTEN TREATED LIKE PAGES FROM THE HOLY WRIT.
THIS COMPRTATIONAL FUNDAMXQTALISM IS, QS MANY
MANAG#&S HAVE FRUND THROU@H COSTLY EXP%R()IENCE,
A DXNGERO$S ASSUMPQXION. RIWWX &#&@N BEFQQR
T¢S%@ XXXXXXXXXXXXXXXXXXXXX SYNTAX ERROR
RETURN TO LINE ONE

If you put tomfoolery into a computer, nothing comes out but tomfoolery. But this tomfoolery, having passed through a very expensive machine, is somehow ennobled and no one dares to criticize it.

—Pierre Gallois

hard copy

The same as "printout"—the actual paper that comes out of the printer, as contrasted with the words appearing temporarily on the screen.

hardware

The actual physical equipment in a system: the computer, disk drives, printer, as contrasted with the software, the disks or programs.

high-density

Even more information per square inch of disk space than double-density.

import

Bringing data in from another program. "My bookkeeping program can import numbers from my sales records."

ink jet printer

A printer that prints by squirting ink onto the page, with great precision, from tiny nozzles that move rapidly back and forth across the paper.

input

As a noun, that which is entered into a computer. "The input consists of monthly sales figures. The output will be annual sales comparisons." Alas, seems to be becoming a verb: "Jones, here, will input the latest figures."

interactive software

A program that, in effect, carries on a conversation with the human. Games are a common use. In business programs, interactive software might, for instance, prompt for responses ("Now enter zip code") or point out errors ("zip code cannot have four digits. Try again.").

interface

Technically, the connection between two parts of a computer system by cable, plug and socket, or phone lines. Commonly, any connection between or among elements of a system: the interface between the marketing and production departments. Also used as a verb. Everything is used as a verb these days. ("Will your IBM system interface with my Macintosh system?")

K

Short for "kilo" or "1,000" although technically, in computers only, 1,024 (2 to the 10th power). A computer with 640K of memory really has 655,340 bytes of memory.

laser printer
Printer that produces near-typesetting-quality output, 300 dots per inch or more.

letter-quality
Said of a printer if the quality is as good as an old IBM Selectric typewriter or equivalent.

load
The act of electronically transferring a program from a floppy or hard disk where it is stored into the temporary memory, or RAM, where it can be used. "Please load the inventory control program."

machine language
The most elemental programming language, dealing with the very logic of the machine itself. Few programmers work in machine language.

mainframe
The noun or adjective applied to a very large computer. "We replaced our mainframe with microcomputers and an abacus."

megabyte, meg, MB
One million bytes of information, or 1,000K. Used to refer to the storage capacity of a hard or floppy disk, or the size of the RAM or ROM memory of a computer. "My hard disk has 65 megs."

memory
The place in a computer where information is stored, either temporarily (RAM) or permanently (ROM).

microcomputer
A small computer, more commonly called a PC or a personal computer. Everyone agrees that a microcomputer is smaller than a minicomputer, but no one agrees where to draw the line between them. Anything that costs less than $5,000 is probably a micro; anything that costs more than $20,000 is probably a mini. In between, fight it out.

minicomputer
Bigger than a micro, smaller than a mainframe.

modem
A device that translates the output of a computer into sounds that can be sent over ordinary telephone lines to other computers.

monitor
The device containing the screen on which the words, numbers, and pictures appear.

motherboard
The main circuit board in a computer. Memory that attaches here is faster than other add-in schemes. Many motherboards can be expanded (more memory added) by adding chips.

MTBF
Mean time between failures, a measure of the reliability of hardware, which might have an MTBF of 50,000 in-use hours, or more.

multitasking
Running more than one program at a time. Tremendously helpful for assembling reports, newsletters, and any document with more than one source of input.

multiuser system
A computer system in which two or more computers are connected together so they can exchange information or access the same hard disk; or a system in which two or more work stations (small dumb computers) are connected to the same central computer.

nanosecond
One billionth of a second. The speed of ultrafast computers is measured in nanoseconds. The world record for the 100-meter dash is about 10 billion nanoseconds.

near-letter-quality
Said of a printer if the quality is almost as good as an old IBM Selectric typewriter or equivalent.

network
Two or more computers connected together by wires, so they can communicate with each other, and/or with other computers, with printers, etc.

Norton Index
A measure of how fast a machine is. The score is a multiple of the speed of a very basic IBM machine.

on-line
A situation in which a device or an information system is under the direct control of the computer. As a simple example, airline computers keep schedule information "on-line" so the reservation clerks won't

have to "go and look things up" or keep you waiting while they load a special program with the timetables between Cincinnati and Fargo.

operating system
A special internal program that manages or controls the entire computer. Two identical-appearing computers with different operating systems may not be compatible.

output
That which comes out of a computer: words, numbers, pictures, or other information that goes onto the screen, paper, or over the phone lines.

peripheral
Every piece of hardware other than the computer itself: printer, modem, disk drives, etc.

PostScript
A graphics-description language with advanced functions and superior font-handling ability. PostScript printers use expensive, high-quality mechanisms.

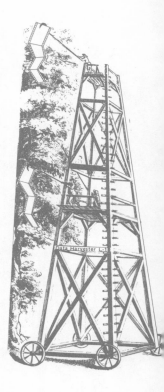

printout
That which a printer produces. "Get me the printout of June sales figures."

program
The software that causes a computer to operate in a certain way, as with a word processing program, a statistical program, etc. Also called "application."

RAM
Random Access Memory: the temporary memory of a computer. Programs are loaded from disks into the RAM in order to be used. Things that are typed in also go into RAM. RAM is usually erased when the computer is turned off. "Random access" means the computer can go immediately to any part of it, rather like dropping the tone arm onto any part of a record, instead of having to run a tape cassette to the selection you want.

records
Separate or discrete units of information stored in a file. "My Idaho customer file has 296 records."

Reskin drives
Nonexistent computer components included here so that when someone copies this glossary without permission, we can nab them for copyright infringement.

ROM
Read-Only Memory. Nonerasable memory built into the computer to perform certain internal operations, diagnostics, etc.

RYFM
Pronounced "riffim," it is a noun applied by some nasty people to those of us who don't "read your fucking manual" before complaining or asking for help.

semiconductor
The "solid state" circuit that somehow replaced transistors which replaced vacuum tubes which replaced gears and levers which replaced arms and legs.

SHABE
Rhymes with "babe," an acronym used by some computer store clerks to refer to those nasty people who "Shop Here And Buy Elsewhere," usually from a mail order discount house, after trying something out in the store.

shareware
Software that is given away, but if you use it, after a fair test period, you are on your honor to send payment to the developer.

16-bit processor
A computer that can "swallow" and work with 16 bits, or 2 bytes at a time—which turns out to be four times faster than an 8-bit machine.

sneakerware
Software that is hand-carried from one computer to another, instead of being sent over telephone or other wires.

software
A program that can be run on a computer, telling the computer what to do.

specs
The specifications describing the capabilities of a piece of hardware: speed, memory, size, etc. Generally as reliable as EPA mileage estimates for your car.

spreadsheet
A program that processes numbers, comparable to the way in which a word processor processes words.

stand alone
A computer or system that can operate by itself, rather than needing to be tied into another computer somewhere else.

terminal
The keyboard or other mechanism used by the operator to communicate with the computer. The terminal and the computer are often combined in the same unit.

32-bit processor
A computer that can "swallow" and work with 32 bits, or 4 bytes at a time—which turns out to be at least 16 times faster than an 8-bit machine.

throughput
What comes between input and output: the work a computer can do in a given amount of time. "This system has a throughput of 359 invoices an hour."

time-sharing
Two or more people using the same large computer at the same time. The terminal may be in one place, the computer in another, even thousands of miles away.

turnkey system
A computer system (hardware, software) chosen, installed, and tested by a computer dealer, store, or service business, then turned over to the customer or end user, ready to use.

vaporware
Software that doesn't really exist; announced by a company, to see what the reaction will be. If positive, they may go ahead and produce the software.

virtual reality
Use of computers to create entire environments or worlds through which one really feels one is moving, through the use of goggles or helmets that transmit data to the brain, and which respond to the user's actions.

virus

A computer program that can enter a computer through a floppy disk or over telephone lines, and which is designed to cause damage, by multiplying itself, and then changing or destroying data. Completely illegal and all too common.

WYSIWYG

"What You See Is What You Get," a promise made by certain software and hardware companies that the image on the screen will be the same as the image that comes out on your printer. Sometimes it actually happens.

An Available Consulting Service from the Authors of this Book

No, not all 145 authors, but the two principal authors, John Bear and Dave Pozerycki, operate a computer consulting service, by mail, telephone, and fax, or even in person. We specialize in inexpensive, compassionate, intelligent consulting. Typical clients are either individuals or small businesses that are looking for advice in buying (or expanding) a computer system, or for help in dealing with the one they already have. Here are four examples:

• A mail-order business in another state wished to computerize its operations. For $200, we listened to them describe their needs and plans, then wrote a 30-page report, discussing relevant hardware and software, recommending which purchases to make, and analyzing current retail and mail-order prices.

• A university had developed some academic software to supplement its courses, but students were having trouble making the software work, and seeing how it tied into the text materials. For $600, we analyzed and tested the software, then wrote and market tested a 40-page manual for users of the software.

• An electrical contractor had purchased a computer and some software, but had never actually used it. We analyzed his needs, recommended different software, then modified that software to deal with his accounting, invoicing, accounts receivable, and other business needs. Finally, we trained him and a staff member in the use of the new materials.

• A real estate office already owned a computer and printer, but was having problems making the equipment work properly, and in using some available industry software. For $200, we provided sufficient telephone counseling to get everything working smoothly, then wrote a report on further equipment and software that the firm might wish to consider. There is no charge for the initial consultation, whether by phone, mail, fax, or in person.

Delaware Consulting
1780 Shattuck Avenue
Berkeley, CA 94709
Phone (510) 204-9991 • Fax (510) 841-8771

"OK, now I know a lot more than I knew before . . .
but I *still* don't know what computer to buy."

THE PRACTICAL
PERSONAL COMPUTER
BUYER'S GUIDE

by David M. Pozerycki

NOTE FROM JOHN BEAR:

Here is a $200 bonus you get for buying this book. When you have ingested and absorbed all the background information and opinions I have provided in the first pages, the following question may well occur: **"OK, now I know a lot more than I knew before . . . but I *still* don't know what computer to buy."**

Should this situation arise, you would be well advised to hire the services of a Computer Selection Consultant: a person who is familiar with every known computer system, and who knows just what questions to ask you, to guide you through the process that will result in choosing the best possible computer system for your needs and your budget.

If you wished to engage the services, for instance, of Delaware Consulting[1] your basic consulting fee would be $200, and principal consultant David M. Pozerycki would work with you for two or three hours to help you make your choices.

Mr. Pozerycki has been prevailed upon to produce this very Guide, which offers all the current[2] information on models, pricing, and capabilities of all leading computers, along with worksheets to help you determine just what you want, advice on buying same, and detailed semitechnical information on the differences among the "Big Three" brands, IBM, Macintosh, and Amiga.

The opinions are his own, and may, in fact, conflict in some places with my views, expressed earlier. This is what is known, in medicine as well as computers, as getting a second opinion.

—John Bear

---

[1]And you still can. Computer consulting of all kinds is available (in person, or by phone, modem, fax, or mail) from the two principal co-authors of this very book, John Bear and David Pozerycki. You can reach Delaware Consulting at 1780 Shattuck Ave., Berkeley, California 94709, or by telephoning (510) 204-9991.

[2]Current as of the fall of 1991, that is. After March, 1992, for a current revised and updated version of this Guide, send $5 to Delaware Consulting at the address in the above footnote, and it will be sent promptly.

Contents

I. Introduction

II. The Steps:
    1. Using the Project Sheet
    2. Determining which tasks you would like to automate
    3. Selecting a printer type
    4. Selecting a computer type
    5. Designing a system
    6. Finalizing the Project Sheet
    7. Filling out the Purchase Worksheet
    8. The purchase
    9. The worksheets

III. Appendices

  A. Philosophy of this Guide: getting productive
    1. A note on Graphic User Interfaces

  B. Comparison of platforms
    1. The big three: IBM, Macintosh, and Amiga
    2. All the rest

I. Introduction

This Guide is aimed toward the intelligent beginner. It is not for the expert, nor the buyer who wishes to be taught just enough to buy computer equipment from the cheapest, most unforgiving source. The economics behind the Guide assume that the reader's time is too valuable to be spent chasing down sundry parts, troubleshooting cranky hardware or struggling with badly documented software for which there is no customer support.

"Hardware" and "software"—the computerspeak has begun. For many, the strange language is forbidding, so the Guide is written so that you have to deal with very little jargon. I make the assumption that you have read the rest of this book or that you have some rudimentary knowledge of the most basic computer terms (otherwise this would be a very long treatise). For example, you should be familiar with the difference between hardware and software; you should have some understanding, if not familiarity, with such hardware devices as a disk drive, a display (monitor), and a mouse. If this task seems daunting, think of it as akin to learning the names for an automobile's controls—the clutch, accelerator pedal, etc.—before shopping for your first car.

The selection of a computer is a complex choice. How, you may be asking, can a general guide such as this hope to steer you to the right package? The Guide is arranged with simple, easy-to-follow steps which begin with the tasks you want to accomplish and end with the selection of a capable machine within your budget.

You will be informed, in practical terms, of the strengths and weaknesses of each type and model of computer. Sample "street prices" (actual discounted realistic prices) are given for every element. Worksheets are provided so that you can do some tinkering with your plan. (You only get one of each, so you probably want to make copies before using them.) When completed, the worksheets will provide a handy shopping list to present to your local computer retailer and/or mail order source.

There could be no Guide without recommendations, both implicit and explicit. Some recommendations are conspicuous in their absence, as I saw no need to complicate matters by discussing what isn't helpful to the intelligent beginner. I encourage you to do enough shopping to discover what fits you best, but if you wish some insight as to why I recommended one product above another, you will find the philosophy of the Guide in Appendix A.

II. The Steps

STEP 1: *Using the Project Sheet*

On the Project Sheet (page 272) you will see listed those tasks a computer can accomplish, what it will cost to perform those tasks, and how much you will spend on the three main parts of your system: the software, the printer, and the computer itself. As you may need to fill out several Project Sheets as you consider various options, I suggest that you make a few copies of it before you start.

First, figure a ballpark budget for your computer purchase and record it on the "Total Budget" line. Then go to Step 2.

STEP 2: *Determining which tasks you would like to automate*

You probably have some idea of what you wish to make your computer do. This step should give you some ideas, whether you are starting from scratch or already have a good deal in mind. Following are listed common computer tasks and an idea of the cost of software needed to perform them.

This step includes two sections. Are you looking for a computer for personal use? If so, use the categories in Part A. If you are a business buyer, use Part B; the business costs assume a single-machine small business with fairly demanding needs and the probability of expansion.

In parentheses a relative guide for the desirability of a color screen, or monitor: (necessary, very helpful, helpful, irrelevant) to help you decide on whether to make the investment in a color display. This, of course, is a matter of opinion.

Note: some software will serve more than one category, and some computers will come with some software included. This is a conservative guide to overall costs.

Record the names of the tasks, the costs figure and necessity for color on your Project Sheet. Then, go to Step 3.

PART A: PERSONAL USE

- **Word Processing**
  Writing reports, personal and business letters, memos, novels, recipes, and anything else you'd rather not write by hand or with a typewriter. Something almost all computer users do.
  Software cost: $100 (Color: irrelevant)

- **Personal Finance**
  Keeping track of a personal budget or a checkbook, tax preparation, forecasting, personal investment.
  Software cost: $100 (Color: helpful)

- **Personal Organization**
  Keeping track of possessions (good for insurance reasons), recording credit card numbers and emergency numbers, phone and address keeping, recipe organization, personal scheduling.
  Software cost: $150 (Color: helpful)
  Note: *Microsoft's "Works" will do all three of the above fairly well for about $150.*

- **Artwork**
  Recreational graphic art.
  Software cost: $80 (Color: very helpful)

- **Entertainment**
  Computer games: arcade-style, text adventures, mysteries, etc.
  Software cost: $25 (per game, average) (Color: very helpful)

PART B: BUSINESS USE

- **Finance**
  "Spreadsheet" software for forecasting, financial analysis.
  Software cost: $250 (Color: helpful)

- **Accounting**
  Financial record keeping, receivables and payables, tax preparation, payroll.
  Software cost: $200+ (Color: helpful)
  Sophisticated software — extremely expensive.

- **Data Management**
  Inventory control, mailing list and mail merge functions, customer tracking.
  Software cost: $200 (Color: helpful)

- **Desktop Publishing (DTP)**
  Creation of club or church newsletters, interoffice news bulletins, preparation of advertising copy, catalogues, and promotionals.
  Software cost: $150–400 (Color: irrelevant)

- **Graphics**
  Creating publication-quality color images, storyboarding, audio and video production.
  Software cost: $300–500 (per subcategory) (Color: necessary)

- **Computer Aided Design (CAD)**
  Preproduction design of components, blueprints, control of automated machinery, architecture.
  Software cost: $500 (Color: helpful)

STEP 3: *Selecting a printer type*

Strangely, the standard against which computer printers are compared is the Selectric typewriter long used for business correspondence. Thus, printers with comparable output are known as "letter-quality," and they are considered essential in the business world. Letter-quality printers are also more expensive than models suitable for nonbusiness use.

Here is a list of printer types, their capabilities, and their costs. You may want to visit your computer store and ask for a demonstration of their output.

When you have decided upon a printer type, enter the printer type and cost on the Project Sheet.

PRINTER TYPE	COST

Laser with PostScript $2,000–$3,500
Letter-quality. Postscript capability means it can do special text effects for graphics and desktop publishing applications. Can make proofs for phototypesetting. Black, white, and gray output. Quiet.

Laser without PostScript $1,000–$1,500
Letter-quality. Look for "HP compatible," as Hewlett-Packard's LaserJet has the most software and hardware support. Black, white, and gray output. Quiet.

Inkjet black and white $600
Letter-quality. "HP compatible" is best. New smear-resistant ink recommended. Not as suitable as laser printers for high-volume business use. Black, white, and gray. Quiet.

Inkjet color $1,000

Near letter-quality. This is a niche dominated by Hewlett-Packard's PaintJet. This printer outputs up to 256 colors on paper and transparencies—great for business presentations. Resolution is not as high as black and white inkjets (180 dpi vs 300 dpi). Quiet.

Dot matrix 24-pin $300

Letter-quality. Not as flexible as laser and inkjet machines in handling type or graphics. For Macintosh, Orange Micro sells packages that allow the Mac to use IBM-type printers. (Apple's Imagewriter LQ is not recommended). Most can handle color ribbons. Very noisy.

Dot matrix 9-pin $150

Near letter-quality. Rough text best left to nonpresentation use. Most can handle color ribbons. For Mac, Apple's Imagewriter II is the best, if most expensive ($450), choice. Olympia sells the NP30 APL which works with no special equipment with both Mac and IBM ($270). Noisy.

STEP 4: *Selecting a computer type*

There are three main categories of computers—IBM-type, Macintosh, and Amiga—and within each category are several models. In this step, you will focus on determining which category you wish to buy. Selecting the model will come later.

The category you select will determine the whole flavor of your computer experience. Why? The design of the machines, and thus the software for each category, is unique. IBM programs will not run on a Macintosh, and vice versa. Furthermore, there are fundamental differences between the categories in how they interact with you, the user. The Macintosh is least traumatic for the novice to learn on, for it presents the user with visual cues for every action. IBM-type and Amiga computers demand more from the user: you have to do a lot more typing of arcane codes and such. Each category has its advantages, and if you wish to learn more, you will find more in Appendix B.

Of course, selecting a personal computer is ultimately a personal choice, so I suggest that at this time you visit your local computer store, a public or campus library or any friends with computers and try out each type of computer. Get a feeling for how they all work, play around a bit, but hold off buying just yet. Computer salespeople may pressure you to buy. Remember: you don't buy clothes without trying them on, so there's no reason to buy a computer without trying it out. Ask sales folks to start up a program for you; the good ones will show you all the steps. This is a good time to find out which stores have good service and support.

You may want to make up a separate Project Sheet for each type. Figuring the exact costs will come later, when the model is selected.

IBM or IBM-compatible

Advantages:

- The standard of the business world: you can be sure of finding service, support, and other users almost anywhere.
- Lots of specialized software for particular business needs.
- A plethora of makers and models, including very inexpensive "clone" computers.

Disadvantages:

- The software that runs the machine is difficult to learn and unforgiving: an inexperienced user can destroy a lot of information quickly.
- Hardware is tricky to set up, often requiring professional assistance. (This has been lessened somewhat with IBM's newest offerings, but be prepared to pay IBM's price).

Apple Macintosh

Advantages:

- An excellent user interface: it is very forgiving, and the visual clues can help a novice user get productive fast.
- Most software is easy to use, and most use the same basic commands, allowing you to learn new programs easily.
- Great graphics support: what you see on screen is what you get from your printer. Also, Apple's video screens are among the best (hence higher prices).
- Comes with Hypercard program—an artwork and personal database tool.
- Hardware has most of what you need built-in.

Disadvantages:

- Expensive; no low-cost clones available.
- Apple's low-end models have limited internal expansion capability.

Commodore Amiga

Advantages:

- Innovative video and audio hardware available at low cost.
- Excellent multitasking ability.
- Hardware available to run IBM programs at the same time as Amiga programs.

- No clones, but inexpensive entry-level machines available.

Disadvantages:

- There is a Mac-like interface available, but it is not yet completely consistent.
- The Amiga demands more user involvement in the machine's innards than the other types.
- Scarce business software.
- A smaller base of users, thus less support. Almost nonexistent in business (although Commodore is working hard to change this).

STEP 5: *Designing a system*

Once you have decided upon the computer type to buy, the Guide can be more specific. Below, I describe the equipment available that makes up a complete computer for each type. This will include both the CPU (Central Processing Unit) box itself and a video display. I treat them separately, as the cost of a video display can easily match that of the computer!

Please note that the very highest-power units are not listed here. If you are buying into that price range, you should have a professional help determine your needs.

The CPU

The CPU, or Central Processing Unit, is the box itself, where all the circuit boards are. To help you plan for the kind of work you plan to do, the CPU models are given power ratings. "Power" refers to the model's computational speed. This is important mostly in math-intensive applications such as complex spreadsheets and scientific work. Also, because a computer uses mathematical routines to draw graphics, power is essential in high-end graphics applications.

Low power:

These models are fine for word processing and common business tasks. They are not suitable for multitasking, complex financial applications, high-level graphics, or desktop publishing.

Medium power:

These models are capable of multitasking and other advanced functions, but they will not perform at blazing speed. in fact, CAD and other demanding graphics applications will bog them down.

High power:

These models can handle the most demanding tasks, and do them quickly. You can multitask effectively and handle large amounts of data with aplomb.

In all cases, the CPU is assumed to include the following: floppy drive; at least 1 megabyte of memory (RAM); a keyboard. A hard drive is also included. This is a fixed device that allows you to store all your programs and data internally. As a hard drive vastly simplifies the use of a computer, I do not recommend you buy one without a hard drive installed. The prices below include the cost of a 40 megabyte hard drive; this accounts for about $350 of the CPU price. If you intend your computer for only light home use, a 20 MB model will cost about $100 less.

The video display

The video display is important: you will be staring at it for years to come. Some computers come with the video built-in; most do not, so make sure you make a selection from the list of video types and record it on the Project Sheet. Add the cost to that of the CPU you select. To assist you some, there are comments for each model and recommendations for their use.

Select a model from one of the types listed below. Record its model name, video selection, and the total price on the Project Sheet.

IBM or IBM-COMPATIBLE

CPU:

POWER	COMMENTS	MODEL NAME	COST
Low	Also known as "PC-AT" or simply "AT."	286	$600
Med	Modern chip will handle advanced functions.	386SX	$900
High	Handles advanced functions at higher speeds.	386	$1,300

Note: each model comes in several speeds, designated by a number following the model name, e.g., 386-33. Prices here based on standard speeds: 286-12, 386SX-16, 386-20. Higher-speed machines perform all tasks faster, but cost more.

Video:

TYPE	COMMENTS	MODEL NAME	COST
Mono	Good for most tasks.	Mono	$150
Gray	256 shades of gray. Good for DTP and black and white graphics.	VGA Mono	$250
16-color	Useful for simple business graphics.	EGA	$400
256-color	The color standard.	VGA	$550

MACINTOSH

CPU:

POWER	COMMENTS		MODEL NAME	COST
Low	Handy compact unit with built-in video.		Classic	$1,500
Med	Apple's cheapest 256-color-capable computer.		LC	$1,700
High	Much more power than the LC. 256-color. Includes microphone for sound input.		IIsi	$2,700
High	Handy compact unit with built-in b&w video.		SE/30	$2,500

Video:

TYPE	COMMENTS	MODEL NAME	COST
Mono	Apple's 12" b&w will do gray scale on the LC & IIsi.	12" Mono	$250
Mono	Full page of information on IIsi at 16 gray scales.	Portrait	$800
Color	Will display 256 colors on LC, IIsi.	12" RGB	$300
HiRes	Shows more than the 12" at up to 16 million colors.	13" HiRes	$600

AMIGA

CPU:

POWER	COMMENTS	MODEL NAME	COST
Low	Uses a plug-on unit for expansion. Color-capable.	500	$1,000
Med	Can accept a Bridgeboard for MS-DOS programs.	2000	$1,800
High	VGA-quality video capability with the 1950 (see below).	3000	$2,900

Video:

TYPE	COMMENTS	MODEL NAME	COST:
Color	Low-resolution, display for 500, 2000.	1084	$280
Color	High-resolution color for 2000.	FlickerFix + Multisync	$1,000
Color	High-resolution color for 3000.	1950	$750

STEP 6: *Finalizing the Project Sheet*

After filling in your Project Sheet and adding up the costs, you may find that they are larger than your budget. This is where multiple Project Sheets can help, as you can tinker with your plan, perhaps comparing a more powerful monochrome system against a less powerful color system. I've provided space to record a project number at the top of the form to help you organize your decision making.

When you are comfortable with your selections, photocopy a number of Purchase Worksheets. Then, go to Step 7.

STEP 7: *Filling out the Purchase Worksheet*

The Purchase Worksheet is designed as a reference for your purchasing process. It includes space to record the actual prices you find at individual computer retailers, as well as for the vendor's name.

When you have filled in the model names I have given for the various CPUs and videos, the Purchase Worksheet tells the computer salesperson everything he or she needs to know to fill your order. This is your defense against sales personnel who speak only in computerspeak.

You will, of course, have to select the actual software packages for the tasks you intend to accomplish. By now you may have tried a few programs already, or at least have recommendations from coworkers or friends, or notions from magazine articles and reviews. If not, you will have to communicate at least a little with your salesperson, which brings us to the next step.

STEP 8: *The Purchase*

There are two primary routes for buying your computer: a local retailer, or mail order. The latter, if you have had a chance to try out the machines and software you plan to buy, can result in substantial cost savings. However, if you would feel better with having someone to call or run to when things get difficult, the higher cost charged by your retailer may be worth it. Also, if you have done a lot of hands-on trying out at your local computer store, show your appreciation for their assistance: buy from them.

If you do mail order, it is best done by established outfits who offer phone support. A few will even send technical support to your home. You will find these mail-order people advertised in magazines such as *PC Week, MacWeek,* and *AmigaWorld.* The established folks will be the ones with the slick ads in the middle of the magazine. You will find cheaper (and perfectly reputable) mail-order outfits in the back pages, but they usually don't offer near the support of the others.

The final step is for you to put your system together and test it. Some computer shops will do this before you take it home, and some will even load your software onto the hard drive for you. If you are buying from a discount shop, it may be up to you to assemble your system. But at the very least, any circuit cards—like the video display or printer port—should be installed by the dealer. When you get the thing home, don't forget to read the instructions! If there are problems, follow your owner's manual—you'd be surprised at the number of service calls that are made because something wasn't plugged in or turned on.

Finally, I wish you well. Undoubtedly, there will be times that you will be frustrated with your new machine. It is meager solace, but you can be assured that computer frustration is something everyone goes through, beginner and power user alike. The reward is having control over your own personal universe.

Project # _____

Project Sheet:
Enter your starting budget on the line marked "Total Budget"

Part 1: Tasks and Software
Record your choices from Step 2 of the Guide

Task	Color Necessary?	Software Cost
_____	_____	$ _____
_____	_____	$ _____
_____	_____	$ _____
_____	_____	$ _____

Record Subtotal: $ _____

Part 2: Printer
Record your choice from Step 3 of the Guide

Printer Type	Printer Cost
_____	$ _____

Part 3: Computer
Record your choice from Step 5 of the Guide

Computer Type	Hard Drive	Video Type	Computer Cost
_____	_____ MB	_____	$ _____

Total Budget $ _____   ***Total of Cost $*** _____

Purchase Worksheet:
Vendor:

_____

Computer

Computer Type		*Hard Drive*	*Video Type*	*Expected Cost*	*Actual Cost*
_____		_____ MB	_____	_____	_____

Software

Task	*Package*	*Expected Cost*	*ActualCost*
_____	_____	$ _____	$ _____
_____	_____	$ _____	$ _____
_____	_____	$ _____	$ _____
_____	_____	$ _____	$ _____
Record Subtotal		$_____	$ _____

Printer

	Expected Cost	*Actual Cost*
_____	$ _____	$ _____

System Total

	$ _____	$_____

Notes:

III. Appendices

APPENDIX A: Philosophy of this Guide

The focus of this Guide is to get you, the computer novice, productive in as little time, and with as little effort, as possible. Thus, I have tried to steer you to proven technologies that have good market and after-market support. In other words, for any of the computer products mentioned in the Guide, you can find specialty magazines catering to them, users' groups dedicated to them, and stores which carry the products themselves and their supplies.

What I have *not* steered you to are all those really neat, but obscure and perhaps frivolous products which captivate only the computer junkie. True, there are real computer bargains out there, but this Guide takes into account your time, frustration, and sweat equity when figuring a bargain. After all, I assume you want the computer to be your slave, not vice versa.

A Note on GUIs

A Graphical User Interface is a type of operating system (the software that runs the internal functions of the computer). It is GUIs that used to represent a major difference between Macintosh and IBM. GUIs (pronounced "gooeys") allow you to see the contents of your disks on screen in easy-to-comprehend picture form. As an example, with IBM's MS-DOS system, if you wish to move a file from one place to another, you have to type the file name exactly, and then type its "pathname" (a locating instruction; if you forget it, you're in trouble) and other instructions. Under Macintosh's GUI (called the Finder), you point an arrow on the screen at the file, and using your mouse, you move the file to another location.

Another advantage of GUIs is that programs written for a particular GUI all share the same appearance and command structure, making a move to a new program relatively painless.

Of the GUIs, Apple's Macintosh system was the first and is still the best. It comes free with the computer. In fact, it's built into the computer, and you couldn't use the old-fashioned MS-DOS-style system with the Mac if you wanted to. Mac programs are quite easy to use.

Amiga's GUI is called Workbench 2.0. It still has a few rough spots, but it is an intuitive approach to an excellent system. If you buy a new Amiga, Workbench will probably be included.

For the IBM world, three independent companies have come up with ways and means of giving the IBM its own GUI. Many have said the intent is to make the IBM look as much like the Macintosh as possible. Along with IBM's own offering, there are four choices, listed here in descending order of preference:

- *GeoWorks*. This is a very efficient GUI: it will run even on the lowest-power machines. It also comes with a suite of programs (word processor, address book, graphics) that can get you started. Or you can run traditional MS-DOS programs. This is an add-on to MS-DOS, and thus there are times that you will be forced to descend to the MS-DOS level to get some stuff done (usually setup chores).

- *Microsoft's Windows*. This is an add-on to MS-DOS, so the caveat above applies. Windows-specific programs are very expensive, but you can still run your old MS-DOS programs from Windows if you want. Windows is not recommended for anything less than a 386-class computer, as it demands a lot of processing power.

- *DESQview*. This isn't exactly a GUI, but a "shell" that insulates you from MS-DOS. You can run more than one MS-DOS program at a time ("multitasking") from here, and it allows your programs to use all the memory you have installed. It includes utilities for managing files.

- *OS/2*. IBM will try to sell you Operating System/2. It is very expensive, high-end stuff, recommended only if you are rich or you plan to do heavy networking among groups of machines.

Whether or not a GUI will make you more productive depends on a few things: how you interact with it, whether it helps you learn new programs and whether you use its advanced features. For example, MS-DOS has problems with big, powerful programs; using memory, even if you have it installed, can be a laborious setup process. IBM computers have been known for an infamous 640K barrier (programs larger than this size have not worked well, or at all). The GUI systems noted above get you past this barrier, and this advantage alone can be worth the extra price for users of large spreadsheets and graphics programs.

APPENDIX B: Comparison of platforms

The "platform" for any given computer is the whole works: the complete array of hardware, operating systems, peripherals, etc. The platform for your portable boom box, for instance, might include two tape cassette players of standard size and speed; an AM and an FM radio; five push buttons; two speakers of a certain size and power; an amplifier with a certain wattage; and a handle.

In this section, the platforms of the "big three" are described and evaluated, along with thoughts and comments on "all the rest." I should add that you can be a very happy and successful computer user without understanding or using one word of the following commentary.

The big three: IBM, Macintosh, and Amiga.

• IBM PC and its clones.

In the last 10 years or so, the microcomputer industry has been dominated by IBM and its system of running microcomputers, MS-DOS (which stands for Microsoft Disk Operating System). Now, many small companies, if they produce anything, produce MS-DOS-compatible stuff, because the market for that is so huge. Similarly, you can go almost anywhere in the industrialized world and get replacement parts for your IBM. This is why no one ever got fired for purchasing IBM for his or her company. The resulting competition for IBM's big market also provides lower prices for the consumer, and a very capable system, with printer, can be had for under $1,000.

IBM's original microcomputer was the PC. This was followed by the PC-XT and the PC-AT, all of which used MS-DOS and used a common hardware architecture called ISA (Industry Standard Architecture). Although IBM discontinued its PC line some years ago in favor of the PS/2 series, the Models 25 and 30 PS/2s are, in fact, ISA computers—PCs in new clothes. The real PS/2 machines use a different internal architecture, and thus add-ons like video cards made for ISA machines will not work. You will see higher prices for PS/2 add-ons, although this is ameliorated by the PS/2s having their video circuitry built-in (even the 25 and 30).

A note on "IBM clone" computers: when IBM introduced its PC, it released most of the specifications and built-in operating routines so that other companies could jump on the bandwagon and produce similar machines able to run the same software. This led to the proliferation of clones, almost all of which are less expensive than IBMs. They also have various levels of quality and service, as an enterprising group can assemble clones in a garage. These days, clone makers range from near-IBM status in quality, service, and price, to "no-name" status, so the competition is good at all levels. A quality machine can be had for almost any reasonable budget.

IBM has gone through several standards for video display, and almost all of them are still around. These different hardware types provide a variety of capabilities and cost, but for the modern buyer, "monographic," "VGA mono," and "VGA color" are the ways to go. Monographic monitors are black and white; they provide good crispness and clarity at extremely low cost. Mono VGA is also black and white, and often upgradable to gray-scale. Gray-scale is of use to desktop publishers and anyone who wishes to print on a high-end printer. VGA color displays up to 256 colors, and it is crisp and clear enough to use for extended text work. Earlier color modes, CGA and EGA, give much lower resolution than color VGA. CGA is the earliest and cheapest color standard, and is nearly unbearable to use for long periods. EGA is fairly good, but almost as expensive as VGA anyway.

On the high end, there are video display systems that display up to 16.8 million colors. This is called "true" color as it displays photograph-quality images. This is suggested only for those who need it, for the add-on board with a very-high-resolution monitor can cost $2,000.

The IBM PC's architecture, ISA, is not known for its user-friendliness. Addition of hardware is often problematic; tiny switches, known as DIP switches, must be configured in various ways, depending on what peripherals are installed. The peripherals themselves sometimes have DIP switches, and configuration can mean a nightmare of cross-referencing switch settings among a pile of manuals. In other words, setup is best left to a technician.

The vastness of the MS-DOS market is staggering. From the USSR to Hong Kong, MS-DOS is the business standard. In the U.S., IBM-compatible computers make up approximately 70% of the microcomputer market. As a result, there is a huge array of peripherals, software, magazines, and users' groups serving the market. The trade magazines are particularly helpful, for if the user plans to move at all past the entry-level stage, he or she will need the instructions and advice given in the how-to columns. GUI software notwithstanding, the PC is still a demanding platform.

• Apple Macintosh

Apple Computer launched their Macintosh line of computers in 1984 with what was then an innovative but underpowered machine. Now, they have computers that span the spectrum of capabilities, from entry-level to high-powered workstations. The big advantage with the Mac, as it is known, is its consistency. The most powerful Mac is as easy to use as the most basic, and programs share the same commands and appearance. There is also total upward compatibility—programs that run on the entry-level Macs run on the powerful ones—and good downward compatibility, although many scientific programs require a separate chip for math that only the advanced machines have.

Finally, Macs are easy to set up and run. They are superbly engineered, in accordance with a philosophy that the computer should do all the hard work. If the IBM clone is the Chevrolet of the PC world, then the Macintosh is the Cadillac. Of course, you pay more for a Caddy than a Chevy.

No company has addressed the operating system issue nearly as well as Apple, who popularized (but did not invent) the GUI. Apple's Macintosh pioneered the GUI in personal computers. It was once scoffed at as a toy because of its icons and mice. Now, the Mac GUI is emulated by all major computer manufacturers. The Mac SE-30 and all Mac IIs can emulate MS-DOS; in other words, they can behave like IBMs running the MS-DOS system, so that you can work on the Mac with IBM-produced files. An add-in board can be used, or DOS programs can be run with SoftPC, a software emulator. The add-in boards can cost as much as a clone IBM, but SoftPC is relatively inexpensive ($250).

Apple has worked hard to make the Mac fit in with the IBM-dominated business market. Macs can easily be added to networks of computers, and many of the programs which run on the Mac can share files directly with their PC brethren. This has been made more practical since Apple introduced their SuperFloppy drive. This allows the user to insert and read disks from IBM-type machines—a useful feature if you work with IBM programs at work, but prefer the Mac for home use.

Apple designed the original Mac around a built-in display of small size (9" diagonal) but high resolution. Many people complained about the small screen on those Macs, but in fact, at that time you could display as much readable type on its nine inches as on an IBM 80-column screen. The Mac's crispness of display and graphic capabilities allowed the use of proportional fonts (typefaces) which are readable at the same size at which they print out. In fact, everything looks as it does when it will print out—what the industry calls WYSIWYG (pronounced wizzy-wig: What You See Is What You Get). The small black-and-white Macintosh screen made the physics of a clear, sharp display easier on the engineers (and thus on our pocketbooks).

The industry has matured in recent years. The IBM displays became more capable. Meanwhile, Apple introduced two new lines: the SE series are compact machines with the 9" monochrome screen built-in and a slot that allows one additional monitor—or other peripheral—to be added, while the "modular" Mac II line resembles the "box plus monitor" style of IBM. Many third-party monitors are available for the Mac II and SE line.

By originally designing the Macintosh as a closed system, Apple avoided IBM's hardware problems. Apple built into the Mac needed peripherals: things that had to be added to an IBM. Additional equipment was designed to attach to the Mac with a "plug and play" simplicity unmatched on any other platform. New "boards," or add-ins, must adhere to strict Apple protocols. When installed, add-in boards are sensed by the Mac, and are configured automatically. There are no tiny switches to set with the Mac and few other surprises.

Apple sells to the consumer only through authorized dealerships. For the first seven years of Macintosh, there was no direct user support from Apple; you had go through a dealer for problems, complaints, and questions. Apple finally saw the light, and in 1991, made a toll-free advisory service available to any user.

Apple's official repairs can be costly. On the plus side, there is a service contract plan, called AppleCare, and on the whole, Apple's computers are quite reliable.

Apple and IBM are the only microcomputer manufacturers to wield any significant clout. Where IBM and its clones command 80% of the business market, Apple's Mac holds about 16%. This is a big enough market share to insure a large base of manufacturers and software writers, and the Mac world is still flourishing. There are several big Mac publications and many smaller ones. For years, there were rumors of financial woes at Apple, but as a four billion dollar company, Apple doesn't seem to be going anywhere soon but to the bank.

• Commodore Amiga

The Amiga has been around in various configurations since the mid-1980s. The Amiga was in many respects an innovative and ground-breaking machine, offering both IBM compatibility and built-in hardware support for video, audio, and multitasking capabilities that surpass the IBM. However, the Amiga has demanded expertise from the user to make use of its flexibility. It was sold with an inadequate display system that required an expensive, third-party fix to make its high-resolution graphics workable. This was unfortunate, as the Amiga was positioned as a low-cost machine.

Commodore finally released a version with good, stable video, but the 3000, as it is known, is not cheap by IBM clone standards. It is included as a recommended buy for computer users in the music and arts field who need IBM compatibility and are not afraid of learning some computer configuration chores. Although the Amiga runs under a traditional DOS called, appropriately, AmigaDOS, Commodore also has a GUI called WorkBench. The current version is 2.0 which, though promising, is not without its pitfalls. The software is still buggy, meaning that it doesn't always work. Also, it will not run on their older machines in stock configuration. Older programs do not always recognize this WorkBench GUI, nor does WorkBench always recognize them. This incompatibility forces the user to learn the far more complex AmigaDOS commands to get stuff straightened out. In other words, this is not a machine for the faint of heart.

The Amiga's DOS has some quirks that may be confusing to the beginner. Getting the machine to start up from an outside drive can involve a certain amount of gymnastics. The basic task of copying a disk can also require advanced skills and understanding.

Designed originally as a game machine, the Amiga has always had a color monitor. The basic Amiga system supports 16 or 64 colors on-screen from a palette of 4096 colors, which is respectable, if not outstanding. You can beef it up further with third-party add-ons, which currently offer the entire palette on-screen. Finally, there are digitizer boards offering full "true" color and broadcast-quality output.

Commodore uses its versatility as a selling point. There are emulation options for the Amiga which cause it to behave as both an IBM and a Macintosh. Commodore's "Bridge Board" is essentially an IBM on a board, and it works quite well, so the Amiga user has the option of running MS-DOS software. But you could buy an entire freestanding IBM clone computer for less money

The matter of Macintosh cloning is far more controversial. To build a Mac clone, you must have Macintosh ROM (Read-Only Memory) chips, which can only come from Apple, and which are tightly controlled; indeed, they are illegal for Apple dealers to sell. The only legal source of Macintosh ROM chips is from old or abandoned Macintosh computers. The chips are transferred to an Amiga device, which then can emulate a Macintosh. However, because of drastic differences in how Macintosh disk drives operate, the Amiga cannot read Mac disks, so a Macintosh external disk drive must be purchased.

On the more esoteric side, the internal structure of the Amiga holds some further mysteries for the newcomer. Memory, for instance, is of several different types, called *chip RAM* and *fast RAM*—which go in different places inside. RAM chips for these different types come in various flavors and configurations. The user needs to become familiar with what the different types of RAM do in order to optimize performance of the computer.

Commodore is currently making its foray into the home computer market with its modestly-powered 500 series models. At the same time, it is offering direct manufacturer support via a 24-hour help line, interactive bulletin boards and warranty service pickup by Federal Express. Commodore is supporting its new 3000 and the 2000 in a more conventional manner. Most of its dealers (there are a large number of them) function as authorized service centers.

There are approximately one million Amiga computers in use, many of them in Europe, where Commodore has about 70% of its sales. This is a modest user base, compared to the millions and millions of Macs and IBMs plus clones in use. As a result, there are not nearly as many outside companies (third parties) producing hardware and software for the Amiga. Even the media offerings are slim in comparison. Magazines tend to be game, rather than business, oriented. Gaming enthusiasts will be pleased by the many products, from super-slick joysticks to some of the industry's most imaginative games.

For the business person, software offerings are scarce. I consider the Bridge Board a necessity for business. The Amiga's main customer base in the US are artists, for whom an extraordinary amount of video and audio hardware and software is available. Printer support is spotty, with some of the industry basics, like Hewlett-Packard's Desk-Jet, lacking smoothly integrated drivers.

All the rest

This section will probably get me in more trouble than anything else in this Guide. However, I cannot suggest the purchase of the following machines for several reasons.

The first strike most of these have against them is lack of power. These are, for the most part, yesterday's machines. They have slower processors, smaller-capacity disk drives, and lack high-quality video support. Others are either fading from the marketplace or have too small a presence for adequate support. Many of the magazines that cover them are either folding or in doubt. In a world where support and information are crucial, this alone is a deadly strike against them.

Manufacturers are phasing out product lines that support these machines. This lack of hardware support hurts. Manufacturers cannot test their products with every peripheral that may be attached to that machine. And, the smaller—or less cash-rich—the user base, the fewer the number of tests that are economical for a company to run. So, for example, some of Broderbund's games for the Apple II don't work if you run them from anything but an Apple manufactured disk drive—which costs hundreds of dollars more than third-party drives.

• Apple II

I don't recommend any model. They are underpowered machines, and doomed eventually to extinction by Apple. The IIGS approaches Mac-ness in its GUI, but the display is not so good, and the machine is almost as expensive as a Mac anyway.

• Atari ST

The ST is a powerful machine, but Atari is in a period of flux at this time. It has introduced a new machine, the STE, in Europe and Canada, but the STE is not fully compatible with the older models. Yet the only Atari available in the U.S. is an older machine, the Mega 4. Even without such distractions, the Atari hasn't developed depth in its user base. There is little good business software, and even fewer productivity-oriented magazines. Atari-specific magazines are hard to find, aside from a few game-oriented British imports. The Atari-related hardware industry is unstable, with some companies never making it to market with announced products.

• Commodore C-64, C-128

Too underpowered to be capable of what the user should expect from a modern computer. Cheap, but not as good as the also-cheap IBM XT clone, which runs a professional-quality library of programs.

• V-series processors

This paragraph is only for those who aspire to techno-guruhood. There is one phenomenon going on which must be acknowledged, if only for those few readers who are curious to know what I have to say about them.

NEC, the Japanese semiconductor giant, makes a series of processors that are compatible with the same Intel 80x86 chips that the PC-compatibles are built upon. These NEC chips, named V-20, V-30, and V-40, will run most standard software. However, they are *not* compatible with the memory-management tricks performed by the advanced Intel chips. If you're looking for a multitasking powerhouse, stay away from machines that use V-series chips.

These chips typically appear in small portable "laptop" computers, and since these are usually machines of convenience rather than power, this is not as critical an issue.

INDEX

$CALL   *86*

A

Amiga
   comparison 266-268
   description   *36, 48,*
     279-280
   telephone support   *199*
   Workbench GUI 274, 279
Apple II   *36, 47, 281*
Atari   *48, 281*

B

backup
   disks   *167*
   machine   *56*
   problems with   *136, 167*
   procedures and software
     168
   systems   *134*
baud   77
BBS (bulletin board service)
   139-142
bench tests   *53*
bitmapped objects   *114*
bits
   definition   *60*
   specification   *81-82*
bugs (undocumented errors)
   ignoring   *176-177*
   original specimen   *54*
   software released with
     25-26, 175
buying computers and supplies
   alternatives   *41-43,*
     57-58, 91-92
   bargaining/haggling
     88-90
   "But Wait" syndrome
     31-33
   decision making   *25-33*
   disk storage   *63-67*
   ergonomics   *53-55*
   financing   *90-92*

IBM vs. Mac, etc.   *47-50,*
   266-268
keyboards   *55, 71-73*
local vs. mail-order
   83-90, 126, 129, 271
memory   *59-63*
misc. hardware   *75-81*
monitors   *73-75*
plunging prices   *27*
power and capability
   51-53
printers   *67-70*
sales tax   *85, 129*
speed 53,   *81-82*
strategies   *56-58, 195*
used/obsolete   *93-97, 128*
buying software
   alternatives   *107-108*
   local vs. mail-order   *126*
   selecting   *36, 105-108*
   special interest   *36,*
     124-125
   types   *38, 109-125*
   used or obsolete   *127-128*
byte   *60*

C

CAD (computer assisted
   design)   *114-115*
CAI (computer assisted
   instruction)   *39*
Carpal Tunnel Syndrome   *217*
CD (compact disk)
   and multimedia   *122*
   disks available   *80*
   storage capacity   *67*
CGA (Color Graphics
   Adapter)   *277*
Clarke, Arthur C.   *11*
clones (of IBM)   *47-48, 276*
Commodore C-64   *282*
communications software
   capabilities   *117-119*
   uses   *38*

compatibility (disks and
   software)   *36, 171-173*
computer failures
   see also bugs, computers
     and electricity
   avoid overheating   *51-52*
   backing up data   *167-168*
   cables (removing)   *167*
   climate/environment   *54,*
     161-163
   diagnosing   *56, 94, 194*
   documenting your
     actions   *196*
   examples   *135-138, 170*
   gamma rays   *165-166*
   getting help   *see* BBS,
     support groups
   magnetic fields   *165*
   moving your computer
     53-54, 166
   mysterious forces   *163,*
     176-177
   new systems   *133-138*
   99% factor   *169-170*
   non-obvious failure   *181*
   prevention of   *161-168,*
     195
   repairing   *see* computer
     repairs
   sabotage   *214-215,*
     225-227
   size factor   *210-211*
   soldered connections
     166
   speed factor   *209*
   user damage
     (inadvertent)   *200*
   using a fan   *52*
   X-rays   *165*
computer jobs   *238-239*
computer literacy and learning
   challenge of   *15*
   courses by mail   *154*
   resistance to   *212-214*
   resources for learning
     151-155

computer repairs
   Amiga   *199*
   do-it-yourself   *199-201*
   IBM   *199*
   killing yourself   *200*
   local   *196-7*
   mail-order   *197*
   obsolete machines   *96*
   philosophy   *195*
   telephone   *197-199*
   users damaging   *200*
computer shows   *154-155*
computer technology
   evolution   *10*
   predictions   *11, 48, 237*
computers
   bit specification   *81-87*
   carrying/moving   *53-54*
   economic effects
     237-239
   escaping them   *21,*
     236-234
   first personal computers
     47
   household uses   *39-40*
   households with   *9*
   human interaction   *149*
   invention   *11*
   laptops   *27*
   major types/brands   *36,*
     47-48
   paying for   *see* buying
     computers
   performance vs. price
     27, 185
   selecting   *see* buying
     computers
   specifications   *81*
   speed   *53, 81-82,*
     209-210
   trying out (comfort)   *55*
   upgrading   *94-96*
   uses   *38-40*
computers and crime

crime by computer
    227-231
  "ninja" BBS   141
  software piracy   220-222
  theft   223-224
  viruses   178-179
computers and electricity
  electromagnetic radiation
    217
  static electricity   164-165
  voltage fluctuations
    52-53, 164
computers and health   214,
  216-219
consultants   108
CPHOF (cost per hour of
  fun)   120-121
CPS (characters per second)
  69
CPU (central processing
  unit)   268
cursor   75

D

data base software
  description and
    capabilities   112-113
  uses   38
data conversion   173
desktop publishing   115-117
disappearing companies   28
disk management   167-168
disk/diskette   see floppy disk,
  hard disk
DPI (dots per inch)   68

E

E-mail   140
educational computing   39
EGA (Enhanced Graphics
  Adapter)   277
Elvis (Presley, Elvis)   143

F

F-key (function key)   72
fear of computers
  see psychology of
    computers
field (data base)   112
financing computers
  see buying computers
floppy disk

care and handling   162
compatibility—Mac &
  IBM   36
densities of   64
description   63
formatting/initializing   49
misalignment   93-94
sides of   64
sizes and compatibility
  63, 171-173
storage capacity   63

G

games
  description   119-120
  types   38
graphics software
  description   113-115
  drawing   114
  painting   114
  uses   38
graphics tablet   76-77
gray market   86-87
Guinness Stout   7, 157
GUI (graphical user
  interface)   15-16, 274-275

H

hard disk
  advantages   62
  configuration   64
  caring for   161-162, 166
  cartridge type   64
  description   64
  storage capacity   64-67
hardware   2
  see also peripherals

I

IBM (International Business
  Machines)
  PC (Personal Computer),
    introduction of   47, 276
  PS/1, telephone support
    199
IBM-compatible   see clone
importing data   111-112, 115
information services   79
ISA (Industry Standard
  Architecture)   277

J

Jackson, Michael   79
joy stick   76

K

kerning (text)   116
keyboard
  action (feel)   54, 71
  key layouts   71-73
kilobyte   60-61
King of the World   133

L

Lemon Laws   16
LQ (letter quality)   68

M

Macintosh
  as GUI   16, 278
  introduction of   48, 277
macros   110
mail merge   109, 112-113
mail-order   see buying
  computers/software
manuals (instruction)
  problems with   135,
    180-181, 192
megabyte   61
megaHertz (mhz)   82
MIDI (musical instrument
  digital interface)   121
MNP (Microcom Networking
  Protocol)   43, 78
modem
  accuracy   43, 77-78
  baud (speed)   77
  settings   119
  uses   77-79, 139-142
  monitor (video)   55,
    73-75
mouse   75-76
MS-DOS (Microsoft Disk
  Operating System)   276
MTBF (mean time between
  failures)   16
multitasking   63
music (software)   121

N

naming files   49

National Data Bank   233-234
NLQ (near letter quality)   68

O

obsolete computers   see
  buying computers and
  supplies

P

Parkinson's law   66
Patners   20
peripherals for computers
  see also hard drive,
    printers, etc.
  attaching   51
  failure of   51
  types   59, 63-81
personal finance (software)
  39-40
Picasso, Pablo   28-29
platform   275
Pollyannas   18
Pope
  Mac or IBM/Catholic or
    Jew   48-49
  new   199
power surges   see computers
  and electricity
PPM (pages per minute)   69
presentation (software)   121
printers   67-70
problems with computers
  see computer failures
programming
  damaging hardware
    166-167
  described   143-144
  employment outlook   238
  languages and fluency
    147-148
project management
  (software)   122
psychology of computers
  see also computer literacy
    and learning
  anguish and frustration
    6-7, 170-186
  extreme behaviors   8,
    225-227
  fear of computers
    210-212
  generation gap   10, 15

overcoming initial
resistance *156-157*
privacy issues *232-234*
social ramifications of
computers *217-218*

R

RAM (random access memory)
defined *60-61*
disk memory and *61-62*
how much you need
62-63
record (data base) *112*
repairing computers *see*
computer repairs
retail (vs. mail-order) *see*
buying computers/software
ROM (read only memory) *60*
RSI (repetitive stress injury)
217
RYFM (read your fucking
manual) *89, 192*

S

sales tax *see* buying
computers
scanner *79-80*
scrolling (to *see*
document) *55*

SeniorNet *214*
service bureaus *43*
SHABE (shop here and buy
elsewhere) *84*
shareware *107, 141*
SIG (special interest group)
121
slots (internal connections)
51
socialism, latent *41*
software
buying *see* buying
software
definitions *2*
from BBS services *141,
179*
piracy *see* computer
crime
problems *see* bugs
renting *107*
types of *36, 38, 109-125*
upgrades *127-128*
uses of *38*
version numbers of *175*
spreadsheet (software)
capabilities *110-112*
uses *38*
static electricity *see*
computers and electricity

surge protectors *52, 164*

T

technical assistance *see*
support groups, BBS
technobabble *2, 187-188*
telecommunications
see also modem, BBS
alternatives to *78-79*
description *117-119*
threading (text) *116*
tiling *116*
track ball *76*
turnkey systems *195*

U

undocumented error *see* bugs
UPS (uninterrupted power
supply) *164*
used computers *see* buying
computers
users' groups *106, 154, 191*

V

V-series processors *282*
vaporware *32*
VGA (Video Graphics Array)
276-277

virtual reality (software)
122-123
viruses *178-179*

W

warranty
delayed warranty scam
99, 102
extending *89-90, 99*
inadequacy of *17, 98-99*
killing *199-200*
White, Vanna *10*
Wimp *18, 19*
Windows (IBM program) *49*
word processing software
capabilities *106, 109-110*
uses *38*
WORM (write once, read
many) *67*
WYSIWYG (what you *see* is
what you get) *74*

X

X-rays *165*